CLIMATE WARS

CLIMATE WARS

WHY PEOPLE WILL BE KILLED IN THE TWENTY-FIRST CENTURY

HARALD WELZER

TRANSLATED BY PATRICK CAMILLER

polity

First published in German as *Klimakriege: Wofür im 21. Jahrhundert getötet wird*
© S. Fischer Verlag GmbH, Frankfurt am Main, 2008.

This paperback edition © Polity Press, 2017

The translation of this work was supported by a grant from the Goethe-Institut which is
funded by the German Ministry of Foreign Affairs.

Polity Press
65 Bridge Street
Cambridge CB2 1UR, UK

Polity Press
350 Main Street
Malden, MA 02148, USA

ISBN-13: 978-0-7456-5145-3
ISBN-13: 978-0-7456-5146-0 (pb)

A catalogue record for this book is available from the British Library.

Typeset in 10.75 on 14 pt Janson Text
by Servis Filmsetting Ltd, Stockport, Cheshire
Printed and bound in Great Britain by MPG Books Group Limited, Bodmin, Cornwall

For further information on Polity, visit our website: www.politybooks.com

Contents

ACKNOWLEDGEMENTS

The idea of writing a book about the link between climate change and violence goes back to the run-up to the Year of the Humanities in 2007, the eighth in a series of years officially named in Germany for a branch of the sciences. When the weekly newspaper *Die Zeit* asked me to submit a programmatic text on the future of social and cultural theory, I took it as a welcome opportunity for an appeal that colleagues should pay greater attention to the far-reaching changes taking place in the life of society. 'What we today call "climate change"', I wrote there, 'will be the greatest social challenge of the modern age, especially since there will be no way of escaping the question of how to cope with the masses of refugees who can no longer survive in their land of origin and wish to enjoy the opportunities available in better-off countries. We know from the study of past genocides how quickly an attempted solution to social problems can turn into sweeping definitions and deadly actions, and whether societies can avoid such things is a test of their ability to learn from history.' Those lines, written with a certain ardour, soon turned into a strange challenge to carry my thinking further. So, in fact it was Elisabeth von Thadden at *Die Zeit* who gave the first impetus for *Climate Wars*. A further major stimulus was my collaboration with Tobias Debiel on a 'Failing Societies' project, in which I learned a great deal about the subject of our research. Some of the graphics in the present book originated in the hugely important journal *Globale Trends*, which Tobias Debiel edits together with Dirk Messner and Franz Nuscheler – and for these too I am deeply grateful. Many other individuals made their research available to me: Scharsad Amiri, Karin Schürmann, Jacques Chlopzyk, David Keller, Christian Gudehus, Bernd Sommer, Alfred Hirsch and above all Sebastian Wessels deserve my thanks here for their time, effort and commitment. My gratitude too to Romuald Karmakar for discussions and suggestions. The Kulturwissenschaftliches Institut in Essen, especially in the persons of Claus Leggewie, Ludger Heidbrink, Jörn Rüsen and Norbert Jegelka, offered me not only the inspiring collegial atmosphere one needs for such a hazardous project as *Climate Wars*, but also many occasions to discuss and try out various themes and ideas. Special thanks are due to Dana Giesecke, who painstakingly contributed to the book with intensive research, editing and indexing, and whose gentle criticism spared the reader many a redundancy or rhetorical flourish. Her constant involvement was a source of infinite help. And, finally, my thanks to my trusted publishers, Peter Sillem, Anita Jantzer and, above all, Heidi Borhau and Walter Pehle.

Preface to the 2017 edition

The first *Jurassic Park* movie stars Jeff Goldblum as a philosopher who speaks out against resurrecting the dinosaurs: Nature is indomitable, he argues, and will always take what it is owed. An hour later into the movie, he finds himself sitting in a Jeep, a T-Rex breathing hot steam down his neck, and he exclaims: 'Boy, do I hate being right all the time!'

I have had a somewhat similar experience with my *Climate Wars*, albeit in a less fictional context. When the book was first published a decade ago in Germany, it drew a good deal of criticism: there is no scientific evidence of a correlation between the repercussions of climate change and increased levels of violence, my critics said; the book is alarmist. I wish they had been right! Yet today we are seeing more extreme weather events, more refugees, more terrorism than a decade ago, and increased as well as more radical isolationist tendencies among the rich countries. A quarter of a century after the fall of the Berlin Wall, building walls is all the rage again, as is the politics of fear and a yearning for autocratic – which always means violent – problem-solving. Europe is faced with large numbers of refugees and has chosen isolationism, while the causes of displacement are on the rise around the globe. These include usurpation of land, loss of land, violent expulsion, environmental catastrophes, terrorism, war, failed policies, failed states.

In all this, climate change is not the single cause of violence but, rather, a source of conflict, a reason for poverty, a trigger of extreme world events and the ensuing migration and conflicts – more so today than a decade ago. Today, there are 65 million people around the globe who have been forced to leave their homes, each minute statistically adding another twenty-four, and the most significant difference is that, proportionally speaking, the poorest societies take in more and more refugees while the richest nations accept fewer and fewer. While ten years ago they took more than a quarter of the world's refugees, today's percentage is only 14 per cent – even though they doubtlessly contribute far more to the causes of displacement than the poor ones.

Overall, we could say that the world in the early twenty-first century is under more environmental and climate-related stress than ever, but we are not really looking for ways to mitigate these stresses in a civilized manner. Our main motivation in addressing the issue is mostly to maintain and secure our assets, which is why isolationism is the formula of choice. This doesn't exactly bolster the rich societies' credibility, and it also increasingly devalues the societal model of a democratic nation under the rule of law. Globally, this type of society is currently on the retreat after a long period of success, and there are few conceptions as to how the Western model of democratic society could actually be modernized to preserve its level of freedom, security and democracy while at the same time developing a less destructive and, from a global perspective, less unjust relationship with nature.

The path towards greater isolationism and increased violence is not inevitable; perhaps the ever more visible repercussions of climate change and the social consequences it entails will trigger this wave of modernization that is so long overdue – at least since *Limits to Growth* called for it almost fifty years ago – and that, for reasons of short-sighted utilitarianism and political foolishness, has thus far failed to materialize. There is a lot of grassroots activity: the transition town movement is afoot all over the world; a degrowth movement has gained traction, particularly in rich countries; people are discussing social innovations, such as the unconditional basic income, and political means such as the successful divestment campaign. To ensure such developments aren't thwarted by new and old autocrats and their utterly backward-looking notions of society and politics, we must elevate our ecological and climate-policy discourse onto a new platform. For controlling climate change and an intact ecosphere is not an end in itself: it is about preserving the very prerequisites of the social environment that allows us to live well and in freedom. Looking at it this way, it is high time for the climate and eco-policy movement to repoliticize and to force the question of how we want to live and what kind of society we want to put on the political agenda – and to be ready to fight for it. We can no longer afford the luxury of leaving these issues to the agents of reactionary economic interests.

Harald Welzer, March 2017

1

A SHIP IN THE DESERT: THE PAST AND FUTURE OF VIOLENCE

> A slight clinking behind me made me turn my head. Six black men advanced in a file, toiling up the path. They walked erect and slow, balancing small baskets full of earth on their heads, and the clink kept time with their footsteps. [. . .] I could see every rib, the joints of their limbs were like knots in a rope; each had an iron collar on his neck, and all were connected together with a chain whose bights swung between them, rhythmically clinking.

This scene, from Joseph Conrad's *Heart of Darkness*, is set in the heyday of European colonialism, a little more than a hundred years ago.

The pitiless brutality with which early industrial countries satisfied their hunger for raw materials, land and power, and which left its mark on whole continents, cannot be seen in the landscape of the West today. The memory of exploitation, slavery and extermination has succumbed to democratic amnesia, as if the countries of the West had always been as they now are and their superior wealth and power were not built upon a murderous history.

Instead, the West prides itself on its inventiveness, its observance and defence of human rights, its political correctness and humanitarian stance when a civil war, flooding or drought threatens human life in some part of Africa or Asia. Governments order military intervention to spread democracy, overlooking that most Western democracies rest on a history of exclusion, ethnic cleansing and genocide. Whereas the asymmetrical history of the nineteenth and twentieth centuries has translated into luxurious living standards in Western societies, its violence still weighs heavily on many parts of the second and third worlds. Quite a few post-colonial countries have never made it to real statehood, let alone achieved prosperity; many have continued to experience the old exploitation under different conditions, and the signs often point towards further decline rather than significant improvement.

Climate change resulting from the insatiable hunger for fossil fuels in the early industrial countries hits the poorest regions of the world hardest – a bitter irony that flies in the face of any expectation that life is fair. Figure 1.1 shows the remnants of the *Eduard Bohlen* steamer, which were dug up after almost a hundred years from the sands of the Namibian desert. It played a minor role in the history of major injustice. On 5 September 1909, it ran aground in thick fog off the coast of the country that was then called German South-West Africa. Today the wreck lies 200 metres inland, the desert having gradually inched its way out to sea in the intervening period. Since 1891 the *Eduard Bohlen*

© *WikiMedia Commons*

had made regular stops in South-West Africa, carrying mail for the Woermann Lines based in Hamburg. But during the German colonial war against the Herero people, it was converted into a slave ship.

In this genocidal war, the first of the twentieth century, a large part of the native population of South-West Africa lost their lives, while concentration camps were built to house prisoners of war sold off as slave labourers. Right at the beginning of the war, the German colonial authorities offered Hewitt, a South African dealer, 282 captured prisoners, whom they had placed on board the *Eduard Bohlen*, not knowing what else to do with them until the Hereros were defeated. Hewitt jumped at the opportunity and managed to drive the price down to 20 marks per head, arguing pertinently that, since the men were already out at sea, he should not have to pay the normal price and customs duties for finished goods. So, on 20 January 1904 the *Eduard Bohlen* left Swakopmund bound for Cape Town, where the men were put to work in the mines.[1]

The Herero opened their campaign against colonial rule on the night of 11–12 January 1904, destroying a railway track and several telegraph lines and killing 123 German men in raids on farms.[2] After talks to suspend hostilities led nowhere, the imperial government in Berlin sent out an expeditionary force under the command of Lieutenant-General Lothar von Trotha, who immediately declared a war of extermination. His aim was not only to defeat the Herero militarily but to force them to fight in the wastes of the Omaheke desert, where he controlled the watering places and could simply watch them die of thirst.[3] This gruesome strategy was so successful that the Herero were reported to be cutting their animals' throats and drinking their blood, then squeezing the last drop of moisture out of the stomach contents. But they died all the same.[4]

The war continued after the Herero fighters were wiped out. The Nama, another native people, were to be disarmed and subjugated once German troops had established a presence in their area. The Nama, unlike the Herero, did not opt for pitched battles but resorted to guerrilla warfare, which presented the colonial army with considerable problems and impelled it to adopt measures that would find frequent application as the bloody century progressed. In order to rob the Nama guerrillas of support, the Germans murdered their women and children or herded them into concentration camps.

Violence occurs when there is pressure to take action that will produce results. If these are not forthcoming, new forms of violence are devised – and, if found to be effective, are repeatedly applied. Violence is innovative: it develops new forms and new conditions. Nevertheless, it took the German colonial army more than three years to crush the Nama people. The concentration camps, by the way, were not all under state control; private companies such as Woermann also ran a line in forced labour.[5]

This war was not only an example of the ruthlessness of colonial power but also a blueprint for future genocides; its strategic intent was total extermination, by working prisoners to death in concentration camps. At the time all this could be written of as a success story. The History Department of the General Staff proudly reported in 1907 that 'no trouble, no deprivation was spared to rob the enemy of the last remnants of his capacity to resist. He was driven from water-hole to water-hole like a beast hounded half to death, until, having lost all will, he fell victim to natural forces in his own country. The waterless Omaheke would complete the task begun by German force, the annihilation of the Herero people.'[6] That was a hundred years ago. The forms of violence have changed since then, and even more the ways of speaking about them. The West now uses force directly against other countries only in exceptional cases; today's wars involve long chains of agency, in which violence is delegated, reshaped and invisible. The conflicts of the twenty-first century are post-heroic, seemingly waged against the will of their actors. And since the Holocaust it has been impossible to speak with pride of exterminating whole peoples.

The *Eduard Bohlen* rusts away in the desert sands, and perhaps the whole Western social model, with all its democracy, freedoms, liberalism, art and culture, will appear to a historian of the twenty-second century as an equally strange relic from another world. If there are still historians in the twenty-second century . . .

This social model, so remorselessly successful for a quarter of a millennium, is becoming global and even drawing once-communist (just barely communist) countries into the intoxication of a standard of living complete with cars, flat-screen TVs and travel to faraway lands. But, at this very moment, it is also running up against operational limits that scarcely anyone has allowed for. The emissions caused by the energy-hungry industrial heartlands, and increasingly also by emerging economies, threaten to knock the climate out of kilter. The consequences are beginning to make themselves felt, but it is impossible to predict what lies ahead. The only certainty is that the unrestricted use of fossil fuels cannot continue for ever – not so much because they will eventually run out (which has been assumed for a long time) as because the climatic effects are uncontrollable.

When global warming due to atmospheric pollution rises above 2 degrees, the Western model will reach its limits of controllability. But there is more. An economy based on growth and resource depletion cannot function globally, since it logically implies that power is accumulated in one part of the world and applied in another. It is in essence particularist, not universal: everyone cannot exploit everyone else at the same time. Astronomy has not revealed any other planets within reach that might be colonized, and so the conclusion is inescapable that Earth is and will remain an island. Humans cannot simply pack up and move on when the land has been grazed bare and the mines have been phased out.

As resources start to run out, at least in many parts of Africa, Asia, Eastern Europe, South America, the Arctic and the Pacific islands, more and more people will have fewer and fewer means to ensure their survival. Obviously this will lead to violent conflicts among those who wish to feed off the same area of land or to drink from the same trickling water source, and just as obviously, in a not so distant future, it will no longer be possible to distinguish between war refugees and environmental refugees. New wars will be environmentally driven and cause people to flee from the violence, and, since they will have to settle somewhere, further sources of violence will arise – in the very countries where no one knows what to do with them, or on the borders of countries they want to enter but which have no wish at all to receive them.

This book is concerned with the question of how climate and violence go together. In some cases, such as the war in Sudan, the link is direct and palpable. In many other contexts of present or future violence – civil wars and simmering conflicts, reigns of terror, illegal migration, border disputes, unrest and insurgency – the connection between global warming and environmental conflicts is only indirect; it

makes itself felt mainly in the impact of climate change on global inequalities and living conditions, which varies enormously from country
to country.

But, whether wars in the twenty-first century are directly or indi-
rectly due to climate change, violence has a great future ahead of it.
We shall see not only mass migration but also *violent solutions to refugee
problems*, not only tensions over water or mining rights but also *resource
wars*, not only religious conflicts but also *wars of belief*. A hallmark of
the violence practised by the West is an effort to delegate as much of it
as possible to mercenaries or private security companies, or, in the case
of border control, to agencies operating in economically and politically
dependent countries that are the source of likely immigration. Security
policies designed to catch criminals before they commit a crime – to
shift the offence 'upstream', as it were – are part of this increasing trend
towards the indirect use of force. Whereas the West prefers this to the
kind of open war it has had to fight in Iraq or Afghanistan, social conditions in other countries are such that violence is a permanent and central factor that people have to face in eking out an existence. All this is
an expression of the asymmetry that became decisive for world history
two and a half centuries ago and has been deepened by the processes of
global warming.

Crystal ball gazing at future wars and conflicts would be an idle
pursuit, since social processes do not develop in linear fashion. We
cannot know today which migrations will cause the Siberian permafrost
to thaw, or which outbreaks of violence will trigger the flooding of a
megacity or a whole country. Still less can we know how people will
react in future to perceived threats, or what effects their reactions will
unleash. The same caveat applies to scientific attempts to understand
climate change and its likely consequences. It is all too easy to overlook
the fact that the arguments employed by climatologists – for example,
when they use precisely datable ice or rock layers to measure carbon
dioxide concentrations in the air or water – usually highlight processes
of change that can be shown to have occurred in history.

The future scenarios of greatest concern to the public therefore rest
upon data from the past. Similarly, this book will not so much speculate
on possible futures as analyse how and why violence has been exercised
in the past and present, in order to gauge what future lies in store for

us in the twenty-first century. Since violence is *always* an option for human action, it is inevitable that violent solutions will also be found for problems that have their origin in environmental changes.

The following pages will therefore not only offer accounts of climate wars but also investigate how people decide to kill others in war, or how their perception of the environment itself changes. For it is not objective circumstances themselves that determine how people behave, but the manner of their interpretation. It also needs to be asked why there are some wars that no one is interested in ending, and why increasing numbers are willing to trade their freedoms for promises of security.

The book starts by presenting a case that problems push for solutions when they are perceived as threatening. After a three-part investigation of killing – yesterday, today and tomorrow – it describes the 'shifting baselines' – that is, the fascinating phenomenon that people change their perceptions and values along with their environment, without even realizing that they are doing it.

The book naturally ends with a consideration of what might be done to prevent the worst from happening, or – put more loftily – to draw some practical lessons from history. Chapter 11, the first concluding chapter, examines the possibilities for cultural change that might permit an escape from the deadly logic of unstoppable growth and limitless consumption, one which does not make people feel that they have to sacrifice something. Optimists should stop reading at the end of this chapter and reflect on how a start might be made with the concept of a *good society* that is developed in it.

The second concluding chapter, chapter 12, outlines my own view of how things will shape up in the wake of climate change – a rather bleaker view, it must be said. The consequences will not only change the world but establish different social conditions from those we have known until now; they will also spell the end of the Enlightenment and its conception of freedom. But some books one writes in the hope of being proved wrong.

2

CLIMATE CONFLICTS

THE WEST – I

In 2005 a 'European Agency for the Management of Operational Cooperation at the External Borders of the Member States of the European Union' was brought into being. Behind this cumbersome, bureaucratic-sounding name lies a highly dynamic institution, which is supposed to make the EU's external border controls more robust and effective. At present it has a staff roughly a hundred strong and is planning for a pool of 500 to 600 border police, drawn from the member states and – a legal novelty – empowered to take on functions *outside* the EU. The agency also has at its disposal more than twenty aircraft, thirty helicopters and over a hundred ships, as well as elaborate equipment such as night vision devices and state-of-the-art laptops.

Since the official name is obviously too unwieldy, a catchier and evocative abbreviation has now been agreed upon: Frontex (from the French *frontières extérieures*). It works closely with other agencies such as Europol, advises local border police at key areas of illegal migration, and assists in 'joint removal operations of third-country nationals illegally present in the Member States'.[1] Such persons are those who, having somehow reached an EU/Schengen country and been refused asylum, are liable to be shipped back or, in official parlance, 'repatriated' to their country of origin.[2]

The Schengen Agreement, which came into force on 26 March 1995, has concentrated the frontier problem in states on the outer edges of the EU, passport-free travel now being the rule within the Schengen area. The 'country of origin regulation', however, requires asylum-seekers to give proof of political persecution if they come from a country classi-fied as 'safe'; and the 'third country regulation' provides that individuals who have, for example, managed to reach southern Spain from Sierra Leone and then moved on to Germany may be summarily sent back to Spain and refused the right ever to apply for asylum in Germany. Not surprisingly this has stepped up the pressure on the EU's Spanish and Portuguese as well as East European frontiers, while applications for asylum in Germany have fallen by a quarter since 1995. But it also raises the question whether, in view of the rising numbers of refugees (set to rise even more as a result of future climate change), it will be possible to secure the EU's external frontiers as effectively as this is done at present.

Frontex, established by a decree of the European Council, chalked up some early successes – for example, a major cut in the number of refugee boats landing in the Canary Isles. The refugees who make the 1,200-kilometre journey, mostly by dinghy, across the open sea from West Africa to Gran Canaria or Tenerife come from countries where the existing conditions make life virtually impossible. Displaced by dam projects or civil war, they have drifted into megacities like Lagos, where 3 million people live in slums and there is neither running water nor a sewage system. There they pay smuggling gangs an exorbitant sum for a place on an overcrowded, barely seaworthy boat, with no return ticket and a high risk of not surviving the trip.[3] Even so, some 30,000 made it alive to the Canaries in 2006, posing considerable problems for the authorities and the tourism industry there.

Other refugees try the Straits of Gibraltar, which, though only 13 kilometres across, have strong currents and dense traffic that make them no less hazardous. Many fail to reach the shores of Spain or Portugal, and those who do are usually shipped straight back; it is estimated that some 3,000 drowned in the attempt in 2006 alone. Frontex takes account of this, by defining one of its important tasks as 'preventing illegal entry in life-threatening conditions'.[4]

Since the reasons why refugees want to reach Europe at any price remain the same, and since their routes become more dangerous as Frontex increases its efficiency, the ideal form of control is to project the EU's borders outwards, preventing refugees from ever leaving the African continent. As long ago as October 2004 Otto Schilly, then German interior minister, suggested building reception camps in Africa and verifying there whether an asylum application was valid or not.[5] Most other EU interior ministers were not at all keen on the idea, and it also ran into protests from human rights organizations. The search for other solutions has been tough, as have negotiations with the African Union, so that there is still no alternative to the further tightening of border controls if such people are to be kept out of Europe. The situation in the Spanish exclaves of Ceuta and Melilla perfectly symbolizes the problem: border installations are continually being reinforced there, while refugees take ever more desperate measures to climb the fences; a mass storming in September 2005 involved approximately 800 people.

In the medium term, innovative technologies have given affected countries some relief: for example, a \$2 billon system on the US border with Mexico will make it possible to locate intruders by GPS and to livestream the information to the next police patrol, dramatically reducing the number of illegal entrants. In 2006 no fewer than 1.1 million people were arrested in this frontier zone. In September 2006, the House of Representatives approved a plan to build a 1,125-kilometre high-tech fence to bolster security further. It is true that the total length of the frontier is 3,360 kilometres, but it is assumed that such measures will deter many potential violators, since the remaining areas consist of barely negotiable desert or mountain; the shortest distance across on foot is 80 kilometres. Between 1998 and 2004, a total of 1,954 people died along the US–Mexican border.

America and Europe will have to do more in future to protect themselves from the inrush of the millions of refugees who are expected to follow climate change. Hunger, water problems, wars and desertification will exert incalculable pressure on the islands of West European and North American prosperity. The German government's Scientific Advisory Committee on Global Climate Change (WGBU) has pointed out that '1.1 billion people currently lack secure access to drinking water in sufficient quantity and quality'. This situation 'may grow worse in some parts of the world, because climate change may lead to great variations in precipitation and water availability.'[6]

In addition, some 850 million people around the world are under-nourished – a figure which experts think will grow considerably in the wake of climate-induced shrinkage of farmland. The ensuing distribution conflicts point to a greater risk of violent escalation, since further population movements will increase the number of so-called migration 'hot spots'. In this light, the WGBU urges, the promotion of development should be understood as a form of 'preventive security'.

Such trends give a foretaste of what will happen when climate change boosts the flow of refugees. Space and resource conflicts due to global warming will fundamentally alter the shape of Western societies in the next few decades; Frontex is a nugatory harbinger of things to come. Climate change is therefore not only an extremely urgent issue for environmental policy; it will also be the greatest social challenge of the modern age, threatening the very existence of millions of people and forcing them into mass migration. The question of how to cope with such flows will become inescapable as refugees of whatever provenance seek to enhance their survival chances by moving to better-off countries.

THE OTHERS

Over the past forty years, the desert in northern Sudan has moved 100 kilometres towards the once fertile south. The causes are, on the one hand, steadily decreasing rainfall and, on the other, the overgrazing of grassland, deforestation and ensuing soil erosion that makes the land infertile. Forty per cent of Sudan's forest has been lost since the country became independent, and at present a further 1.3 per cent is vanishing each year. For many regions, the United Nations Environmental Programme foresees total deforestation within the next ten years.

Climate models for Sudan point to a temperature rise of 0.5 degrees Celsius by 2030 and 1.5 degrees by 2060, while at the same time rainfall will decrease by an annual average of a further 5 per cent. This would mean a decline of 70 per cent in the grain harvest. Some 30 million people live in northern Sudan, and to appreciate what these figures mean we need to bear in mind that the country is already one of the poorest in the world; it also faces major ecological dangers, and a civil war has been simmering for the past half-century. There are 5 million so-called Internal Displaced Persons (IDPs), who have been systematically driven out of their native villages. Hostile militias not only kill people but also burn villages and forest, in order to prevent the return of those they 'displace'.

Most IDPs live in camps with virtually no infrastructure: no electricity, no sewer system, no running water, no medical care. The food supply is largely provided by international aid agencies. In order to cook, people there have already cut down all the forest for as much as 10 kilometres around. The bare land is dangerous: many women are raped and killed on their way to fetch wood. They are not robbed, because they have nothing anyone could take.

The Darfur region in the west presents a similar picture, perhaps even worse since fighting has spilled over the border from Chad and the Central African Republic. There are another 2 million IDPs in Darfur, most of whom live in rough and ready camps on the edge of large settlements and towns. In some areas the population has swollen by as much as 200 per cent since the outbreak of open war. The United States and the EU have been unable to agree whether it should be described as genocide, but somewhere between 200,000 and 500,000 people have been killed so far.

Sudan is the first case of a war-torn country where climate change is unquestionably one cause of violence and civil war. It used to be assumed that the violent effects of climate change were indirect, but where survival is at stake even small shifts can acquire explosive force. Then it is a question of struggle for existence. In a country where 70 per cent of the population lives on and from the land, there is a real problem if pasture and arable land begin to disappear. Nomadic herdsmen need pasturage for their animals, just as small farmers need land to grow cereals and fruit for themselves and their families. When the desert expands, livestock breeders use the land of farmers, or vice versa. There is a critical threshold below which survival interests can be asserted only by force.

From 1967 to 1973, and again from 1980 to 2000, Sudan suffered a series of catastrophic droughts, which were one reason for the major population movement and thousands of deaths from starvation. Of course, apart from ecological factors, there are many other causes of conflict – so many, in fact, that an attempt to present a historical overview leaves one feeling helplessly confused.[7] Varying in intensity and geographical location, war has marked the country's life throughout the half-century since 1955. Only between 1972 and 1983 was there a fragile state of peace. An agreement was finally signed in 2005 that ended hostilities in the south, but since 2003 war has been raging in Darfur, in the west of the country. Everyone agrees that the war situation is disastrous – though little or nothing is said about the shortage of drinking water, the catastrophic floods, wastewater contamination and rubbish mountains, or the environmental destruction caused by expansion of the oil industry. There is a direct link between climate change and war. To look at Sudan is to look into the future.

THE WEST – II

In Western countries, the public agitation that followed the three reports of the Intergovernmental Panel on Climate Change (IPCC) in early 2007 has since subsided. Yet, if anything, the global scenarios have become grimmer. We now know that some parts of the world will be winners as a result of climate change, since they will become more favourable for agriculture and more attractive as a holiday destination. Hotel managers on Germany's North Sea coast are happy enough, and the potential for wine-growing is expanding ever northward. The Stern Report, which considered the economic implications of climate change, seems to have caused a moment of horror, only to be rapidly followed by contemplation of the new economic prospects for the technologically advanced countries.[8] Lord Stern, the World Bank's former chief economist, calculated that the costs of unrestricted global warming would amount to between 5 and 20 per cent of world income (probably towards the upper end of this range), whereas the stabilization of CO_2 emissions until the year 2050 would cost no more than 1 per cent of GNP, well within the capacity of normal economic development to absorb it.

Naturally there are variations between branches of the economy: producers of renewable energy would benefit, while ski tourism would lose out. But all in all an immediate change in climate policy is thought to offer an economic opportunity for the West. Improved energy production, more efficient appliances of every kind, hybrid vehicles, biofuels, solar panels and much else besides promise a rosy future. There is even talk of a 'third technological revolution', although this overlooks the fact that the first and the second are the causes of today's problems.

Citizens show an environmental awareness when they use aircraft with a bad rather than a good conscience. But thinking about climate change can lead to unexpected reactions. Car drivers might go for a more powerful model than they originally intended, for the simple reason that the time for twelve-cylinder SUVs with 500 HP might soon be over.[9] So-called climate and sustainability funds advertise themselves with the argument that climate-related lines of business fare better in the long run than the equity market as a whole. Nor are the benefits only financial; it gives investors a good conscience to feel that they are doing something ecologically useful.[10]

What do such examples show? They show that people adapt to new environmental conditions – and that the adaptation may be rooted not in a general change of behaviour but in a modified perception of the problems. A study was published in 2005 on how fishermen relate to the continual decline in fish stocks in the Gulf of California. Despite sharp falls in the fish population and massive overfishing, the younger men tended to be less concerned than their older colleagues, because they no longer knew how many kinds of fish used to be caught in abundance off the coast.[11]

One can see the coming climate problem as an opportunity here and now, as a vague distant possibility or as a matter of no consequence, positioning oneself accordingly in relation to the diffuse threat. As in the case of the southern Californian fishermen, people's perceptions change within the changing present of which they are part, and when, nonetheless, dissonances arise there are many and various ways to overcome them. For that it may well be enough to have an awareness of the problem, which creates the sense that one is not indifferent, heedless or powerless in relation to it. One then changes one's attitude to the problem, not to its root cause.

We also need to realize that attitude and behaviour are two different things, linked to each other only loosely, if at all. One can have attitudes independently of the situation, beyond any reality checks or decision conditions, but actions generally take place under pressure and are determined by the requirements of the situation. This is why people often act in ways that contradict their attitudes – although, interestingly, they rarely have major difficulty in integrating such contradictions. One then compares one's own behaviour with the still worse behaviour of others, finding it absurdly trivial beside the scale of the problem or deciding to act differently in the future. All this serves to reduce the dissonance between what is morally recommended and what one actually does.[12]

Such dissonance reduction is not unimportant: it may be effective even in extreme situations – for example, when people are asked to kill other human beings and find it difficult to reconcile their task with their moral self-image. In a study of mass murderers, I tried to show how the men in question manage to bring murder and morality into harmony with each other.[13] They do this by operating within a mental frame of reference that allows no doubts to form about the necessity and rightness of their actions.

In Nazi Germany such men acted in groups, far from their usual social contexts, developing and ratifying common norms that were not subject to external criticism. They acted in what we might call 'total situations',[14] without the heterogeneity of everyday life in which changing roles, social contacts and demands exert a corrective or conflictual influence on one another. Even killing was regarded as a necessary task, but it caused them considerable problems, since the murder of defenceless men, and especially women, was totally at variance with their customary self-image. However, precisely because they could think of themselves as men with a task they were expected to fulfil, they were able to reconcile their grisly work with their moral image of themselves as 'good guys'.[15] For this reason, scarcely any of them developed massive feelings of guilt in later years, and most were able to integrate successfully and inconspicuously into postwar German society.

The most striking and depressing feature of the testimony given by SS mass murderers is that there is never any personal acceptance of guilt, only pointed remarks to the effect that they were put in the position of having to do gruesome things against their will and feelings – and that they themselves suffered from this. Here we find a hint of Himmler's ethic of 'decency',[16] which in its time not only directed action but enabled the perpetrators to see themselves as human beings capable of suffering from the unpleasant aspects of their work. After the war, this self-perception underpinned the biographical seamlessness that so strikes the reader of their statements.

Such examples of extreme violence show that, for people in real situations, what is in principle decisive are not the objective circumstances but their perceptions of reality and how they interpret them. Only interpretation leads to a final conclusion, and then in turn to action. Hence an action that appears from outside to be totally irrational, counterproductive or purposeless may be highly meaningful for those who perform it, even when they are damaged as a result. Mohammed Atta, for example, saw a point in flying an aircraft into the Twin Towers, and the Red Army Faction terrorist Holger Meins in starving himself to death in a prison hunger strike. Overly rational images of human beings, such as those which underlie many action theories, allow no space for such forms of *particular rationality*. Only when we investigate how individuals perceive reality can we understand why they draw conclusions that appear from the outside as completely bizarre.

This may also give us more insight into the peculiar fact, on the one hand, that there is little scientific doubt about the danger of climate-induced breakdown facing many societies in the years or decades to come, and, on the other, that no one really believes it.[17] There are a number of weighty reasons – apart from the remarkable capacity of human beings not to be troubled by contradictions in their behaviour – for this curious form of 'apocalypse blindness' (Günther Anders). The most important is the complexity of modern action chains and the incalculability of their consequences. Zygmunt Bauman calls this phenomenon 'adiaphorization': the disappearance of responsibility as a result of the division of labour in human action.[18]

One prerequisite of responsibility is that the parameters for methodical action are known. In modern, functionally differentiated societies, with their long action chains and complex webs of interdependence, it is in principle difficult for individuals to relate the eventual consequences of their actions to the controlled acts of volition for which they can take practical responsibility. For this reason institutions such as courts, mental hospitals or advisory centres have arisen to facilitate and regulate the production of such a relationship – which has a dynamic of its own, since here too a division of labour may mean that, as Heinrich Popitz put it, lack of staff competence 'fatally [compounds] lack of involvement on the part of those whose cases are being dealt with. The two together lead to the smooth excesses of indolence that we know.'[19]

The problem of fading responsibility thus appears hand in hand with processes of social modernization, as a kind of price for the development or rebuilding of the institutions in question; responsibility is converted into competence, and hence automatically also into incompetence. Perhaps more serious, however, is the fact that people can take responsibility only in so far as the temporal relationship between an action and its consequences allows for them to be held responsible. If the cause-and-effect relationship does not stretch beyond the lifetime of the actors involved, then one finds a certain kind of limited allocation of responsibility, such as the verdict of the International Court of Justice that, although Serbia did not commit genocide against the Bosnian Muslims, it failed to intervene to prevent it. Other examples would be damages for product liability, as well as certain areas of criminal law, insurance law, and so on. In each case, the question is how far someone was responsible for the consequences of an action and how far he could have anticipated them.

But what if the person who brought about the consequences of an action cannot be held responsible because he or she is no longer alive? In company law this problem is regulated by the recognition of a legal successor,[20] but the same does not apply when private individuals are involved. Moreover, things become considerably more complicated in the case of climate change, since the causes of the problems looming today go back at least half a century and could not have been foreseen in the state of scientific research at the time, and since strategies in the present to deal with consequences that cannot yet be anticipated may themselves have highly uncertain consequences that stretch into a distant future. The relationship between action and consequence is here trans-generational and can only be foreseen through the mediation of science. Its imperceptibility decreases the motivation for action and does not make it easier to allocate the blame for today's problems.

For it would logically imply holding a forty-year-old person responsible in 2012 for a problem whose causes predate his birth and whose solution can only come after his death – a person, therefore, who can have no direct influence on either the causes or the solution. Although he should be required to deal responsibly with the problem, it must be asked whether he is *able* to do this in any traditional sense and, if so, what form such responsibility might take in practice.

This question has an important bearing on democracy. What does the blurring of cause–effect chains imply for policy decisions and the general development of political awareness? How does the inbuilt lack of responsibility influence perceptions of the social consequences of, and possible solutions to, climate change? Which solutions that are now unthinkable to us will we consider possible in a few years' time?

ATTEMPTED SOLUTIONS

In the first third of the eighteenth century, when no one could imagine that in a couple of centuries the 'modern age' would convert its ideals of progress, rationality and efficiency into industrial mass murder, Jonathan Swift put forward a proposal for the eradication of poverty in Ireland. As things stood, the statistics showed a constant increase in the numbers of the poor, as well as a disproportionately low return for the economy from the sums invested in each child. Neither the children of the poor nor their parents would any longer have to face a grim existence of hunger, theft and begging or become a burden to others; 'instead of being a charge upon their parents, or the parish, or wanting food and raiment for the rest of their lives, they shall, on the contrary, contribute to the feeding, and partly to the cloathing of many thousands.' His solution?

I do therefore humbly offer it to publick consideration, that of the hundred and twenty thousand children, already computed, twenty thousand may be reserved for breed, whereof only one fourth part to be males. [. . .] That the remaining hundred thousand may, at a year old, be offered in sale to the persons of quality and fortune, through the kingdom, always advising the mother to let them suck plentifully in the last month, so as to render them plump, and fat for a good table. A child will make two dishes at an entertainment for friends, and when the family dines alone, the fore or hind quarter will make a reasonable dish, and seasoned with a little pepper or salt, will be very good boiled on the fourth day, especially in winter.

Swift then lists a whole series of positive effects that would ensue if children were treated as raw material for trade, gastronomy or the tanning industry; there would even be moral benefits, since abortion and infanticide would decline. In conclusion, he insists that he has no other motive in putting this forward than 'the publick good of my country, by advancing our trade, providing for infants, relieving the poor, and giving some pleasure to the rich'.[21]

This 'modest proposal' is not Swift's best-known satire, and its eerie quality comes from the way in which it logically develops a solution unthinkable in the moral climate of the West at the time. Given the twentieth-century rationalizations of genocide, however, complete with statistical material and moral arguments, we might think that Swift looks ahead to a time when all morality is no more than a residual category, which serves at best to reassure people before and after they act but sets no limits to their inhumanity.

The modern age has already witnessed many radical solutions to perceived social problems; how far these can go is shown by the 'final solution of the Jewish question', which involved straightforward annihilation of the Jews. Although we know from Turkey, Germany, Cambodia, China, Yugoslavia, Rwanda and Darfur, and from many instances of ethnic cleansing,[22] that radical solutions are always an option even for democratic societies, there is a tendency to interpret mass homicidal processes as a departure from the 'norm', as 'special cases'.

The few attempts to reverse the perspective, by asking what such catastrophes actually mean for the theory of society, have remained marginal and lacking in influence, whether philosophical (Günther Anders or Hannah Arendt, for example) or sociological (Norbert Elias or Zygmunt Bauman) in their approach. It is true that the sociology of catastrophe has found its way into homeland security thinking, but it has little place in social theory and is rarely met in either historical or political theory.

The social catastrophes of the twentieth century have clearly shown, however, that ethnic cleansing and genocide are not a deviation from

the path of modernity but possibilities that first arose with the development of modern society. From this point of view, such cataclysms as
the Holocaust should be understood not as a 'breakdown of civilization'
(Dan Diner) or a 'relapse into barbarism' (Horkheimer and Adorno)
but as a result of modern attempts to produce order and to solve perceived social problems. As Michael Mann shows in an extensive study,
ethnic cleansing and genocide are closely linked with modernization
processes, even though one would not think so at all from their displays
of seemingly archaic violence. The same might be said of Islamic terrorism, which is a reaction to modernization and therefore closely, if
negatively, bound up with it.

In *Modernity and the Holocaust*, Zygmunt Bauman explained why the
Holocaust has never become a systematic object for social science: first,
its perception as an event in Jewish history has defined it as a patho-
logical, rather than normal, problem of modernity;[23] and, second, it has
been attributed to an unfortunate set of circumstances, which, though
not so explosive in separation and usually tamed within the social order,
came together disastrously in interwar Germany. If, instead of reassur-
ing themselves in this way, sociologists had methodologically studied
the phenomenon, they would have discovered industrial mass extermination as a 'test case' for the latent potential of modernity, which provided new insight into its character and motive mechanisms. Bauman
notes the paradox that 'the Holocaust has more to say about the state
of sociology than sociology in its present shape is able to add to our
knowledge of the Holocaust.'[24] He therefore argues that the Holocaust
should be seen as something like a 'sociological laboratory', in which
'attributes of our society' are revealed which 'are not empirically
accessible in "non-laboratory" conditions'.[25]

Hannah Arendt impressively incorporated modern institutions such
as the concentration camp into the theory of society.[26] In her account,
the camps show that totalitarian societies and the dynamics of force
create new realities, in which the actors in question can integrate particular rationalities that otherwise appear meaningless or deranged into
comprehensive semantic systems. The standard instruments of social
science, geared to rational models of behaviour, are not calibrated for
the explanation of such systems.

Faced with such problems, historians read meaning back into events that may not have been there for people living at the time. One reason for this is that social history takes its bearings from the concept of understanding used in the human sciences, which involves 'empathetic observation of an earlier state of culture' and has 'its roots in an idealistic, culturally optimistic, conception of history'.[27] This kind of understanding proves ineffectual in relation to the criminal activities of modern totalitarian regimes, because the reality it has to deal with there is not understandable in any conventional sense.

KILLING MAKES SENSE

Nazi extermination policy took over from colonial warfare a variant of killing that did not simply eliminate individuals regarded as superfluous or damaging, but extracted maximum utility in the form of 'extermination through labour'. Thus, in the construction of giant underground facilities for the production of V-2 rockets or Me- 262 jet fighters, prisoners were worked so hard that they could expect to live no more than a few months. Labour could be used simultaneously both for exploitation and as a means of killing because there would always be a fresh batch of people who could be worked to death.

This naturally required planning and execution, so that killing in turn became work. 'Extermination through labour' had to be organized logistically and technically; there had to be a camp, with prisoners' barracks, sanitary facilities, staff accommodation, means of transport, electricity, water, railway tracks and wagons, and so on. For engineers and architects involved in this infrastructural development, extermination took on the form of a complex, business-like activity, with all the professional skills and efficiency concerns found in other contexts. This was also apparent in the organization of mass murder, such as that which took place in conquered Russian territories after 1941; here the normalization of killing meant that it was seen as a job like any other, and the need for professional problem-solving became part of an overall context of systematic tasks. The process was based on a division of labour: no one actually had to feel like a murderer, even though the killings were direct acts, not involving remote-controlled techniques such as gas chambers.

In the Nazi war of extermination, killing appeared rational to the perpetrators precisely because they saw it as 'dirty work', which could even be distressing to execute. The pressures that these 'necessary' duties placed on those who performed them were, as we have seen, a constant theme in Himmler's speeches as well as in their own conversation. Their very distress spared them a murderous self-image, both at the time of the killings and after the war was over. Instead, they were able to embed their acts in a meaningful frame of reference: 'I kill in the service of a higher cause'; 'I kill for future generations'; 'I kill differently from other people'; 'I get no joy from this *work*'. It is a psychological mode that makes people capable of doing unimaginable things – of doing just about anything, in fact. Human action, unlike that of creatures incapable of self-consciousness, is not subject to any instinctual or constitutional limitations.

Human beings exist within a social universe and should therefore consider *everything* to be possible. There are no natural or other limits on their behaviour, even when – as in the case of suicide bombers – it puts an end to their own life. We should therefore consider it sociological folklore when impressive-sounding anthropological claims are made that people develop hunting instincts, flock together and experience a lust for blood. In reality, violence has historically and socially specific forms, and it takes place in equally specific contexts of meaning.[28]

In the Nazi period, the higher meaning of killing was to help the racially pure society to achieve world domination. Rapid advances in technique led to the detachment and displacement of violence, replacing mass shooting with special extermination camps; the perpetrators no longer killed with their own hands, but transferred the task of killing to technology and the task of processing the dead to so-called functional prisoners. Zyklon B, in specially designed gas chambers, made it possible for the killers to exterminate without using violence *directly*.

Commemorations of the Holocaust are always associated with the idea that we can learn from history, that historians can provide the knowledge required to ensure that what happened then 'never happens again'. But why should it 'never happen again', when the evidence shows that human beings – even those of unquestionable intelligence and with a liberal education – are able to find meaning in the most anti-humanist theories, definitions, conclusions and actions, and to integrate these into their familiar conceptions of the world?

When we look at the wide historical panorama of violence and of people willing to kill, should we not assume that the Holocaust made it more, not less, likely that such things will happen again? In 1994 the majority in overpopulated Rwanda thought it made sense to kill 800,000 Tutsis in the space of three weeks. It is a modernist superstition that allows us to keep shrinking from the idea that, when people see others as a problem, they also think that killing them is a possible solution. This often has less to do with aggressiveness than with purposive thinking. According to Hans Albert, the production of weapons has 'in many cases been more useful than the production of tools' for problem-solving.[29] So, where does that leave us with 'learning from history'?

3

GLOBAL WARMING AND SOCIAL CATASTROPHES

In late August 2005 Hurricane Katrina hit the South-east of the United States, causing $80 billion of damage and flooding most of New Orleans. It was a catastrophe foretold: *Scientific American* had predicted the flooding back in October 2001.

After a number of levee breaches, 80 per cent of the city lay in water up to 7.60 metres deep; power cuts made it impossible to pump this away, while roads into and out of the city were blocked. The disaster relief effort was completely overstretched, and it was not long before looting began. The Superdrome, officially allocated as an emergency centre for the homeless, was soon crowded to overflowing, while the area around it witnessed outbreaks of violence that led the authorities to consider declaring martial law. The governor of Louisiana, Kathleen Blanco, called in the National Guard on 1 September and authorized them to open fire: 'These troops know how to shoot and kill', she said, 'and they are more than willing to do so if necessary and I expect they will.'

At New Orleans railroad station, cages were linked together with chains to form a temporary jail that held 700 prisoners, but for all their efforts the police and the National Guard were at first unable to get a grip on the situation. There were attacks on relief teams, shootings, rapes, shop looting, break-ins, and so on. It eventually took the army, with a force of 65,000 men, to restore law and order. There were also problems in evacuating people from the city.

The flood did not strike equally: while many prosperous residents were able to flee, it was the poor, mainly Afro-American, population who made up the bulk of those remaining. The effects also varied by neighbourhood. John R. Logan, who studied the social impact of Hurricane Katrina, confirmed that damaged areas of New Orleans were 45.8 per cent black, compared with 26.4 per cent for undamaged areas. Similar proportions were apparent in terms of poverty indicators.[1]

Altogether the destruction was so severe that some questioned whether the city should be rebuilt. The cataclysmic events saw the coining of the term 'climate refugee', to denote someone in flight from a weather-related disaster. It is estimated that 250,000 former residents of New Orleans settled elsewhere in the country; a year after the hurricane, roughly a third of whites and three-quarters of blacks had not returned, with the result that the population structure is today markedly different from before. This is also true of the city's political geography.[2]

What is usually known as a natural disaster – for example, flooding as a result of severe weather conditions – proved to be something quite different in the case of New Orleans. From the ignorance of the dangers to the woeful adequacy of the flood defences, from the barely controllable outbreak of anarchy to the extreme reactions of the security forces, from the social inequality in the aftermath of Katrina to the creation of a new category of refugee and a new social demography of the city: the whole concatenation of events would be much more accurately described as a *social disaster*.

Actually 'natural disaster' is a bit of a misnomer, since nature does not experience anything as a disaster. But it can produce events that are disastrous to humans and have unexpected social consequences that exceed people's capacity to control them. Two points should be made in connection with New Orleans. First, similar extreme weather events, related to global climate change, will affect other coastal cities in the years and decades to come, and the management of them will not everywhere be better than in the spectacular failure we saw in New Orleans. The fact that, early on – when the effects of the hurricane still seemed manageable – the richest country on earth was forced to solicit help from abroad shows that disasters quickly reveal weaknesses, gaps and makeshifts that are invisible in normal times.

This brings us to the second interesting lesson. Social disasters lay bare what goes on behind the scenes in society, revealing its combination of functionality and dysfunctionality; or, to change the metaphor, they open a window on life beneath the surface of society and the assumptions of normality on which it rests. Disasters light up inequalities in life chances that are institutionally cushioned (and sealed off in respective neighbourhoods and sectors of work) in the normal run of events; they uncover administrative shortcomings that exist even when unchallenged; and they demonstrate that violence is always available as a possible course of action. All this becomes visible at a time when the usual forms of social interaction break down. As New Orleans shows, there do not even have to be many dead and injured.[3]

Close observation of social disasters can thus afford greater insight into the real functioning of society than one would gain from the thesis that its essence is displayed in normal situations. For what we see in disasters is not an exceptional state of society but simply a dimension that remains hidden in everyday life. This being so, we should study not only what holds societies together but also what makes them fall apart.[4]

Climate change will increase the frequency of social disasters, which will bring about temporary or lasting states of society, or social formations, about which nothing is known because too little interest has been taken in the subject up to now. Social and cultural theory is fixated on normality and blind to disasters,[5] but a glance at the cultural history of nature is enough to convince us that it must bring climate change within its purview.[6] Present-day social changes – from the climate war in Darfur to the Inuits' loss of habitat – highlight the startling immateriality of social and cultural theory, and it is high time that it modernized itself and found a way back from the world of discourse and systems to the strategies through which social beings try to control their fate. The fact is that a considerable part of the world's population will face increasing difficulties in the future, as desertification, soil erosion and salination, oceanic acidification, river contamination, aggradation and overfishing limit their survival chances.

All these disastrous trends are manmade in origin and fraught with social consequences. Conflicts break out between those who put too much pressure on scarce resources and those who have to leave the affected areas and settle elsewhere. There is no future for many devastated industrial regions, such as the area around the Aral Sea in the former Soviet Union, where pollution has sent cancer rates rocketing and life expectancy has fallen since the 1990s from sixty-four to fifty-one.[7]

Such palpable evidence makes it all the more astonishing that nearly all academic studies, models and prognoses regarding the phenomena and consequences of climate change have been in the *natural sciences*. In the social and cultural sciences, it is exactly as if such things as social breakdown, resource conflict, mass migration, safety threats, widespread fears, radicalization and militarized or violence-governed economies did not belong to their sphere of competence. In the history of science there has probably been no comparable situation in which a scenario of such change in large parts of the world, based on solid scientific evidence, has been regarded with such equanimity by social or cultural theorists. It points to analytical deficiencies as well as a lack of a sense of responsibility.

UNDERCOMPLEXITY

This lack of interest shifts the responsibility onto the shoulders of natural scientists, who have neither the professional competence nor the authority to measure the social dimension or consequences of climate change. They may be familiar with complexity, indeed admirably so, but not with the processes through which human beings construct reality or with the role that the most diverse frameworks, cultural forms and social-historical models play in the perception of problems and solutions. Professionally speaking, natural scientists do not have a clue about such things, nor does anyone expect them to. But, as members of society, they have an ordinary awareness of social problems and solutions, and they regularly bring this to bear in the final chapter of their otherwise profound and enviably helpful books about social collapse, the drying up of rivers, the melting of ice, and so on – where, after presenting all the apocalyptic facts, they consider what can be done about them.

The idea that human beings can produce situations about which *nothing* can be done is completely alien to scientists and technologists. Moreover, they are usually unable to grasp how different levels of action knit together, how collective reason may combine with individual unreason (or individual reason with collective unreason), how feelings intrude into the rational goals of action, how society may do things that no individual intended, and how these may form part of new realities and generate new problems requiring action.

In the books of such authors as Tim Flannery,[8] Fred Pearce[9] or Jill Jäger,[10] one is therefore struck by the disturbing contrast between their sharpness of analysis and the paltriness of their proposed solutions. When Flannery, for instance, at the end of his disheartening study of climate change, recommends buying a smaller car or sticking to a good old hand drill instead of a power-driven device, his advice falls hopelessly short of the complexity of the problems he has been describing. Nor could it be otherwise, since Flannery's professional competence covers the physical, not the social, aspects of the problem. Climate change – and here Flannery's study is a perfect case in point – is an object for natural science when the question is how it came about and how it is likely to develop. But its consequences are a question for social and cultural theory, since those consequences *are* nothing other than social and cultural.

WHO ARE 'WE'?

Another example may serve to make this clearer. Apart from neuroscientists, no one makes more use of the first person plural than the authors of books on climate change and other topical environmental questions. 'We' have caused this or that; 'we' must stop doing such and such if 'our' world is to be saved. But no one knows who lies behind this 'we'.

At a very high level of aggregation, the word 'we' stands for the whole of humanity, though 'humanity' is not an actor but an abstraction. In reality there are billions of subjects from different cultural backgrounds, endowed with highly diverse economic opportunities and political resources, who act within a number of complex life-communities. No socially identifiable 'we' links together a landless

Chinese farm labourer and the chairman of a multinational energy corporation; they inhabit completely different social worlds, each with its particular demands and, above all, its particular rationality. Does the company chairman share a future in the first person plural with his own grandchildren, not to speak of the Chinese labourer's? Of course not – any more than he shares the same social reality with a child refugee in Darfur, a mujahideen in Afghanistan or a child prostitute in Tirana.

The use of 'we' assumes a collective perception of reality that does not actually exist, even in relation to a global problem such as climate change. For global warming affects people very differently: while some have long-term fears for the future of their grandchildren, others watch their own children die here and now. If 'all of us' (and therefore the readers of this book) decided overnight to live in a 'climate-neutral way', never causing more CO_2 emissions than are strictly necessary, another 'we' – let us say, the group of Chinese energy supply officials – would sabotage 'our' efforts with each of the 1,000 megawatt coal-burning power plants that are coming into service in China each week, which emit 30,000 tonnes of carbon dioxide per day.[11]

The political evasiveness of the abstract 'we', blithely unconcerned with effects or the influence of power relations, turns into ideology. An account of the world in the first person plural is anyway not possible, since we know how the cultural history of nature has led to radically diverse conditions of life around the globe.[12]

OLD ENVIRONMENTAL PROBLEMS

By the seventeenth century, only a few insignificant remains of the erstwhile forests survived in the islands, most of them untended and decaying. The great fires were now lit on the other side of the ocean. It is not for nothing that Brazil owes its name to the French word for charcoal.

W. G. Sebald, *The Rings of Saturn*

Climate change not only intensifies existing global asymmetries that may result in wars and outbreaks of violence; it also strengthens environmental trends that originally had nothing to do with climate change. The current debate, vitalized by the Fukushima disaster, focuses on the question of energy production and CO_2 emissions. Other environmental issues that must now be described as 'classical' – sea pollution, soil contamination and declining biodiversity, the burning of rainforests, drying up of rivers or disappearance of lakes – have taken a back seat, although the cause of them too is the insatiable hunger for resources in societies fixated on growth. As Dennis Meadows, one of the authors of the legendary *Limits to Growth*, repeatedly stressed, climate change should therefore not be understood only as a symptom of the resource overuse that is leading at ever greater speed to disaster. The difference with the ecological debates of forty years ago is that they referred not only to energy but also to the social practices in which it was employed and had an impact. Theorists such as André Gorz, Ernst Friedrich Schumacher, Hans Jonas, Petra Kelly, Carl Amery or Ivan Illich always had the political dimension of ecological issues in mind – a viewpoint which, given the often narrowly technological focus on sufficiency and efficiency, should be reintroduced in today's world. Efficiency gains alone do not solve any resource problems, and indeed they are often achieved at the cost of a higher input of material. Since they never do more than limit the rate at which natural resources are plundered, even a 'greener' growth-oriented economy would systematically destroy the foundations on which it is built. Thus, 2010 was the year with the highest energy consumption in the history of mankind, up 5.6 per cent on 2009 – but such records do not last long and therefore pass unnoticed. Next year will be another one with the highest-ever energy consumption. The same goes for the other side of the use of fossil fuels: emissions that have an impact on the climate also rose again in 2010, by 5.8 per cent.

The targets of the Kyoto Protocol, which is due to be replaced in 2012 with a new emissions regime (though the deadline is likely to be extended), will not have been met by many of the countries that ratified it. But public opinion is less aware of this than of America's, Australia's or China's stubborn refusal to accept supranational regulation in general.

Whichever classical theme of the environmental movement one takes – loss of countryside to motorways or new towns, growth of individual transport, global increase in greenhouse gas emissions, ocean pollution, misshapen infants in specially affected areas such as the Aral

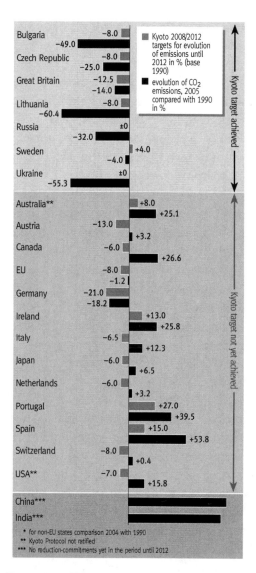

Figure 3.1   Kyoto targets: the 'is' and the 'ought'
Evolution of greenhouse gas emissions, % (2005 compared with 1990)

Sources: United Nations Framework Convention on Climate Change, Deutsches Institut
für Wirtschaftsforschung.

Sea – the problem is becoming worse as a result of globalization, yet it appears largely remote from everyday consciousness. This is not the place to dwell on the sometimes hair-raising ecological trends in the former Eastern bloc, as well as in the United States,[13] but it should be noted that some American states (California, for example) and European countries (e.g., Germany and Austria) have been playing a pioneering role. They have sometimes scored major local successes, although they cannot change the global trend towards greater resource consumption and environmental pollution.

What has mainly improved in the past thirty years is not the problem but consciousness of the problem. This raises the question of how the necessary changes in behaviour can be brought about if the ecological problems such as global warming appear so insurmountable; the very limited scope to control these always produces a motivational block, especially as the results of any individual action are negligible. There is also the far from minor point that the world's population is gener-ally expected to reach 9 billion by the middle of the century[14] – which would mean that increasing numbers of people will be in competition for dwindling resources. There are currently as few solutions to the related problems as there are to those resulting from global inequality and injustice.

All of these trends – from manmade climate change, through non-renewable resource consumption and ongoing habitat destruction, to demographic growth – are *social* problems. So too are all other ecologi-cal problems social, in so far as they affect the conditions for human life and are perceived as problems only by human beings. Shrinking biodiversity in the world's oceans, rivers and lakes, in rainforest and savannah, is not a problem for nature, which is completely indifferent to whether polar bears and gorillas or jellyfish and green algae are part of it. Plants and animals have no awareness that their habitat is disap-pearing; they simply die. Human life communities register ecological problems, however, because humans are unique in being conscious not only of the past but also of the future. This alone creates a faint hope that their insight into what has gone before will lead them to think about what they will no longer be able to do.

4

A BRIEF SURVEY OF CLIMATE CHANGE

The decisive factor for the violence and other social problems that may result from climate change is not the rise in average temperatures or sea levels over the coming decades (these consequences are already with us and will become more intense to a degree that will vary with the scale and drama of the change); nor is it the extent to which climate trends are manmade or represent a natural fluctuation such as has often happened before in the history of the planet.

As a social scientist, I shall base myself in this section mainly on the reports of the Intergovernmental Panel on Climate Change (IPCC), since these were subject to pre-publication policy debates that filtered out anything thought to be exaggerated. As is well known, such negotiations among governments are concerned less with the truth than with interests – for example, with the obligations that a particular finding might entail for individual countries. What emerges at the end of this process, after it has brought the scientists involved to the brink of self-suppression, is therefore the most conservative imaginable assessment. Since the policymakers are engaged in warding off obligations and constraints, the analysis is geared to that which is virtually beyond doubt and contains the least possible speculation.

Furthermore, the public discussion has mostly overlooked the fact that the IPCC reports make scant use of models, prognoses and assumptions but rest their case on *existing* measurements of rising temperatures and ocean levels or shrinking glaciers. The reports are therefore empirically focused more on the past and present than on the future, leaving what will happen much more open the further they look ahead. In most regions in question, however, the effects of climate change are already palpable, even without the complicated measurement methods and results of oceanologists, meteorologists and palaeobiologists. So, from today's vantage point, what are the main aspects and likely consequences of climate change?

The IPCC report published in February 2007 assumed with 90 per cent probability that the currently observable climate change is the result of human activity, mostly caused by emissions of so-called greenhouse gases throughout the period since the Industrial Revolution. Fossil fuel use for industry and transport produced the CO_2, while agriculture (especially livestock farming) emitted the methane and nitrous oxide. Both carbon dioxide and methane levels in the atmosphere are now higher than at any time in the past 650,000 years.

The warming of the global system is beyond all doubt, the authors write; it can be read from the increase in air and ocean temperatures, the melting of glaciers and permafrost, and the rise in sea levels. Average yearly temperatures since 1850 (the year when measurements first began) show that the eleven warmest years were all in the period from 1995 to 2006.[1] Ocean temperatures have increased down to a depth of 3,000 metres.[2] And the rise in sea levels has been compounded by the effects of climate change, since higher temperatures enlarge the water surface and the melting of polar ice and glaciers increases the amount of seawater. This is one of the simplest interactions; the fact that there are much more complex ones, some with feedback mechanisms, makes prognoses intrinsically difficult. The observable effects of climate change already include displaced rainbelts and more frequent rainfall, desertification and extreme weather events such as heatwaves, storms and heavy downpours, including in regions where they have not previously existed.[3]

The last time that known temperatures in the polar region were so high was 125,000 years ago. The IPCC forecasts that, at present rates of emission, average global temperatures will rise by 0.2 degrees Celsius per decade – more if emission rates continue to increase. The various scenarios would result in a temperature increase by the end of the century ranging from a minimum of 1.1 degrees to a maximum of 6.4 degrees. What that implies is not a gradual drift but sharp changes in ways of life. The rise in ocean levels will be between 18 and 59 centimetres.

The future will bring a further melting of ice cover, glaciers and permafrost; typhoons and hurricanes will occur more frequently and in unusual places; rainfall will become more likely in the North and less likely in the South; and ocean currents will probably change direction as a result of interaction among these processes.[4] Although, for understandable reasons, it is not possible to say exactly what will happen when and where, it is evident that all this will have consequences for plant and animal life, and therefore for human nutrition and survival chances.

In April 2007 the IPCC published its conclusions about the highly varied impact that climate change is expected to have on societies around the world, depending not only on its direct consequences but also on the capacity of each society to cope with them. Northern Europe, for example, with its high living standards and good levels of nutrition, is well protected against disasters and in a position to repair any material damage. But a region like the Congo, which already suffers from poverty, hunger, deficient infrastructure and violent conflicts, will be hit much harder by environmentally determined negative changes.

A number of factors come into play. The worst-affected countries will probably be those with the least capacity to deal with the consequences, while the ones that will escape most lightly, or even profit from the climate changes, will be the ones with the greatest resources to cope. What is more, the hardest-hit populations will probably be those with the lowest greenhouse gas emissions in the past, whereas the big polluters will suffer the least from the consequences. Here we see the signs of a historically new global injustice: climate change will deepen the existing asymmetries and inequalities of life chances.

Africa is the continent most vulnerable to climate effects, on account of its widespread poverty and tendency to political chaos and the presence of violent conflicts in a number of regions. The IPCC predicts that, by the year 2020, a total of 75 to 250 million people will not have sufficient access to safe drinking water. In some regions only a minority

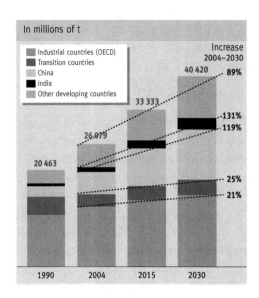

Figure 4.1   CO$_2$ emissions by region, in millions of tonnes (including trapped)

Source: International Energy Agency.

of the population has this today: 22 per cent in Ethiopia, 29 per cent in Somalia, 42 per cent in Chad.[5] Agriculture will also suffer from lack of rainfall and declining groundwater levels; some estimate that by 2020 as much as half the normal yield will be lost in certain regions. Nor does the state of fishing look any better; species are dying out in lakes and rivers, while coastal regions are at risk from flooding.[6] Diseases such as malaria and yellow fever will spread in previously unaffected areas in East Africa and elsewhere.

In *Asia*, as many as a billion people may be affected by shortages of drinking water by the year 2050; and in addition the melting of Himalayan glaciers will lead to ecological changes, floods and avalanches. Food production may rise in many parts of East and South-East Asia, but fall in a number of other areas (Central and South Asia). Diarrhoeal diseases due to flooding will increase, and rising water temperatures will make cholera epidemics more likely in coastal regions. Coping capacities vary from country to country, but are often completely inadequate.

Australia and New Zealand will also suffer (to some extent they already do) from considerable water problems. The main effect here of climate change will be on biodiversity. But, since both countries have good capacities for controlling and coping with disasters, the social consequences will not be as great as in Africa or Asia.

South America is affected by falling groundwater levels and desertification. Clearing and burning of rainforest, which results in soil erosion, will accentuate the effects of climate change, as will the decline of biodiversity. Coastal regions will be at risk of flooding as in all other parts of the world. Capacities for controlling and coping will vary from country to country.

In the *polar regions* the social consequences of climate change will be comparatively minor, since scarcely anyone lives there. On the other hand, the effects of warming will be especially acute. The melting of sea ice, the thawing of permafrost and increased coastal erosion will have an impact not only on human and animal life but also on sea levels, evaporation, and so on. Warming will have a number of positive effects: improved land use potential, greater access to raw materials beneath the ice, and the opening of new shipping routes. But conflicts over sovereignty claims and exploitation rights are already beginning to loom.

The population of *island groups* in the Caribbean and the Pacific is at massive risk from climate change – not only because it will lose income from fishing and tourism, but above all because many islands will become uninhabitable. Compensation claims will be problematic, and, as we know from history, resettlement will carry a major potential for conflict.

For *Europe* the consequences of climate change will be relatively benign, although melting glaciers, extreme weather events, landslides and floods will not be good for agriculture and the tourism industry. Here too a North–South gap will be apparent. Whereas Northern Europe may benefit from new possibilities for growing fruits, cereals, wine, and so on, Mediterranean regions will be increasingly liable to drought and water shortages. In general, however, European countries have an excellent capacity for limiting or offsetting the effects of climate change, or even for turning them to advantage. Countermeasures such as improved coastal defences have already been introduced. Here the social consequences will be mainly indirect, especially in relation to pressure on borders, greater insecurity, and so on.

The same is true of *North America*. Agricultural prospects will improve in many regions, but many others will face flooding, water shortages, worse conditions for winter tourism, and so on. Heatwaves may also become a common problem, and coastal areas will suffer from hurricanes and floods. Here, as in Europe, measures are already being taken to prepare for the future.[7] As for coping capacities, the same remarks apply as for Europe, with regional variations.

The overall picture, then, is of an uneven distribution of the social consequences of global warming. The resulting injustice, both geographical and generational, contains a serious middle-term potential for conflict.

TWO DEGREES MORE

Climate researchers are agreed that the social and economic consequences of climate change may still be controllable, if global warming can be restricted to 2 degrees in excess of levels before the industrial age – that is to say, 1.6 degrees higher than today. As Fred Pearce calculates, there were 600 billion tonnes of carbon dioxide in the atmosphere at the end of the last ice age, and that level remained more or less constant right up to the Industrial Revolution. Manmade emissions have since raised the figure to 800 billion tonnes, and without further acceleration it would probably rise no higher than the tolerable maximum of 850 billion tonnes. At present, however, another 4 billion are being added each year, which means that the sustainable maximum will be reached in the next ten years – without even allowing for higher rates of emission in newly industrializing countries. So, to keep the temperature rise to 2 per cent is a realistic goal only if global emissions 'peak within five years or so, falling by at least 50 per cent within the next half-century, and carrying on down after that'.[8] Whether one thinks this achievable will depend on one's confidence in the power of collective reason.

5

KILLING YESTERDAY

APOCALYPSE

The years around AD 520 were catastrophic for the Eastern Roman Empire. Constantinople and other cities were devastated by a series of earthquakes, the Euphrates brought repeated floods, and the empire had to endure military conflicts with the Persians, the Bulgars and the Saracens. It also had to contend with internal revolts, and to cap it all the appearance of Halley's Comet spread open panic. Mischa Meier, the German historian of antiquity, lists all these cataclysms and notes something very strange: contemporary sources paint a detailed and dramatic picture of the disasters, both local and wider in scale, but do not give the impression that they came out of the blue or were seen as particularly threatening.[1]

Twenty years later, around AD 540, a whole cascade of disasters poured over the same area. Again a comet of ill omen appeared in the skies, again Bulgar raids and natural devastation took place in conjunction with each other. The Ostrogoths reconquered large parts of the empire in the prelude to a gruelling war that caused numerous civilian casualties. The capital was once more hit by earthquakes, and plague caused 'death on a scale never seen before. Trade and crafts came to a standstill in Constantinople and other cities. The infrastructure of the empire broke down, whole villages were emptied of people.'[2]

Here the sources give eloquent testimony of the panic, fear and dramatic sense of threat. What, Meier asks, explains this striking difference in perceptions over such a short space of time? His answer is astounding but illuminating. People expected the world to end sometime around the year 500; it was an idea based on the calculations of Christian chroniclers, on the experience of the fall of the Western Roman Empire, and on the reign of Emperor Anastasius (whose very name meant 'resurrection'). This was the frame of reference in which the disasters of 520 to 530 were interpreted; people were mentally prepared for the Apocalypse and explained events as harbingers of it. The patterns of interpretation and orientation, Meier notes trenchantly, probably ended in dissonance only when 'the charted disasters had not come to pass, when external conditions had not changed'.[3]

Of course, the fact that the world did not come to an end ensured that the reference framework was different twenty years later. Impending apocalypse was no longer seen as the reason for the increased number of disasters: 'the perception of events', Meier writes, 'could no longer be matched with the prevailing patterns of orientation.'[4] This led to considerable criticism of the emperor, who was held responsible for the threatening events.

This is an interesting example, which convincingly shows that disasters are not events predefined in certain ways; it is only in the perceptual horizon of those affected by them that they are interpreted, or not interpreted, as full of menace. Erving Goffman's classic *Frame Analysis*[5] presents in detail this argument that certain socially moulded patterns or 'frames' are available for the understanding of events and their emotional significance – that it is not the sheer objectivity of an event, but these principles organizing its perception, which shape how people respond to it.

Psychology, social psychology and the cognitive brain sciences are in agreement that people take decisions on the basis of complex assumptions, only a small number of which reach the level of conscious reflection. Their reference framework, then, includes not only conscious and unconscious perceptions and interpretations but also background assumptions ('this is so', 'this is how it is done', etc.), socialized habits and forms of behaviour, situational requirements, the actions, demands and orders of others, and so on.

The interpretation of perceived threats and the motivation for conclusions and decisions are therefore shaped by cognitive appraisals that may be confirmed and strengthened by interactions and group processes, and vice versa. Relevant in this respect are the situations in which the players find themselves, their socially acquired patterns of perception and interpretation, and the changes that various threats, wars or other disasters bring about in these patterns. More abstract conceptions and reality models also come into play, concerning the end of the world, what is and is not to be expected, war and peace, justice and injustice, responsibility, retribution, and so on. Such factors, at different levels of specification, form the reference framework for the situational perceptions, conclusions and action decisions of the individuals concerned. Hence, one and the same situation may be perceived and interpreted completely differently by different persons, or at different points in time. Since the chain of disasters in AD 520 was generally thought to confirm what people expected at the time, they did not give rise to interpretive endeavours; those around 540, however, did not conform to expectations and triggered widespread panic. Only when events, experiences or developments can no longer be understood within the prevailing frame of reference do orientation problems arise and create a need to explain what is going on. In what is felt to be a climate of disorder, a desire naturally grows for overviews and transparency – and, of course, for order.

DEFENCES

'I do not remember the date. But people said the president was dead, and he was our parent. Then the Tutsis immediately fled. We saw houses burned here and there. We were angry after the death of our parent. The war began. The Tutsis were killed.'[6] These words refer to one of the shortest and most terrible genocides of the twentieth century, when 500,000 to 800,000 people were killed in Rwanda between April and July 1994. Most of the victims belonged to the Tutsi group, which was reduced by three-quarters in the space of just thirteen weeks. But the mass murder did not strike only at Tutsis; Hutus who were critical of it, or who were considered traitors because they were married to Tutsis or for some other reason, suffered the same fate.

It has now been well documented that the sharp differentiation between the two groups was largely a product of the colonial age, and that in particular the Tutsi minority owed its better social position to the higher value that the colonial authorities attached to it. In the years before the genocide, a widespread sense of social discrimination among the Hutus turned into a perception of threats and finally culminated in a total enemy-image of the Tutsis. At some point the Hutu majority came to perceive a genocidal threat from the Tutsis and, feeling that they had to do all in their power to resist it, actually turned it into its opposite. When President Habyarimana was assassinated on his aircraft on 6 April 1994, the mass killing began.

'After the crash, people said our parent was dead. . . . Since he loved us and we loved him, when he was dead, everyone was affected, and we thought we were finished. People said the enemy had attacked us and that we had to defend ourselves.'[7] As we see, both this participant and the previous one were able to attach a meaning to the mass murder: there was a deadly attack that had to be resisted. The genocide of the Tutsi was perpetrated by ordinary members of the Hutu majority, although it was mostly army officers, senior state officials and administrators who gave the orders and compiled the lists of those to be killed. The number of murderers was in the six figures; they usually killed with machetes handed out to them beforehand.

A number of violent conflicts and massacres between Hutus and Tutsis had already taken place since the 1960s. It is remarkable that the two groups were not at all segregated from each other – on the contrary, their daily coexistence was largely unproblematic, and they worked together and made friends with each other. So why this outbreak of mass murder along ethnic lines? The quotations have already suggested that Hutus felt there to be a problem, but it may well be that these two killers were not aware of the deeper reasons for their feeling.

Both explain the mass murder by the same personal event: the assassination of their president. They saw him as *one of theirs*, like a family member, a father-protector who had responsibility for them; they therefore logically saw the assassination as a life-and-death crisis for themselves. However unjustified this sense of threat may seem from outside, it plays the most important role in the subjective motivation of perpetrators of genocide, mass killings and massacres.[8] Even if the real majority–minority relationship shows this to have been a grotesque reversal of any actual threat – 90 per cent of the Rwandan population were Hutus – people reacted as if they had to attack and kill in order to save their own and their family's lives. In this way a sense of fear was bent around and itself became a deadly reality. The Hutu *believed* there was a lethal threat from the Tutsis, as anti-Semites in Germany in the 1930s and 1940s believed in a Jewish world conspiracy,[9] or the followers of Slobodan Milošević believed that the Serbs were in mortal danger. Even when the threat perception was totally irrational, it resulted in the real deaths of countless numbers of people. Irrationality of motives has no influence on the rationality of action. The Holocaust is the most disturbing proof of William Thomas's theorem: 'When people define situations as real they become real in their consequences.'

BODY COUNT

During the Vietnam War, American soldiers engaged in several massacres of the civilian population. The best known and most horrific of these, at the village of My Lai, was the subject of several judicial investigations. The interrogation records express in grotesque terms the soldiers' perception that they were killing *enemies*. The following extract gives us a flavour:

A: I held my M-16 on them.
Q: Why?
A: Because they might attack.
Q: They were children and babies?
A: Yes.
Q: And they might attack?
A: They might have had a fully loaded grenade on them. The mothers might have throwed them at us.
Q: Babies?
A: Yes.
Q: Were the babies in their mothers' arms?

A: I guess so.

Q: And the babies moved to attack?

A: I expected at any moment they were about to make a counterbalance.[10]

From the outside such statements appear completely absurd, or deranged. But a reconstruction of how US soldiers saw things in Vietnam shows an extreme underlying loss of orientation and control, which resulted from the fact that they were unprepared for jungle warfare and unable to cope with the Vietcong's guerrilla techniques – and therefore that they experienced the whole operational space as threatening. The fantasy of the grenade-wielding baby, which occurs in a number of statements, evidently had its roots in this perception of a diffuse, all-embracing threat from an invisible enemy. It testifies to extreme disorientation and a sense that the surrounding threat was total and incalculable. Anyone not part of the 'we group' was a disguised enemy ready to do anything.

This disorientation occurred against the background of a military strategy that released soldiers from the rules of conventional warfare, making the killing of civilians a perhaps regrettable but by no means forbidden accompaniment of battle. It was the strategy of 'search and destroy', 'free fire zones' and 'body counts',[11] which measured military success by the number of dead bodies. This deadly mixture makes the fantasy of Vietcong babies less unfathomable. To treat the casualties as an undifferentiated mass can be functional, since it increases the sharpness of vision.

Nor were frontline soldiers the only ones affected by such fantasies. In the US political and military leadership too, the unexpectedly disastrous course of the war spread an irrational perception of reality, so that it was assumed, for example, that enemy fighters would sooner or later desert the Vietcong and hand final military superiority to the Americans. As one contemporary observer wrote, the chiefs of staff and the president's advisers were 'like men in a dream', incapable of making a realistic assessment of the consequences of their action.[12]

'Body count' statistics were supposed to make it possible for the Pentagon to predict the moment of victory (originally set for the end of 1965), when the enemy's fighting capacity would be exhausted. But, in practice, reliance on such figures led to the indiscriminate slaughter of men, women and children; only the number of casualties mattered, in a kind of logic that led one officer to tell his men that pregnant women should be counted twice.

Historians always look in retrospect for causal sequences and for logical connections between action A and outcome B. But things like the above show that outcome B may be quite different from what was intended for action A. US soldiers in Vietnamese villages reasoned differently from those who gave the orders in the Pentagon, and they did so because they faced different problems. The statistical hubris of a 'body count' exit from the war led on the ground to escalations in which the body count became an end in itself: such are the sequences that lie hidden beneath abstract concepts such as 'escalation dynamic'. In extreme situations of perceived threat, certain kinds of reasoning have an autocatalytic effect and generate certain kinds of action and outcomes that subsequently seem even to participants as curiously alien and unfathomable.[13]

Another example from the same war concerns the idea that the North Vietnamese army had a high command in the jungle (COSVN – Central Office of South Vietnam) that had to be located and destroyed. This fantasy fed partly on the inability of the US Army to crush the numerically and technologically inferior forces of the Vietcong, and partly on the assumption that the enemy operated in accordance with the same logic as the Americans. This led to a senseless bombing campaign to burn areas of jungle and uncover the (non-existent) 'nerve centre'. Here too the aim was to allow a clearer overview of the situation. But the result was that world public opinion turned against the American conduct of the war, at the latest after photos were published of a little girl, Kim Phuc, naked and in tears, her hair burnt, fleeing from her bombed village. This too, of course, was a consequence that no one had intended, but it would prove decisive for the future course of the war.

The Vietnam War was also an assault on the ecological conditions under which the enemy lived. False perceptions led to the dropping of '800,000 tons' of bombs on the country, 'more than in all the theatres of the Second World War combined',[14] and to the widespread use of toxic defoliants to expose the jungle to view, which would have long-term consequences for future generations of Vietnamese.

Of all the wars that punctuated the so-called Cold War, the one in Vietnam was certainly the most absurd, costly and long-lasting. Its consequences run deep in both Vietnamese and US society. Official America suffered there its first major defeat, moral, military and economic, as well as in terms of public confidence in the policies of its president.

The underlying causes of the conflict were in many respects psychological: fantasies of superiority jostled panic fears of losing face. Both Lyndon B. Johnson and Richard Nixon publicly declared that they did not want to be the first American president to lose a war, and since it is hard to go back on such a statement they threw everything into winning the war long after that had become an impossibility. Their advisers (including the highly intelligent Henry Kissinger) and most of the top military brass created an unreal space around themselves, analysing the problems as they saw them and developing various solutions that carried them further and further towards the final debacle.

As Barbara Tuchman points out, those responsible for the conduct of the war typically refused to take on board any information that did not match their expectations. First they considered it out of the question that they could ever be defeated by a 'fourth-rate' country like Vietnam; then they went on systematically to overestimate the strength of their own forces and those of the Saigon regime; and, finally, the more they clung to their illusions, the more clearly disaster loomed on the horizon. The familiar mechanism of dissonance reduction was obviously at work here – and, given the obvious parallels with the Iraq War, it is a good example of how psychological phenomena such as hubris and 'groupthink'[15] can be more powerful than the lessons of history.

CHANGED REALITIES

In view of all this, it is not surprising that radically changed realities often bring violent problem-solving in their wake. The unexpected collapse and system change of the Eastern bloc in 1989 proved too much not only for social and political theorists, whose business it was to predict such things, but also for citizens and politicians in the countries concerned. Post-colonial societies are especially prone to violent conflict, and it can take decades before a relatively stable civil society develops in them. 'Thus, after decolonization, only 19 out of 44 African countries were capable of developing a stable state.'[16] Violent conflicts followed independence in most cases, often persisting to this day in varying degrees of intensity (Sudan, Congo, Sierra Leone, Guinea-Bissau, etc.). In Ethiopia, a war that lasted from 1976 to 1991 caused as many as 2 million casualties (more than 90 per cent of them civilians); half a million to a million died as a result of fighting in Mozambique between 1976 and 1992; and war in the Congo has claimed 4 million victims since 1998.

As to the former Eastern bloc, system change and the road to democracy have by no means always been peaceful. In 2007, nearly twenty years after the collapse of the Soviet Union, the list of the sixty most unstable (and therefore violence-prone) countries in the world included Uzbekistan (23rd place), Kyrgyzstan (28th), Bosnia-Herzegovina (35th), Tajikistan (42nd), Russia (43rd), Turkmenistan (45th), Belarus (50th), Serbia and Montenegro (55th), Moldavia (58th) and Georgia (60th).[17] In not a few of these countries there were sharp conflicts among different ethnic groups.

Studies of mass violence and genocide have shown little or no understanding of what happens when people begin to attack or kill their neighbours – as if it were normal for them to love, or to have a close relationship with, their neighbours under peaceful circumstances. In fact, as everyone who lives in a shared house knows, and as Jan Philipp Reemtsma has powerfully reminded us,[18] close proximity may well be a source of violence rather than an obstacle to it; you can end up hating the people you have to live beside.

It is the ambiguity or 'viscosity' of group boundaries that can lead to extreme acts of violence in a crisis. The function of such acts is to establish once and for all who 'we' are and who 'they' are, who should be seen as a friend and who as an enemy. The violence itself draws the boundary line, since 'we' and 'they' are unmistakably clear after an attack or mass killing. One man from the former Yugoslavia explains how he distinguished friend from enemy: 'Civilians are different, civilians don't walk the streets when there's shooting going on [*laughs*]. It's really quite simple: civilians don't walk the streets when there's shooting going on.'[19]

People develop various techniques for identifying and allocating group membership; ID papers are one, racial theories another, mass murder yet another. Thus, perceived threats to a 'we group' from a 'they group' make it more and more necessary to establish ways of identifying others, and in cases of extreme violence the *outcome* itself defines who belongs to which. The result of such self-referential systems is only superficially chaos. For the perpetrators, violence actually creates order.

The most spectacular escalation of violence during the post-1989 systemic breakdown, and the one with the most protracted consequences, took place in Yugoslavia, a country where various ethnic groups had once lived unproblematically side by side in a federation led by the charismatic autocrat Josip Broz Tito. Here too conflicts now became sharper and sharper as these groups felt it necessary to assert their difference through violence. It was happening not in sub-Saharan Africa or Kashmir but in the middle of Europe, at a time when the Cold War seemed to be over and no one thought a hot war was on the cards.

It is also remarkable that no one had foreseen the explosive force of nationalism in the unipolar world that followed the collapse of the Soviet Union, or the disorientation in the republics that had been part of it. The rival forces in Yugoslavia, as well as actors on the international political stage, seemed bereft of ideas amid the turmoil. The disastrous mistakes of the then German foreign minister, Hans-Dietrich Genscher, accentuated the conflict among the republics of Yugoslavia. His decision to recognize the secession of Slovenia and Croatia as sovereign states, which Belgrade saw as sabotage of its attempt to re-establish the federal republic under Serb domination, provided further fuel for the radicalization of Serb nationalism.

This case shows that foreign policy sticks to familiar bearings after a systemic change; it was as if the collapse in the East had changed nothing in the general configuration. As Henry Kissinger famously remarked: 'It is an illusion to believe that leaders gain in profundity while they gain experience ... [T]he convictions that leaders have formed before reaching high office are the intellectual capital they will consume as long as they continue in office.'[20] Not only politicians but also managers, academics or doctors keep to models and prescriptions that have brought them success in the past, even when the conditions for their application have totally changed. This often has disastrous consequences.

But such immobility is not the only dramatic aspect of politics visible in escalations of violence after systemic change. Defective models and concepts are also typical of politicians in the newly formed states themselves, since they tend to be people who lack experience of democratic negotiating processes, market economics and liberal constitutionalism, but are well versed in power politics, corruption, propaganda, personality cults and cronyism. This combination of unimaginative and autocratic ways has the most baneful effect where the polity itself is in turmoil. Moreover, whereas the West still favours and promotes the model of the bourgeois-national state, murky situations in which the state has collapsed and there is a pressing need to act often mean that a new state can be conceived only along ethnic lines of divide, since other elements that might generate a national community are nowhere to be seen.[21]

So, for political actors who take the stage after systemic change, nationalism regularly offers the best promise of success. This in turn intensifies radical tendencies, as we saw in the case of Slobodan Milošević. His efforts to preserve his influence and to keep ultra-nationalist rivals at bay turned him more and more into a nationalist himself.

Changed realities also change those who have shaped them – a process well illustrated by the radical evolution of the Nazi leadership elite. At the level of social psychology, however, one of the reasons why this is such an uncertain process is that people often do not notice how their own mental maps of what is right and wrong, normal and abnormal, predictable and unexpected, undergo change amid the changing realities around them. In other words, as members of a society in the throes of normative change, the fact that they remain constantly in tune with their surroundings means they often do not notice that their own norms are changing. This may be termed the phenomenon of 'shifting baselines' (see pp. 139–143 below).

The deadly violence to which this gave rise in Yugoslavia and elsewhere is well known. Less familiar is the idea that our democratic postwar society stands on the foundations of this process of identification through extreme violence. From time to time it resonates in the somewhat equivocal lament that Germany's non-Jewish majority robbed itself of an essential part of its culture by killing the Jews – as if the main damage was suffered by the society that succeeded the National Socialist *Volksgemeinschaft*. Extreme violence crosses generations, probably persisting even through several systemic changes, and today's Federal Republic of Germany is a society that still displays the consequences of violence (as the retired general Klaus Naumann, former head of NATO, put it). But in this respect it differs only in scale, not in principle, from other postwar societies.

Phenomena such as the Holocaust or the violent break-up of Yugoslavia (the latest European instance of state-building) illustrate the truly horrifying point made recently by Michael Mann: that most of Europe's ethnically homogeneous states are the outcome of processes of ethnic cleansing and mass killing. These murderous options are not simply occupational accidents but the dark side of the democracy that rests upon them. The path to ethnic cleansing and genocide does not follow any master plans and is often strewn with unintended consequences. War and violence intrinsically tend to trigger developments that no one foresaw at the beginning of the state-building process; resettlement can suddenly turn into expulsions, and expulsions into genocide.[22] It is important to realize that such dynamics are not historically random. But escalations of extreme violence are aspects of modernization processes that are subject to cultural amnesia after the successful constitution of a new state. One reason why this is possible is that the victims of homogenization have run away or are dead.

If the ethnic cleansings and genocides of the nineteenth and twentieth centuries are understood as dynamos of modernization – and there is much to suggest that they should be – then the social transformations that come in the wake of globalization will produce a further rise in deadly violence. And, if changes in habitat, system change or the resource needs of other countries lead to increasing instability in various societies, attempts to find solutions through violence will become more and more likely.

6

KILLING TODAY: ECOCIDE

THE FLESH OF YOUR MOTHER STICKS BETWEEN MY TEETH

Environmental historians have a special fondness for remote islands. If, because of distance or limited nautical skills, their exchange with other societies is close to zero, external factors have a close to zero influence on their development and decline. The island is like a laboratory, in which this or that event (not infrequently a disaster) happens under controlled conditions.

Easter Island, 3,500 kilometres off the nearest land mass, South America, is therefore a kind of promised land for environmental historians. It was probably settled around AD 900 by Polynesians, who were masters in navigation and the construction of seaworthy boats, and it then experienced half a millennium of rising prosperity. According to Jared Diamond, the ecological conditions were not as optimal as on other islands settled by Polynesians, but they were sufficient to feed a large population of 20,000 to 30,000 divided into eleven or twelve clans, each with its own chief.

Of twenty-one species of plant that have since disappeared from the island, the tallest, which could grow as high as 30 metres, was especially suitable for large canoes.[1] There were twenty-five species of land birds.

The inhabitants lived not only on what they grew in the fields, but also on birds, dolphins and the numerous descendants of the rats that the original settlers had evidently brought along with them.

The golden age of Easter Island society must have been around the year 1500, when the number of buildings reached its peak before declining by 70 per cent through the seventeenth and into the eighteenth century.[2] Easter was a theocracy; the chiefs, who had a quasi-divine status, exercised the office of high priest and, as in other Polynesian societies, mediated between the gods and men and regulated relations among the clans, chiefs and individuals.[3] Earlier in its history the island may be said to have had the qualities of a medium-grade paradise, but by the time that the first Europeans arrived in the eighteenth century it offered an almost surreal picture. Easter was completely treeless and almost depopulated: the few inhabitants were, as Captain Cook reported in 1774, 'small, lean, timid and miserable'.[4] The only animals were rats and chickens. The landscape made an especially bizarre impression, since hundreds of (mostly broken) stone statues lay around. Many reached a length of 6 metres and a weight of 10 tonnes, but the largest of all was 21 metres long and weighed 270 tonnes.

A heap of half-finished or transport-ready statues was found in a quarry. The puzzle was how the inhabitants had managed to move and raise these giant sculptures, given that the island seemed to have no timber that could have been used to build the necessary wooden platforms and accessories. Today it is assumed that the figures were shown off by chiefs and clans to make an impact on others, and that at some point rivalry began over who could display the largest and most powerful. Historical dating techniques have shown that the average size of the statues grew over the centuries.[5]

Archaeological reconstructions make it likely that the islanders – partly because of the feverish production of statues – subjected their ecological resources to fatal predation. Deforestation seems to have begun soon after the first settlers arrived around AD 900 and was complete by the seventeenth century at the latest. We cannot know what went through the head of the man who felled the last tree; he probably gave it little thought and treated it as a simple necessity of life. When timber had still been plentiful, it had been used for burning and cooking, the extraction of charcoal and the building of houses and canoes, and not least as ancillary material for the deployment of the stone statues.

In sum, Diamond writes, 'the picture for Easter is the most extreme example of forest destruction in the Pacific, and among the most extreme in the world. ... Immediate consequences for the islanders were losses of raw materials, losses of wild-caught food, and decreased crop yields. ... Lack of large timber and rope brought an end to the transport and erection of statues, and also to the construction of seagoing canoes.'[6] There is no way of compensating for such a resource collapse on an island cut off from the outside world; fishing became ever more problematic as the canoes fell into disrepair, while soil erosion on the deforested, wind-swept land made agriculture less and less of a possibility. Without wood there was no longer any fuel, and in winter the inhabitants burned the last plants and grass. Decline spelled change even for the dead, since there was no wood for cremations and corpses were either mummified or buried in the ground.

Evidently this shrinking of the means of survival must have intensified resource competition in relation to food, building material, tools and symbolic representation. If decisive proof were needed that man does not live from bread alone (especially where he has none),[7] the Easter islanders certainly provide it with their persistence in a cultural practice to the point of risking their own survival. But they are not alone in this: standards of shame in the West can induce people to perish in a blazing house because they think it impossible to run naked into the street.[8] Norbert Elias has several times described how excessive emotional involvement can block the detached view of a situation necessary for self-preservation.[9]

In the early seventeenth century, King Philip III of Spain 'died of a fever he contracted from sitting too long near a hot brazier, helplessly overheating himself because the functionary whose duty it was to remove the brazier, when summoned, could not be found.'[10] As we saw in the previous chapter, people's decisions depend on how they perceive and interpret their situation. But it is also clear that there can be self-destructive decisions, even if, as in the case of Philip III, better solutions seem readily available. The fact is that cultural, social, emotional and symbolic factors often play a greater role than the survival instinct: one need look no further than suicide bombings to find a parallel in the contemporary world.

Philip III, like the Easter islanders, used a frame of reference that made it impossible for him to see what lay in store. It was as if the available cultural grids prevented things from being perceived in a different way, as if those involved literally *could not see* what else they might do. Such fatal blocks may also be produced through training and discipline. For example, in the hard-drilled armies of the eighteenth and nineteenth centuries, the order of battle meant that infantrymen had to stand and be killed: 'Men stood silent and inert in rows to be slaughtered, often for hours at a time; at Borodino the infantrymen of Ostermann-Tolstoi's corps are reported to have stood under point-blank artillery fire for two hours, "during which the only movement was the stirring in the lines caused by falling bodies".'[11]

In other words, the perceived problem in all these cases was not at all the danger to one's own survival but the risk of breaching symbolic or traditional codes of conduct linked to status or the obeying of orders. That risk may evidently be so great that no other option is visible. People then become prisoners of their own survival techniques.

Further striking evidence of this is provided by strategies that lasted far beyond their useful life yet continued to bind the energies and imagination of people alive at the time. For example, generations of master builders and military contractors went on constructing fortresses long after technology and forms of warfare had made them obsolete. The ever greater and more destructive power of cannons forced them to extend the external fortifications, until in a city like Antwerp these stretched for 9 miles around the central citadel. The absurdity of this constant outreach was that the actual cities to be defended ran out of space – indeed, they were constricted by their own defensive installations. Nor were there ever enough soldiers to man the fortress, and those stationed inside it cut themselves off from the enemy and were of no use if he decided to attack a position of greater interest. The building of new citadels when they were already known to be pointless was thus a case of ploughing on with formulas and procedures that had been successful under different historical circumstances.[12]

Another aspect overlooked in relation to the power of the forces involved is the decision either to threaten or to employ violence.

Heinrich Popitz vividly illustrated this by means of the following example. On a cruise ship there are a third as many deckchairs as there are passengers. This is enough to go round, because at any one time sufficient people are occupied with something else. But the picture suddenly changes when new passengers come on board with techniques for hogging a deckchair even when they are not using it. The most effective of these is social cooperation: you ask another user to 'keep' your chair until you want to use it again. This has an advantage for the other user, because it is a favour that can be asked for in return.

Gradually a group that is privileged and a (perhaps numerically superior) group that is underprivileged take shape. The former can use the organizational advantage of cooperation for a common interest, in the face of which the other passengers are isolated individuals who would also like to have a deckchair but lack the power to assert their interest. This other interest does not yield an organizational advantage, especially as the disentitled have no cooperative model that might prevail over that of the entitled.

Power arises here out of a simple organizational advantage. This can even be extended at random to a third category – for example, by creating a third category of 'guards', who, in return for keeping order at certain times, are permitted to use a deckchair even though they do not belong to the category of those entitled to one. The fascinating aspect of this example is that the underprivileged group *do not see* that their inferior power is the result of an organizational advantage that the others have exploited, and from which new power can be generated. What they see is that they cannot have a deckchair, and although they may feel angry their very emotion blinds them to the real causes of their inferiority.[13]

Let us return here to the Easter islanders, who can tell us a lot about the importance of problem perception for the decisions that people make. Their case also shows that perceived problems can turn into very real ones and violently push for a solution. At the end of the Easter Island culture there was a terrible war. The resource conflict, due essentially to deforestation of the island, eventually led the inhabitants to become predators towards one another, as we know from the discovery of human bones with teeth marks (made to extract the marrow). This cannibalistic endgame has not only been proved archaeologically;

it also features prominently in the oral heritage. Ecological degradation led to erosion not only of the soil but also of human culture.

Around 1680 the chiefs and high priests were overthrown by military men; the eleven or twelve clans decided to band together into larger fighting groups,[14] and many inhabitants retreated to the protection of caves and tunnels. No more statues were erected, and those belonging to rivals were toppled and destroyed; stone slabs that had served as platforms were now used to protect cave entrances. As a further defensive measure, one group dug a deep trench that created a kind of peninsula, while a further technological advance saw the introduction of deadlier obsidian spearheads. In short, the island sank into a state of surreal destructiveness, which no longer offered a chance of survival to the great majority. John Keegan, military historian that he is, paints the picture of an absolute war that spelled the end first of politics, then of culture, and finally of human life.[15]

The island experiment, which was subject to no external influences, ended when the inhabitants used up their last resource: themselves. Of the few left after the war, the majority were bought up by Peruvian slave traders in the eighteenth century.[16] In 1872 the island had no more than 112 inhabitants. The greatest insult that could be hurled at someone in Easter Island was: 'The flesh of your mother is stuck between my teeth.'

GENOCIDE IN RWANDA

Now let us go back to Rwanda. The genocide there could take place with such dizzying speed because the many were killing the few (Hutus made up 90 per cent of the population). But, this being so, what accounts for the seemingly bizarre feeling among the Hutu that they had to defend themselves at all costs against the Tutsi? Why this sense of a deadly threat that had to be tackled, come what may?

The first part of an answer, as we have seen, is that first the German and then the French colonial authorities had considered the Tutsi to be a racially superior group and placed them accordingly. This better material and psychological position survived the colonial period and continued to have its effects after the country gained independence in 1962. The second part is that the history of conflict after 1962 had been long and bloody. Before the genocide began in April 1994, Rwanda had been the scene of a civil war in which Tutsi rebels had fought to wrest power from a Hutu-dominated government. With the assassination of the Hutu president, Juvénal Habyarimana, the previously rather blurred ethnic conflict acquired deadly sharp contours.

A civil war is a situation of chronic insecurity and extreme danger for the population of a country, and individuals can do no more than try to mitigate the real and perceived threats and do all they can to stay alive. The key issues, then, are orientation, transparency and a lessening of fear and confusion. These too require a clear identification of friend and enemy, of 'us' and 'them'. Tutsi is what the enemy is, and the enemy is anyone who is Tutsi. It is even necessary to kill Hutus who try to protect or hide Tutsis, or who speak out publicly against mass killing. This is the self-referential system that forms the backdrop to the violence.

CROWDING

But the festering civil war was only one part of it. At the time, Rwanda was the country with the highest population density in Africa and one of the highest anywhere in the world; there had been rapid demographic growth, much as there is today in many parts of Africa, despite the disastrous living conditions. Such a situation, especially amid civil war and a general outbreak of violence, is likely to increase the propensity of individuals to act violently. Take, for example, the closely studied Kanama commune in north-west Rwanda, where between 1988 and 1993 the population per square mile shot up from 1,740 to 2,040, the average household size grew from 4.9 to 5.3 persons, and all (!) young men under twenty-five lived in their parents' home. It has been calculated that, on small farms in the area, one person lived off only one-fifth of an acre in 1988 and as little as one-seventh of an acre in 1993.[17] Most members of a family could not survive only on the produce of its farm but had to seek additional income from unskilled jobs, brickmaking, and so on. The percentage living below starvation level (1,600 calories per day) rose sharply, and with it the potential and gravity of conflict.

Even such critical demographic-ecological trends are interpreted with various grids. Thus, in Rwanda the conflicts and massacres of the years preceding the true genocide had already formed ethnically coded images of 'us' and 'them' groups, which guided people's actions when mass violence broke out in the aftermath of Habyarimana's assassination. Ecological, demographic and geographical factors tend to be played down, or simply categorized under 'ideology', in studies of violence and genocide, but in reality the perception of problems and their causes plays a decisive role for the active participants.

The perception of problems and possible solutions also has something to do with how the world is thought about more generally. It may be that murder is not actually defined as murder but regarded and *understood* as (in the case of the Holocaust) 'special treatment', 'fulfilling a law of nature' or a 'final solution to the Jewish problem' or (in the case of Stalinism) 'the dying out of classes' in accordance with the laws of history. The common interpretation of these as verbal smokescreens is a false trail. The Nazis really did consider the Jews to be vermin on the body of the *Volk* – which is why they killed them with Zyklon B, a poison used for pest control. In Rwanda people cut down other people as if they were 'harmful weeds' – which added special meaning to the act of killing by machete blows.[18] (It also suggested to the outside world that the genocide was not a planned operation but a spontaneous outbreak of violence, as if the violence had originated with individuals and the weapons had been lying around in their houses.) Metaphors generally played an egregious role in the Rwandan genocide; the very weapons of murder were known in everyday language as 'work tools' (*ibikoresho*).[19]

Killing as work, mass murder as a kind of agricultural task akin to weeding or pest control: this is also the background to the commonest insult used for Tutsis, 'cockroaches'.

The ethnically pure Rwanda of the Hutu imagination would be a 'field', the Hutus themselves 'children of farmers', their task to keep the 'field' in good order. 'They killed like people go to the fields, going home when they get tired.'[20] This is the deadly logic that justifies the total eradication of the Tutsi: 'In "clearing the bush", care had to be taken not only to cut the "high grass", that is, the adults, but also to tear up the "young shoots", that is, the children and young people. In fact, the extreme cruelty towards the unborn, babies and children was beyond all imagination.'[21]

There should be no mistaking the importance of metaphor for how people behave. Much of what outwardly looks like rationalizing imagery may be a self-evident reality, a tangible fact, for those whom it points towards a certain course of action.[22] The same is true of the extreme paternalist view of politics expressed in the two interview extracts at the beginning of chapter 4. If I regard a president as my 'father', his assassination triggers a different motivational dynamic from the one that arises if I see him as a replaceable member of a functional elite.

Such things need to be understood by anyone who wishes to reconstruct what people see as their problems and how they aim to solve them. The perception of killing as a defensive action is an important element of self-justification for the perpetrators of genocide.

In Rwanda, the 'accusation in a mirror' technique[23] also played a central role: that is, a genocidal fantasy was attributed to the other side, spreading the belief that it was bent on the total annihilation of one's own side. Nor was this by any means only a social-psychological phenomenon; it was explicitly recommended as a propaganda technique, whereby 'the party which is using terror will accuse the enemy of using terror'.[24]

The intended consequence was that Hutus in whom the sense of threat was instilled would be prepared to defend themselves, and would see any kind of homicidal attack or systematic murder on their part as a *necessary* means to that end. A further twist in the spiral came when stories were spread around that Tutsis were actually carrying out murders and massacres – that is, that the stage-settings of a terrifying fantasy world were becoming a reality. All these were well-known devices for the production of a dynamic of escalation, tried and tested most recently in Yugoslavia's terminal wars and the Kosovo conflict.

The social proximity of the two groups, before mass killing separated them in practice, was a potential source of the violence, not an obstacle to it. In the imagined deadly threat of the Tutsi 'them' to the Hutu 'us', it was extremely important that mobility had been blurring the line between the two groups. One function of the murderous violence was to restructure reality by making the boundary crystal-clear.

WHAT DID THE KILLERS SEE?

There were five elements to the killers' perception of society that could make the killing appear meaningful to them. First, there was a high degree of fear and insecurity, and therefore a great need for orientation, that could be addressed through violence. Second, a perception of ever more restricted prospects in work and life led to a considerably greater potential for increased violence. Third, there was a perceived threat of being annihilated if one did not take 'defensive' action against the imagined killers on the other side. Fourth, killing was defined as 'work' that needed to be carried out, within a more general vision of the society and nation as a 'field' that made the task of 'cultivation' seem absolutely useful. Fifth, the killers could assure themselves of the normality and meaningfulness of their action by thinking that everyone else did what they were doing.

Outwardly the genocidal violence seemed to be a primitive, spontaneous eruption, but from the inside it felt amazingly controlled and purposive. Underlying it was not only a history of murder and violence in civil war, with the associated fear and disorientation, but also ecological-demographic problems that made the situation of young men in particular seem more and more constricted and hopeless. This was a key element raising the individual propensity to violence.

The Rwandan genocide was not the result of a climate war, but nor was it due only to political and social-historical factors. Jared Diamond considers that high population density was at least one determinant, and it may well be that this is one of those cases where a problem that plays (or appears to play) no role in our own lifeworld has escaped our notice in a different context. In fact, it is not so long ago that the fantasy of being a 'people without living space' gave rise to a completely new geopolitical orientation in Germany, which made a war of annihilation and conquest seem a desirable and feasible way of opening up space for new German settlements in the East. It would be wrong to think that the underlying perception then was merely 'ideological': Nazi and other ideologies played a flanking role, but the real purpose was to gain new spatial resources, raw materials and slave workers.

The planned conquest of space in the East was different in kind from the problem that the Hutu thought they faced in Rwanda. But the point is that ideologies and 'big pictures' are subordinate to more down-to-earth matters in human perceptions, interpretations and decisions. Just as an early mastermind of annihilation might have had his eye on a dazzling academic career, or an SS Obersturmbannführer on a nice property on the Polish lakes, so might a young Hutu from Kanama have glimpsed the prospect of escaping his cooped-up life in the parental home if he fell in with the government's plan to massacre the Tutsi. Such focused considerations may be much more significant than 'racial fanaticism', 'ethnic cleansing' or 'ethnocide' for the perpetrators of violence. Let us therefore now look at another genocide, which took place ten years after the one in Rwanda – just the other day, in fact.

DARFUR – THE FIRST CLIMATE WAR

First aircraft would come over a village, as if smelling the target, and then return to release their bombs. The raids were carried out by Russian-built four-engine Antonov An-12s, which are not bombers but transports. They have no bomb bays or aiming mechanisms, and the 'bombs' they dropped were old oil drums stuffed with a mixture of explosives and metallic debris. These were rolled on the floor of the transport and dropped out of the rear ramp which was kept open during the flight. The result was primitive free-falling cluster bombs, which were completely useless from a military point of view since they could not be aimed but had a deadly efficiency against fixed civilian targets. As any combatant with a minimum of training could easily duck them, they were terror weapons aimed solely at civilians. After the Antonovs had finished their grisly job, combat helicopters and/or MiG fighter-bombers would come, machine-gunning and firing rockets at targets such as a school or a warehouse which might still be standing. Utter destruction was clearly programmed.[25]

The air raids were not the end of the story. The violence then began in earnest. *Janjaweed* militiamen, riding horses or camels or driving Toyota Landcruisers, would surround the village, then move in to plunder it, rape the women, burn the houses down and kill any remaining inhabitants.[26]

This was the opening act, in July 2003, to the genocide in Darfur, in western Sudan. What was first reported to Western TV viewers as a tribal conflict between 'Arab horseback militias' and 'African farmers' looks, on closer examination, to have been a war by a government on its own population, in which climate change played a decisive role. Ethnically speaking, Darfur is an intricate web of 'Arab' and 'African' tribes, where 'Arab' is usually associated with nomadic lifestyles and 'African' with settled farming. A further complexity is the distinction between 'native Arabs' and those who first entered the country in the nineteenth century, mainly as Islamic preachers and traders. This core group of a quasi-colonial foreign elite, as Gérard Prunier puts it, was supplemented by slave and ivory dealers, who put themselves on the same level as the native Arabs. Although they had come from outside as conquerors, they eventually merged with the indigenous group, but to this day retain an elite position in Darfur society.[27]

The *Janjaweed*, infamous for their brutality, first appeared in the late 1980s at various trouble spots, in a role 'halfway between being bandits and government thugs'.[28] They are recruited from former highwaymen, demobilized soldiers, young men from mostly 'smaller Arab tribes having a running land conflict with a neighbouring "African" group', common criminals and young unemployed. These people receive money for their work: '$79 a month for a man on foot and $117 if he ha[s] a horse or a camel'. 'Officers – i.e. those who could read or who were tribal *amir* – could get as much as $233.'[29] Their weapons are provided to them.

As in Rwanda ten years earlier, then, these were by no means men who killed spontaneously out of hatred or revenge, but rather 'organized, politicized and militarized groups'.[30] At the time of writing, between 200,000 and 500,000 inhabitants of Darfur have died as a result of their work. There had been massacres in the earlier period too, but at least since 1984, when a disastrous famine hit the country, the history of violence has been closely bound up with ecological problems.

There have been conflicts for seventy years or more between Darfur's settled farmers ('Africans') and nomadic herdsmen ('Arabs'),[31] but they have become increasingly severe as a result of soil erosion and greater livestock numbers.[32] Elements of modernization and judicial dispute resolution, which were introduced in more peaceful times thirty or so years ago, swept away traditional strategies for problem-solving or reconciliation without establishing new or functioning forms of regulation.[33] Instead, during the last thirty years, there has been a tendency for weapons to be used straightaway even in small local conflicts.[34]

In the disastrous drought of 1984, the sedentary farmers tried to protect their meagre harvests by blocking access to their fields by 'Arabs' whose pastureland had dried up. As a result, the nomads were unable to use their traditional *marahil*, or herding routes and feeding places. 'In their eagerness to push towards the still wet south, they started to fight their way through the blocked off *marahil*. Farmers carrying out their age-old practices of burning unwanted wild grass were attacked because what for them were bad weeds had become the last fodder for the desperate nomads' depleted flocks.'[35]

Here we see quite clearly that climate-induced changes were the starting point for the conflict. The lack of rainfall – in many parts of Darfur it declined by more than a third for a whole decade – meant that the northern regions were no longer suitable for livestock and that the herdsmen had to tear up their roots there and move south as full nomads.[36] Furthermore, the drought produced large numbers of internally displaced persons (IDPs), who were accommodated in newly built camps; as many as 80,000 starving people were on the move trying to reach one. The government's first reaction was to declare them all 'Chadian refugees' and to order their deportation en masse, in an operation known as 'Operation Glorious Return'.[37]

At the same time, a dramatic rise in population figures, averaging 2.6 per cent a year, led to overuse of pasture and other land and added to the anyway high potential for conflict. Whereas disputes over land and water had traditionally been settled at conciliation meetings chaired by a third party with government support, a different policy came into operation after General Al-Bashir's military putsch in 1989. Now government-backed militias increasingly intervened, making the conflicts sharper and more likely to end in violence.

Today's conflicts are between government troops or militias and the twenty rebel organizations, so that an overview is as impossible for the participants as it is for outside observers. The largest rebel group – the Darfur Liberation Front (DLF), formed in February 2003 – initially campaigned for the independence of Darfur, but soon

decided to go for a country-wide solution and renamed itself the Sudan
Liberation Movement/Army (SLM/SLA). In addition there is now a
Justice and Equality Movement (JEM), which also seeks to weaken the
government in Khartoum.[38]

The war in Darfur began when SLA guerrillas attacked the airport
at El Fasher, and the government retaliated with the raids on villages described earlier. Nomadic Arab tribesmen then used these as
an opportunity to appropriate farmland and animals. 'As the clashes
intensified, the government in Khartoum dismissed the governors of
northern and western Darfur, who had come out in favour of a nego-
tiated solution.'[39] Government aircraft continued to bomb villages
indiscriminately and deployed the *Janjaweed* to fight against the rebels.
These have since engaged in a genocide interrupted only by periodic
attempts to achieve a ceasefire. Violence has become a permanent feature of the situation. Neither the rebels nor the government are capable
of a decisive victory, and nothing suggests that the opposing sides are
genuinely interested in peace. Moreover, not only the *Janjaweed* but
also the regular army and rebel troops have been inflicting violence on
civilians.[40]

The high toll of the brutal fighting in Darfur has all the characteristics of a climate war; it also represents a new type of simmering warfare
to be found in African societies in fragile or broken states. In chapter 7,
'Killing Tomorrow', we shall return to the point that one of the main
differences between the civil wars of today or tomorrow and classical
interstate wars is that the parties have no interest in ending the conflict
and many political and financial interests in keeping it alive.[41] Violence
markets and violence economies have come into being – non-state
areas in which business is done with weapons, raw materials, hostages,
international aid, and so on. Obviously, no trader in violence is keen to
see his business come to an end; he will therefore regard any attempt to
restore peace as an unwelcome disturbance.[42]

A study published in June 2007 by the United Nations Environment
Programme (UNEP) summed up the situation as follows. In Darfur
environmental problems, combined with excessive population growth,
have created the framework for violent conflicts along ethnic lines –
between 'Africans' and 'Arabs'. So, conflicts that have ecological causes
are perceived as ethnic conflicts, including by the protagonists them-

selves. The social decline is triggered by ecological collapse, but this is not seen by most of the actors. What they do see are armed attacks, robberies and deadly violence – hence the hostility of 'them' to 'us'.

The UNEP soberly noted that lasting peace will not be possible in Sudan so long as environmental and living conditions remain as they are today. But those conditions are now marked by shortages that pose a threat to survival (because of drought, desertification, deficient rainfall), and which are further exacerbated by global warming. The road from ecological problems to social conflicts is not one way.

ECOLOGY OF WAR

'Deploying technologies that make our forces more efficient also reduces greenhouse gas emissions.' This bald statement comes amid the final recommendations of the report *National Security and the Threat of Climate Change*, which was written by a number of high-ranking American officers and published by the Center for Naval Analyses (CNA).[43] It may seem surprising that such senior military men should not only warn of the increased security risk due to climate change but also call for more ecological methods of waging war. Yet they do not limit themselves, as in an EU report published in 2008,[44] to water and soil conflicts, violence associated with migration and wars over raw materials; they further outline the implications of global warming for military technology and strategy.

Bad experiences of sandstorms in Iraq, for example, give reason to suppose that military equipment may malfunction in the hot dry conditions of many future theatres of war. The CNA report complains that frequent extreme weather events such as storms and hurricanes limit naval operations and use up equipment at a faster rate, already making it necessary in the hurricane season to station aircraft inland and to move ships away from harbour.[45] It also makes the historical point that extreme weather has not infrequently affected the fortunes of war: the examples range from the typhoons that twice saved Japan from Mongol invasion through to the Scud missiles that Saddam could not fire at Israel because of the stormy conditions.

Logistical problems occur especially when troops rely on oil-fired generators and have to wait for an endless convoy of tankers;

energy-saving devices may thus lead not only to lower greenhouse gas emissions but also to increased battle readiness.[46] Finally, rising sea levels pose a threat to many US military bases: the Diego Garcia atoll, for example, which has a major logistical function for operations in the Indian Ocean, will disappear, and so too will the Kwajalein atoll in the South Pacific and Guam in the West Pacific. The need to abandon such important positions will set up a vicious circle of rising transport costs and increased fuel expenditure.[47] All these dangers, the report concludes, make it essential that the impact of climate change is systematically built into national security and defence planning.

It is doubtful that such collateral damage has already been factored into calculations of the economic costs of global warming[48] – indeed, the whole subject still awaits scientific analysis. Since the causes of violent conflict within and between countries will not diminish, greater empirical and theoretical efforts will need to be invested in the development of an ecology of war.

Neither in civil wars nor in international conflicts do the contending sides pay much heed to environmental concerns. In Afghanistan, for example, the endless warfare of recent decades means that

> eighty per cent of the country has been subject to soil erosion; fertility has declined, salinization increased and groundwater levels fallen dramatically, while desertification has spread over large areas and wind and water erosion is widespread. According to Abdul Rahman Hotaky, chairman of the Afghan Organization for Human Rights and Environmental Protection (AOHREP), other factors alongside war and war-related expulsions are the increasing length of droughts, improper use of natural resources, weak central government and the lack of an environmental policy.[49]

Seventy per cent of forest has disappeared, and nothing has been grown for the last two decades on 50 per cent of agricultural land.

In the Vietnam War, defoliants exposed 3.3 million hectares of land and forest to toxic chemicals; 'the result was immediate and lasting damage to the soil, nutrient balances, irrigation systems, plant and animal life, and probably also the climate.'[50] More than thirty years later the forests have not returned. In 1995 the World Bank concluded that Vietnam's biodiversity has been permanently altered.[51] Moreover, ecosystems have been rendered more unstable and soil erosion has become more intense.

Apart from these direct consequences of resource destruction, including groundwater contamination by oil and other materials of war and the conversion of whole regions into 'no go areas' littered with landmines, the secondary ecological impact has also been devastating. In the outskirts of Khartoum alone, the uncontrolled settlement of nearly 2 million refugees has led to the mushrooming of slums that lack clean water, drainage systems or any other infrastructure; the situation is no different in other towns in Sudan. Areas up to 10 kilometres around the refugee camps have turned into wasteland as people have cut down every last tree for firewood, and of course this affects the future too, since fuel for cooking and burning is one of life's necessities. The *Janjaweed* raiders not only burn down whole villages but usually also fell or torch nearby trees to prevent the return of any refugees who remain alive.

FAILING SOCIETIES[52]

But rapid desertification anyway means that most refugees will never again live in their place of birth, since the soil there is no longer good for anything. Between 1971 and 2001, two-thirds of forest in northern, central and eastern Sudan disappeared; a third had been lost in Darfur by 1976, and 40 per cent is now gone in southern Sudan. The UNEP predicts a total loss of forest in some regions within the next ten years. The dramatic decline in rainfall has already turned millions of hectares of land into desert. A temperature rise of 0.5 to 1.5 degrees Celsius, which is highly likely to happen, would cut rainfall by a further 5 per cent and make the cultivation of cereals even more difficult. In the El Obeid region, for example, yields will fall from roughly half a tonne to 150 kilograms per hectare.[53] At the time of writing, approximately 30 per cent of Sudan's land surface is desert, but another 25 per cent will become so in the years ahead.

Not much imagination is required to visualize what it would mean for a Central European country to lose a quarter of its farmland, even though its economy would be much less dependent on agriculture and it would have many ways of coping with the shortfall through more intensive farming, increased imports, higher-yield plant strains, and so on. In an agrarian society like Sudan, however, with far fewer resources for survival, a change in environmental conditions is felt not as a constraint but as a disaster that directly threatens the lives of individuals and their families. There is no room for manoeuvre if the daily food supply falls below the level that the body needs to maintain itself. Neither psychological nor sociological knowledge is required to understand that violence is an option in such situations, especially where it is already prevalent in the surrounding society. Every square kilometre of new desert may then be a direct or indirect source of violence, since it limits people's *space for survival* whether they realize it or not.

Because of their disastrous political and economic structure, countries like Sudan have no means to compensate for harvest failure or loss of land; they therefore repeatedly depend upon international relief operations, with all the implications that this has for corruption, the economics of violence and the perpetuation of refugee camps (see the next chapter).

Since fragile or failing states like Sudan are considerably more vulnerable to environmental risks, and have fewer means to cope with them, a natural disaster such as a flood affects them much more severely than it does a region like eastern Germany or central England, and climate change hits them much harder than it does Mediterranean regions, where desertification is also rapidly advancing. The European Union makes provision for payments to badly affected agricultural regions, whereas there is no question of compensation to people enduring desertification in Sudan. Their responses to their situation – over-farming of the remaining land, chopping down of the last trees, and so on – which are driven by sheer necessity, mean that the ecological problems will grow worse in the future. Political structures that do not curb violence, resting neither on the rule of law nor on the promotion of social welfare, serve to sharpen and perpetuate the problems rather than to mitigate them. As the example of Darfur shows, conflicts sparked by ecological factors are then seen as opportunities to play off one group against another, to stir up tensions along ethnic lines, and to keep them alive for as long as possible.

In large parts of Sudan, war has been the normal state of things for

much of post-colonial history; the total number of deaths it has caused
is estimated at 2 to 3 million, not counting the genocide in Darfur.
Average life expectancy in southern Sudan is forty-two years, the lit-
eracy rate is 24 per cent, and the mortality rate for children under five
is 25 per cent. That is how things look in a country where war, with a
few breaks, has been the rule for more than forty years.

Unfortunately, Sudan is not the only country whose future will
become still bleaker as a result of climate change. The 'Failed
State Index' for 2006, which lists sixty states threatened with failure,
includes Sudan right at the top. It is based on a number of indicators, social (demographic pressure, refugee numbers, inter-ethnic
conflicts, chronic migration), economic (sharp inequality, economic
problems) and political (delegitimation of the state, deficient public
services, human rights violations, criminal security apparatuses, elite
rivalry, weight of foreign political actors). African societies are the
most highly placed, but holiday paradises such as Sri Lanka (25th) and
the Dominican Republic (48th) appear along with a number of South
American countries.[54]

All told, 2 billion people today live in countries that count as inse-
cure, failing or failed – which in effect means that their lives are in
greater danger than they would be in other parts of the world. Societies
listed in this index are highly vulnerable to *further* negative changes
of a political, economic or ecological kind – apart from anything else
because a further limitation of their scope for development will increase
the risk of wars and violent conflicts.[55] There is a clear correlation
between poverty and military violence. The statistical probability of an
outbreak of war in a country with a per capita income of $250 is 15 per
cent, while for one with an income of $5,000 or more it is less than 1
per cent.[56]

Paradoxically, the prospects are even worse if the country has many
resources such as diamonds, oil or precious woods. The 'curse of raw
materials' makes it especially attractive to rapacious national and international entrepreneurs of violence. Moreover, as the case of Somalia
shows, civil wars and the like create niches or strongholds for organized
crime and international terrorists. We must bear in mind that these
countries have often reached or crossed the critical threshold of ungov-
ernability, and that they have neither administrative or economic buffer

zones nor transnational connections that might ward off crises or soften their impact. Any environmental shock, be it drought, flood, storm or earthquake, may thus lead directly to a social disaster.

Vulnerable societies, particularly those that failed to build stable civil structures in the wake of colonialism and post-colonial wars, are more prone than others to violent conflict resulting from environmental changes – partly because the state does not have a monopoly of force, but private monopolists and oligopolists also engage in acts of violence.[57] Another reason why the security situation in these countries is so serious is that poverty is at its greatest and the costs of violence at their lowest.[58]

Climate change, then, sharpens inequalities within and between countries – between core and periphery, and between developed and less developed regions. It will inevitably result in further migration and refugee flows. That this will lead per se to greater levels of violence cannot be proven in the current state of research, but environmentally determined migration (for example, where land and water run short or, in economic terms, demand outstrips supply) must certainly be regarded as a *potential* source of violence. In such cases, competition breaks out among those seeking to acquire the scarce resource, and when survival is at stake there is always violence in the air. In sum, the social and political consequences of climate change may be seen as cumulative risks and vulnerabilities for fragile societies, whose situation may grow even worse as a result.

Since the 1990s, resource conflicts within and between states have been a central focus of climate change research.[59] Attempts have also been made to correlate various forms of ecological decline with certain social-economic consequences.[60] For a long time, however, researchers have offered no unified approach to analysis of the social and political consequences of environmental change, and no considerations have been presented as to what all this really means for the theory of society and social development. Some local studies have, it is true, investigated how development possibilities have been affected by sudden and sometimes wholly unpredictable outbreaks of violence partly due to ecological changes,[61] but up to now there has been a failure to collate and theorize the existing material. This is all the more regrettable since domino effects appear in these societies – for example, if a developing potential for innovation is disturbed by social disasters, and capacities for long-term adaptation and prevention in the face of climate change are further weakened.

It is becoming clear that path dependence may translate into greater risks and lasting blockages to social development. Roughly thirty countries threaten to collapse in the near future.[62] In view of this, the continuing paucity of research into the links between ecology, violence and development is truly disconcerting.[63] Patently it is false to assume that different national development paths simply mirror different levels in modernization processes; it may be that they do not correspond at all to classical images of advanced or backward development but reflect 'something else' that has found no place in conventional Western theories of society. This is also the case when – as in some Islamic countries – secularization or other elements of modernization are absent or are being reversed. Clearly the OECD countries are no longer the 'blueprint' for state-building; civilizing and de-civilizing processes may take place in quite different ways from those familiar until now.

STATE COLLAPSE

Fragile statehood means first of all that state institutions and organizations do not function adequately because of a lack of political will, a legitimacy deficit or financial shortfall. In extreme cases, a total collapse of state organs such as the army, police and civil service gives rise to lawlessness and obscure power relations.[64] And if state infrastructure implodes, the danger arises that all other social structures will collapse in short order.[65]

Fragile societies often display weak national integration,[66] consisting of a multiplicity of ethnic, cultural, religious, regional or political groups that compete with one another for resources, enter into conflict and form alliances. Modernization pointing towards an ethnically homogeneous nation-state has not taken place. Without a stable monopoly of force and the rule of law, the state can scarcely intervene to mediate and regulate conflicts, so that the action of police or militias may, as in Darfur, actually make these worse. Fragile societies also suffer from other problems: urbanization rates in poor countries are among the highest in the world, and refugee flows and internal migration have led to a huge build-up on the outskirts of cities.[67] In Lagos, one of the world's megacities, 3 million out of the 17 million inhabitants live literally amid the garbage, without fresh water, sewers, streets, electricity, police or medical care.

Some elements of uneven development are simply beyond people's ability to cope. Global media carry fragments of culture and lifestyle into corners where, not many years ago, people did not even realize that they shared the planet with fully industrialized societies. Changed ways of life and new expectations thus clash abruptly with traditional norms; there are no periods of gradual adjustment. At the same time, selective modernization – for example, better medical provision, rising educational standards or new economic forms – creates acute legitimacy problems for politicians and traditional elites. The reduction of infant mortality triggers demographic explosions that lead to the overrepresentation of young people in the population – a phenomenon which contributed to the social disaster in Rwanda and also played a role in the Sudanese debacle.[68]

Fragile societies are therefore under pressure from many sides: traditional structures undergo erosion, without being replaced by well-functioning modern ones; there is no state monopoly of force but a plethora of competing, often private, players; the vulnerability to social, climatic or other natural changes is extremely high, and the ability to handle them extremely low. When things reach a certain point, the state no longer plays an active role but simply provides opportunity structures for political, entrepreneurial and military elites to impose their interests. At the most, it offers the population a paternalistic frame of reference, which, as in Rwanda, is highly suited to violent mobilizations.

The retreat of the state unleashes domino effects: social conflicts, whatever their origin, become ethnicized; power relations shift among clans and other ethnic groups; and violence increases both within and between groups.[69] The collapse of state and society creates space for the brutal assertion of interests and a confusing spectrum of violence and its perpetrators. The organization, rituals and norms of conflict change quickly as the boundaries to violence break down;[70] this may occur at all levels and eventually lead to genocide.

Once again the availability of violence as an option is clear. Local, splintered problems are matched by local, splintered forms of violence; where regulatory institutions are lacking (or have been destroyed), there is generally a dramatic rise in violent conflict.[71] As it is not attractive to live under such conditions, many gamble their all on seeking an improvement – and any such prospects usually exist only in another country.

Political theorists since Hobbes have assumed that a permanent war of all against all is the norm in the absence of the state, but this is not accurate in the case of societies such as Somalia or Sudan. What characterizes them, rather, are repeated flare-ups of selective violence against particular social groups. War and violence are indeed normal conditions there, but this does not mean that everyone is equally affected. Although theory does not provide for them, there are constellations of fragile statehood with a high degree of violence that may last for an unpredictably long time.

VIOLENCE AND CLIMATE CHANGE

The above examples show that, at least initially, the consequences of climate change are not so much wars between states or threats to their territorial sovereignty as shortages of drinking water, declining food production, increased health risks and land degradation and floods that reduce living space.[72] Violent conflicts and climate change are thus linked in a series of stages and only exceptionally present a direct cause–effect relationship. This is why for a long time most researchers have overlooked or denied the connection between the two. Environmental changes due to global warming are treated simply as one variable in the interplay of factors that lead to violent conflicts. But this is trivial in so far as neither individual nor collective violence is ever mono-causal, and it is even questionable in principle whether the origin and development of violent processes could be given such an explanation. The very category of 'climate refugee', so hazy in international law, makes it clear that the decision to flee may result from war, massacre, extreme weather, rising sea levels or loss of a subsistence base; several of these typically come together when people decide to seek salvation elsewhere. Nothing that brings human beings to make a far-reaching decision can be traced back to a single cause.

The main reason why social processes do not operate in accordance with a mechanical causality is that people act within specific social situations and relationships. The various influences impact not causally but *relationally* on decisions to flee or remain, fight or collaborate, and so on: that is, they change the position of the agent within a reality that is itself changing. Moreover, every decision produces new consequences, which may unintentionally or unexpectedly change the action situation. 'If I had known that . . .', people say when they are faced with unintended consequences of their actions, thereby making it clear both that they had other alternatives and that things could have worked out differently. New problems arise and need to be solved in the course of action – problems that no one reckoned with at the starting point in the chain of decisions and actions. Hence the chain of causes that historians construct has a far greater necessity than the relevant sequence of actions *could* have had at the time, and hence too it is never the case that the people who acted at the time could see all the consequences of their actions. For, unlike the historian, they never know how things are going to work out. The origin and development of social processes can never be attributed to a single cause, and they never unfold in accordance with causal laws. It is therefore a banality to say that climate change is not a *direct* cause of armed conflicts.

'Climate change', write Gleditsch and Nordas,

> will probably have many serious effects, particularly transition effects, on peoples and societies worldwide. The hardships of climate change are particularly likely to add to the burden of poverty and human insecurity of already vulnerable societies and weak governments. Thus, climate change can be seen as a security issue in a broad sense, and efforts to halt or reverse it may well warrant a peace prize. However, so far there is little or any solid evidence that we are going to see an increase in armed conflicts as a result of climate change.[73]

One cannot agree with this in the case of Darfur or other African countries, especially as more recent research has identified correlations between temperature rises and violent conflicts and suggested that civil wars south of the Sahara will be 60 per cent more frequent by the year 2030.[74] A study of climate effects on the development of conflicts in the

Middle East also comes to disturbing conclusions.[75] It may be, then, that there is evidence of greater potential violence in the wake of rising temperatures, declining rainfall or lower harvest yields,[76] and there may be cases in which the disappearance of resources has led not to violence but to migration or contractual solutions.[77] But all this shows is that environmental changes due to global warming produce new sources of violence, with which people cope as best they can.

It is ridiculous to claim, however, as Nils Peter Gleditsch does repeatedly, that one can speak of an increased potential for violence only when enough case studies have been published in specialist academic journals. For violence is never monocausal: it always arises in specific social constellations and historical situations, and years spent compiling hundreds of case studies will never establish a direct and straightforward connection between climate change and violence, in the sense familiar from the natural sciences. This is true of any other social fact, moreover. What is lacking is a theoretical framework that makes it possible to describe, or even better predict, factors leading to social breakdown and converting a latent potential into a direct application of violence. Only such a framework can allow one to assess what is specific and what is generalizable in individual case studies; otherwise one just piles up studies and is unable to see the wood for the trees – a practice that Margaret Mead, in her discipline of anthropology, called 'Bongo-Bongoism': 'Yes, it may be that hunger often leads to violence, but among the Bongo-Bongos I studied things are more complicated . . .'

In any event – and this is largely agreed among social scientists – we can say that the consequences of climate change will reinforce and deepen survival problems and the potential for violence; they will interact with political, economic, ethnic and other social-historical factors and may also lead to the open use of force.[78] The pioneering work of a research team under Günther Bächler has established that 'violent actions are not attributable to drought, flooding or sea levels per se, but rather to the weakness of political institutions, the unsustainability of social-economic structures or the dissolution of traditional conditions of life.'[79]

At present, the main climate triggers of conflict are food or water shortages and social breakdown following extreme weather events or

mass migration.[80] In general, climate-driven environmental changes
make survival difficult where failed states and barren conditions leave
little scope for compensatory adjustment. Whether hunger, thirst,
land loss, expulsion, ethnic conflict or warlord rivalry over power and
resources then lead to open violence depends on the exact local balance between existential threats and compensatory opportunities. The
danger of conflicts is never smaller as a result of climate change; and
here too there are intensification effects, such as the special difficulty
of adjusting to climate change where the state is fragile or has failed.[81]
This means that, at a later stage, the resources for a functioning state
in the affected regions will be further weakened by advancing climate
change[82] – a vicious circle that the asymmetry of global society will
make more frequent in the years and decades to come. But here a few
more remarks are in order about the already discernible links between
environmental stress and the potential for violence.

Ecological problems such as *soil degradation* and *resource shortages*
have been widely discussed at national and international level since the
publication of *Limits to Growth*[83] and the emergence of the ecological
movement in the 1970s. All the more striking is it, then, that the social
implications have received so little attention up to now. Only discussion
of the water wars of the early 1990s, and of the ever growing numbers
of refugees on the coasts of Tenerife, Gibraltar, Andalusia and Sicily,
has given subtle hints that climate change may have a social and political side that goes beyond weather trends and snow cover in ski resorts.

Recently, *eco-social linkages* have been seen in the conflicts between
nomads and farmers in Nigeria, Ethiopia and Kenya, and in the genocides in Rwanda and Darfur. Although violent conflicts are always
a product of several parallel, uneven developments,[84] the structural
causes of violence, such as state collapse, the emergence of 'violence
markets' and the exclusion or extermination of population groups, are
reinforced and accelerated by ecological problems and the disappearance of soil, water and other resources. Salinization adds to the problems by reducing areas of farmland and triggering migration flows. It is
then the search for new pastures or agricultural land, rather than ecological decline per se, which may directly unleash conflicts with other
groups.[85] The same applies to the border conflicts that will become
more frequent as waterways that used to constitute natural frontiers run

dry.[86] Internal migration triggered by environmental changes also leads to major conflicts and may be understood as an indirect consequence of climate change. It is estimated that there are currently 24 million internal refugees around the world.

A further threat is the *breakdown of protection systems*. Alongside the increasing intensity and frequency of hurricanes, tsunamis and drought, rising sea levels are the main danger to development and survival in many parts of the world. The 15 to 59 centimetre rise predicted by the year 2100 will cause the flooding of parts of megacities, where the poor will be the hardest hit. In Lagos, for instance, which today has a population of 17 million, the consequences could destabilize the whole of West Africa; western coastal areas of the continent are themselves exposed to flooding, while further south Mozambique, Tanzania and Angola are in particular danger. Nor are these problems limited to Africa. The floods in New Orleans in 2005 put hundreds of thousands to flight and showed that, even in stable societies, infrastructure can be destroyed with lightning speed and relief organizations stretched to breaking point. The disaster also made it clear how quickly social order can break down.

The greater frequency of extreme weather events is already hitting poorer, more vulnerable groups in society, especially slum dwellers, who are the least able to protect themselves or to make the necessary adjustments. Natural disasters may destroy large chunks of existing infrastructure, sometimes on a recurrent basis, so that transport, supply and health systems are weakened and the state is further destabilized.

The spread of *infectious diseases* and *food crises* poses another set of problems. As we said before, development and conflict research has established a clear correlation between poverty and susceptibility to violence,[87] but disease and malnutrition are further consequences of climate change. According to the IPCC, the expected temperature increases will cause infectious illnesses such as malaria and yellow fever to spread faster and to affect previously untouched regions such as East Africa.[88] In southern Africa alone, the total infected areas are likely to double by 2100, when some 8 million people will be infected. Already the number of additional malaria cases due to climate change is thought to be running as high as 5 million, with 150,000 deaths.[89]

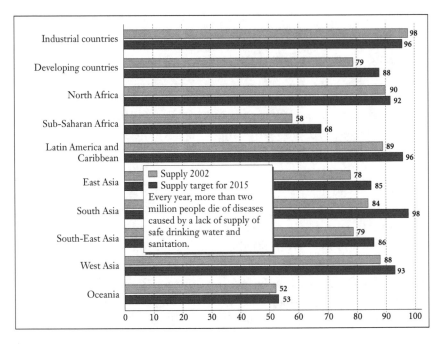

Figure 6.1   Percentage of population with access to safe drinking water, by region
Source: WHO/UNICEF 2004.

Water is, of course, a key factor in the whole issue of health. Sub-Saharan Africa has the worst water supply situation anywhere in the world today,[90] and any improvement is made more difficult by the growing resource shortage.[91] Up to now the greatest effect of climate change in Africa has been the decreased precipitation, especially in West Africa, and in future North Africa too will have to reckon with sharply downward trends. In the last thirty years rainfall in the Sahel region has declined by 25 per cent;[92] we have already discussed the impact on other regions in Sudan. Soil degradation, water shortages and extreme weather events such as drought or floods are already having an effect on productivity, especially in arid and semi-arid regions; this trend will become more pronounced in the years ahead. With the predicted temperature rise of 2 degrees Celsius by 2050, 12 million people in Africa alone would face starvation; a rise of 3 degrees would push the total up to 60 million.[93]

Another future cause of conflict will be the *drying up of rivers and lakes.* A long-smouldering dispute between Iran and Afghanistan goes back to the closure by the Taliban in 1998 of the dam sluices on the Helmand River, which cut the flow of water into the Iranian Hamoun lake region. Soon afterwards all three lakes in the region dried up; the surrounding 'marshes turned to dust bowls. Hundreds of villages on either side of the border were overwhelmed by shifting sand dunes and ravaged by summer dust storms. . . . The old irrigation channels round the lake disappeared beneath the sand.'[94] There are many similar situations where countries lying upstream channel off so much river water that virtually nothing is left for those downstream – a classical instance being the River Jordan, which supplies very little water to the country after which it is named.[95]

Even more spectacular is the disappearance of lakes that mark the boundary between states. Lake Chad, for instance, has by now lost 95 per cent of its original area, owing partly to decreased rainfall, partly to diversion for irrigation projects. Previously, four countries – Niger, Nigeria, Chad and Cameroon – lay on Lake Chad; today neither Niger nor Nigeria has any shores by it. Since people began to settle on the dried-out bed of the lake, border disputes have broken out between neighbouring countries – Nigeria and Cameroon, for example.[96]

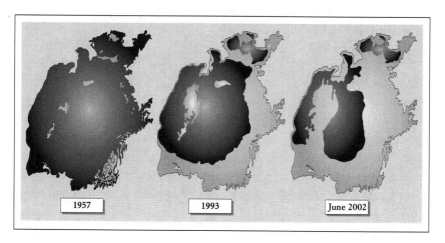

1957   1993   June 2002

Figure 6.2   The shrinking of the Aral Sea, 1957–2002; the sea became divided in two in 1989–90

Source: Philippe Rekacewicz, GRID/UNEP.

Similar things have been happening on the Aral Sea, through which the Kazakhstan–Uzbekistan frontier runs.

The social consequences of climate change give rise to the following conflict scenarios.

- The number of violent local and regional conflicts over access to land and freshwater will increase.
- Migration between countries will grow, together with the numbers of internal refugees, leading to violence at both local and regional level.
- The shrinking of lakes and drying up of rivers, as well as the disappearance of forest and nature reserves, will generate cross-border resource conflicts.
- One country's adaptation to climate change (dam construction, water extraction from rivers and underground basins) will create problems in one or more other countries, again leading to interstate conflicts.

In addition, international trade disputes will increase in relation to such resources as diamonds, wood, oil and gas. Since violent conflicts tend to develop a dynamic of their own, further problems will arise that appear solvable only through the use of greater violence. The scale of the resulting refugee flows cannot be accurately predicted today – forecasts vary between 50 and 200 million so-called climate refugees by the year 2050, in comparison with current Red Cross estimates of 25 million.[97] Social processes cannot, however, be simply projected from existing situations, since it is not possible to predict how countries will react to immigration pressure or how great the conflicts will be that trigger further refugee flows. For example, the war in Iraq alone resulted in 2 million Iraqi exiles abroad (mainly in Syria and Jordan) and 1.8 million internal refugees.[98] It has been calculated that there were already 25 million environmental refugees in 1995 – well above the figure for 'normal' refugees (22 million).[99]

This is another source of disquiet in many governments and international organizations. At the end of 2007, the United Nations Security Council held a debate for the first time on climate change and security, and in 2009 UN Secretary General Ban Ki-Moon was instructed by the General Assembly to produce a report on the issue. In March 2008 the European Union published a joint report by High Representative Javier Solana and the European Commission, under the title *Climate Change and International Security*, which Solana supplemented with further material in December 2008.[100] All the findings concur that global warming will bring considerable security problems in the short, medium and long term, even though these will vary greatly from region to region.

In terms of climate as well as economics and security challenges, the Western countries may remain islands of bliss for another few decades in comparison with less favoured parts of the world. But they too will inevitably be drawn into climate wars – or, to be more precise, into the waging of climate wars. On the other hand, not all of these will look like what have traditionally been thought of as wars.

INJUSTICE AND UNEVENNESS

The consequences of climate change are unfairly distributed, because those who bear the largest responsibility for it are likely to suffer the least harm and to have the greatest opportunity to benefit. Conversely, those parts of the world which have scarcely yet added to the emissions that cause global warming will be the ones hardest hit. The industrial countries emit an annual average of 12.6 tonnes of CO_2 per capita, while the poorest countries limit themselves to 0.9 tonnes. Nearly a half of all emissions worldwide come from the old heartlands, despite the rapid catching-up on the part of the newly industrializing countries.[101]

> Monsoon irregularities will primarily affect the countries of South-East Asia. Floods will mainly hit people in the world's major delta regions, such as those in Bangladesh and India, for example. The impact of rising sea levels will be worst on small island states (the countless Pacific islets, for example) or low-lying coastal cities like Mogadishu, Venice or New Orleans. Rich countries such as the Netherlands will find it fairly easy to improve their dyke defences; communities in Kansas will be able to afford reforestation after storm damage much more readily than those in Kerala.[102]

This relative injustice becomes absolute when whole populations lose their livelihood – for example, if island clusters like Tuvalu are flooded or the homelands of the Inuit disappear. The government of Tuvalu has applied for asylum in Australia and New Zealand on behalf of its population; the Inuit, supported by human rights organizations, want to sue the United States as the chief producer of greenhouse gases.

At present there is little prospect that international disparities will be confronted; international environmental law is still in its early stages, and individual countries are neither compelled to sign up to it nor bound by its provisions. There are no international courts of justice to punish violations of the principles of sustainable development or environmental protection. Binding measures against even higher emissions of greenhouse gases, for example, require the complex negotiation of treaties and agreements, but the main problem is that most of these only provide for signatory states to incur obligations on their own initiative, and that it is therefore difficult or impossible to sanction those which fail to meet their targets. Some countries, moreover – the USA and Australia, in the case of the Kyoto Protocol – tend not to endorse binding declarations that they think will be disadvantageous to them economically.

However distant it seems, the creation of an international environmental organization and court of justice is urgently needed[103] – although the planet will probably be a couple of degrees warmer by the time they take shape.

The unjust distribution of the consequences of climate change, and of the capacity to cope with them, is not only further proof that life is unfair; it has also created considerable potential for conflict, as we can see from the complex human rights issue of how to compensate Pacific island or Arctic dwellers whose living space is *already* disappearing as a result of floods or global warming. Furthermore, the distribution of causes and effects is unjust in the relationship between generations, where the conflict potential is marked in a number of respects.

In the 1950s, the emissions curve generated by the industrial countries rose steeply; the cause of the problem, whose full scale is only now visible to us, is therefore at least half a century old. But the causes of climate change not only go back many decades but have persisted throughout the intervening period and become global as the

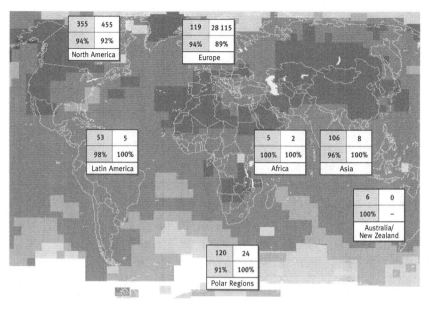

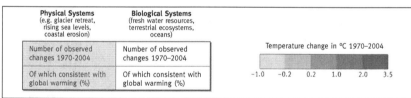

Figure 6.3   World map of climate effects

Source: IPCC.

developing countries have modernized in turn. A reversal is therefore hard to imagine, and for all the mutual promises it even seems utopian to believe that emissions will be held at their present level.

In any case, there is the further problem that the climate is slow to respond. Present and future generations will unfortunately have to deal with a time lag of half a century, whose climate effects would show even if everyone stopped driving a car tomorrow, even if no more aircraft took to the skies, and even if all factories shut down forthwith. Such larger-than-life prospects hardly encourage anyone to do something to counter them.

The global, but very unevenly distributed, effects of climate change also raise considerable problems of justice in interstate relations.[104] It is true that many international programmes are under way to strengthen adjustment capacity – for instance, those coming under the IPCC or the Global Environment Facility (GEF) – but there is reason to doubt their effectiveness. It is certainly frustrating that today's and tomorrow's generations will have to cope with what their predecessors leave behind, especially since, although the effects are already palpable, plans to improve matters remain highly vague.

The measures devised and applied today will yield results, if at all, only in a distant future, while in the meantime the reshaping of lifeworlds keeps running in the background. Since the consequences of what is done will stretch over generations, it may well be asked whether there is any scope at all for people living today to produce outcomes from which they themselves will benefit.

Yet another complication is that, although some effects of climate change are already discernible, the new significance of extreme heatwaves, storms or downpours may be fully intelligible only in a scientific framework. No one today says: 'The weather's gone crazy', but rather: 'It's global warming at work.' Yet knowledge of this comes from scientific research and models; those who lose their livelihood from the melting of Arctic ice and can see for themselves what is happening are few in number, and their special lifeworld is wholly unlike that of Mediterranean peoples, for example. For the moment their experience may still even seem exotic.

Other people, however, can perceive the impending catastrophe only by means of models, and psychologically these arouse little motivation to change personal behaviour or to prioritize activities and interests in a new way. This is true even in prosperous, well-educated Western societies, which can afford the luxury of looking at environmental problems in a time span longer than a quarter of a century. But the *unevenness* of development and especially the moves by non-Western societies to catch up radically undermine the urgent development of environmental awareness and problem-solving strategies.

Arguments based on justice that involve tolerance or acceptance of catching-up modernization play an ambiguous role in this respect. We cannot, it is said, deny to third world societies the kind of technological and economic modernization that the West has to thank for its own locational advantages, high standard of living and relative security for the future. This raises the question of whether justice requires creating the possibility for others to eliminate the foundations for long-term human survival. But the real point here is that questions and arguments centred on justice weigh heavily in discussions of climate change and will become even more explosive in the future; it is already evident that those who profit from a further increase in deadly emissions are already playing the justice card to push through their anachronistic conception of modernization, whereas those who have no chances in their place of birth claim it is just that they should at least be able to live somewhere, even if it is not where they would like to live.

To sum up: the industrial modernization processes in full swing in Asia today, which, as we see from the Chinese case, are not subject to democratic control, give no indication of how they might incorporate a more rational approach to resource conservation and survival interests, or of how the trap of 'catching-up justice' might be dismantled. In fact, the phenomena of injustice and unevenness have considerable significance for social and democratic theory and raise a set of key questions. What does transgenerational injustice imply for the possibility of conceiving oneself as a political subject? Or for the sense that one can achieve something through one's actions? Or for the range of ideas about how something might be changed? What does politics mean in such circumstances, beyond the mere processing of external constraints?

VIOLENCE AND THEORY

As we now know, when societies have practised or endured extreme violence, the effects may last for generations.[105] This persistence allows us to speak of contemporary Germany, Vietnam or Serbia, for example, as societies marked by the effects of violence, and to ask how the experience of extreme violence actually influences their development potential. A further challenge for social theory is the close link between modernization processes and ethnic cleansing or racist campaigns of extermination and genocide. In a curious intellectual blindness, extreme violence and its lasting consequences are nearly always treated as deviations from normal patterns of development, as 'relapses' or 'special cases' isolated from the promise of modernity. Yet Auschwitz and Hiroshima, My Lai and Srebrenica were social catastrophes that became possible only with modern problem-solving strategies, conceptions of order, bureaucracies and technologies. Auschwitz was an industrial installation for the exploitation and murder of other human beings, and that was not in the least archaic or regressive. Such things are invented by industrial, not tribal, societies.

At the same time, the modern idea that social developments follow certain laws and display a regular structure completely leaves out of account the fact that human life-communities always have to face contingency, accident and violence. Often in history earthquakes, volcanic eruptions, hurricanes, floods, climate variations, and so on, have unexpectedly altered or destroyed the conditions of life; and social disasters, unleashed by power and resource conflicts, chance political constellations or even individual personalities, have escalated and taken paths with nothing law-like about them. Just as accident cannot be written out of social processes, violence is an 'occupational hazard of relations in society, . . . "a part of economics in the broad picture of world history", an option for human behaviour that is constantly present'.[106]

In highly complex societies, in particular, developments may depend on how people evaluate the action conditions and opportunity structures, on whether they see a chance to put their special abilities to the test. Instructive in this respect is the case of Kurt Prüfer, an engineer who worked on crematorium ovens for the Topf & Sons firm in Erfurt and, showing particular zeal, developed a 'double muffle oven' that considerably increased the murder throughput at Auschwitz by allowing corpse disposal to take place more quickly than before.[107] Processes of mass murder like the Holocaust are made up of many such particular contributions that often go almost unnoticed; they follow no master plan, but involve a social dynamic whereby people in different places and at different levels within the division of labour see a point in getting things moving and doing their job especially well.

But this does not mean that history *had to* unfold in a particular way, that there was no alternative. The fact that the 'final solution to the Jewish question' ended in mass extermination camps was not a historical inevitability: Hitler might have died earlier, a firmer decision or better conditions might have favoured the 'Madagascar Plan',[108] or a more decisive foreign policy on the British or American side might have opened the way to other options. Thus, developments which appear in retrospect to have been causally determined, logical or even unavoidable could always have happened differently; they arose by chance, in a meandering or self-reinforcing manner, at the time of the action in question. We must thoroughly rid ourselves of any idea that causality is a category of social action.

In social processes, B cannot be said to follow from A. When people do something with or against one another, interpretations and mutual expectations play the decisive role – hence a suspected B is already contained in A, and each actor is part of the other's perception. Social action is not played out in a chain a–b–c–d–e, or as a sequence of action and reaction, but rather as a development of relations. No realistic or rational images of others and their behaviour have to underlie these relations – indeed, it is likely that that happens only rarely. Nevertheless, the mutual perceptions, interpretations and actions change the relations among the players, and in the next move the game is taken a stage further.[109] This means that social action is not causal but recursive – and for that very reason something usually emerges from it that deviates from the original plan.

In this light, categories such as cause and effect, precondition and consequence, structure and function lose some of the glitter that they have in sociological and philosophical theories, while messy categories like accident and feelings push themselves to the fore. Accidents such as Chernobyl may have consequences deeper and longer-lasting than those resulting from any planned action; perceived realities matter more than objective realities for decision-making. Social practices such as the use of force, and action modes such as rationalization, dissonance reduction and the wish to think and act in agreement with others, are not marginal but constitutive conditions of social action.

7

KILLING TOMORROW: NEVER-ENDING WARS, ETHNIC CLEANSING, TERRORISM, SHIFTING BOUNDARIES

Once, I remember, we came upon a man-of-war anchored off the coast. There wasn't even a shed there, and she was shelling the bush. It appears the French had one of their wars going on thereabouts. Her ensign dropped limp like a rag; the muzzles of the long six-inch guns stuck out all over the low hull; the greasy, slimy swell swung her up lazily and let her down, swaying her thin masts. In the empty immensity of earth, sky, and water, there she was, incomprehensible, firing into a continent. Pop, would go one of the six-inch guns; a small flame would dart and vanish, a little white smoke would disappear, a tiny projectile would give a feeble screech – and nothing happened. Nothing could happen. There was a touch of insanity in the proceeding, a sense of lugubrious drollery in the sight; and it was not dissipated by somebody on board assuring me earnestly there was a camp of natives – he called them enemies! – hidden out of sight somewhere.

This image, from Conrad's *Heart of Darkness*, is one of the most arresting and surreal accounts of violence for its own sake. Much as the inhabitants of Easter Island, cut off from the world in an eerie silence, gave themselves up to absolute war, so here the gunboat of a French colonial enterprise fires on a whole continent in a purposeless gesture that has taken on a life of its own. Perhaps the crew think they see an enemy to be fought, but no observer can detect why they are shooting or at what. Military violence creates a *new situation*, a different relationship to the world from the one that existed or was even imaginable before. Conrad's description was based not on the powers of literary imagination but on his own experience. As an employee of the Société Anonyme pour le Commerce du Haut Congo, Conrad/Korzeniowski had travelled up the River Congo to pick up a team of workers from Stanley Falls – although he never made it to his destination. His African experiences threw him into such despair that he switched his life as a colonial trader for that of a novelist. *Heart of Darkness* painted a vision of unfettered violence so powerful that, eighty years later, it provided the basis for a film about a much more recent, though no less demoralizing, form of anonymous violence: Francis Ford Coppola's film *Apocalypse Now*.

In contrast to other objects of social theory – work, media, demography, art, etc. – violence is only to a very limited degree, if at all, part of the experiential world of the academics who concern themselves with it. As a result, little explicit research has been devoted to this central area of human action, and even that is overloaded with moralism and fantasy. Being seen as something *alien*, violence is an unclear and threatening theme to tackle. In recent decades it has mainly been historians who have focused on it, dealing with processes that are now over and done with and therefore less dangerous than present-day or likely future events. Besides, the history of human violence, unlike that of other cultural phenomena, is fairly well documented. This speaks for its fundamental importance for social relations.

WARS

We are cultural animals and it is the richness of our culture which allows us to accept our undoubted potentiality for violence but to believe nevertheless that its expression is a cultural aberration. History lessons remind us that the states in which we live, their institutions, even their laws, have come to us through conflict, often of the most bloodthirsty sort. Our daily diet of news brings us reports of the shedding of blood, often in regions quite close to our homelands, in

circumstances that deny our conception of cultural normality altogether. We succeed, all the same, in consigning the lessons of history
and reportage to a special and separate category of 'otherness' which
invalidates our expectations of how our own world will be tomorrow
and the day after not at all. Our institutions and our laws, we tell ourselves, have set the human potentiality for violence about with such
restraints that violence in everyday life will be punished as criminal by
our laws, while its use by our institutions of state will take the particular
form of 'civilized warfare'.[1]

John Keegan is doubtless right when he notes the peculiar refusal to
come to grips with today's war and violence and to accept that it is
closely bound up with characteristically modern forms of communication. It may be the fact that 90 per cent of wars since 1945 have
been fought outside Europe and North America which has led to the
Western notion that they should be viewed as a problem for *other* societies, especially ones whose forms of statehood have not yet reached the
level of OECD countries. Military violence can thus be regarded as an
anomaly, although the murderous twentieth century is only just over
and war clearly has a great future.

In any event it had a great past after 1945. Since then there have been
more than 200 wars in the world,[2] with a tendency to become more
frequent until the early 1990s and a reverse tendency in the years since
then. There have been roughly fifty wars each in Asia, Africa and the
Middle East since the end of the Second World War, thirty in South
and Central America, and fourteen in Europe. Only North America
has remained free of armed conflict through this period. However, the
fact that wars in Europe have made up only 7 per cent of the post-1945
total tells us nothing about the frequency with which Western countries have taken part in violent international conflicts; for Britain has
been involved in nineteen, the United States in thirteen, and France in
twelve. We should remind ourselves that in 1982 Britain waged a classical interstate war against Argentina over the Falkland Islands, which
included the most important naval battle since the Second World War
and led to the loss of more than 900 lives.

A sharp rise in the number of wars seemed to be looming in the
1990s, but in reality the figure has since declined by roughly 40 per

Table 7.1 Wars and armed conflicts

Wars	Start date	Situation in 2005
Africa		
Angola (Cabinda)	2002	Armed conflict
Burundi	1993	War
Chad	1996	Armed conflict
Congo-Kinshasa (East Congo)	2005	War
Ethiopia (Gambela)	2003	Armed conflict
Ivory Coast	2002	War
Nigeria (Niger Delta)	2003	Armed conflict
Nigeria (North and Central)	2004	Armed conflict
Senegal (Casamance)	1990	Armed conflict
Somalia	1988	War
Sudan (Darfur)	2003	War
Uganda	1995	War
Asia		
India (Assam)	1990	War
India (Bodos)	1997	War
India (Kashmir)	1990	War
India (Nagas)	1969	Armed conflict
India (Naxalites)	1997	War
India (Tripura)	1999	War
Indonesia (Aceh)	1999	War
Indonesia (West Papua)	1963	Armed conflict
Laos	2003	War
Myanmar	2003	War
Nepal	1999	War
Pakistan (religious conflict)	2001	Armed conflict
Philippines (Mindanao)	1970	War
Philippines (NPA)	1970	War
Sri Lanka (Tamils)	2005	Armed conflict
Thailand (southern Thailand)	2004	War
Near and Middle East		
Afghanistan (anti-regime war)	1978	War
Afghanistan ('war on terror')	2001	War
Algeria	1992	War
Georgia (South Ossetia)	2004	Armed conflict
Iraq	1998	War
Israel (Palestine)	2000	War
Lebanon (southern Lebanon)	2004	War
Russia (Chechnya)	1990	Armed conflict
Saudi Arabia	1999	War
Turkey (Kurdistan)	2005	Armed conflict
Yemen	2004	War
Latin America		
Colombia (ELN)	1964	War
Colombia (FARC)	1965	War
Haiti	2004	Armed conflict

Source: AKUF, 2007

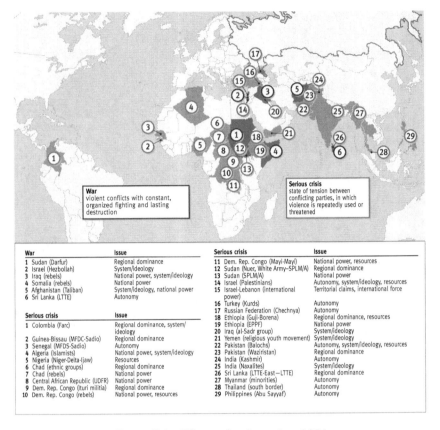

Figure 7.1   Wars and serious crises, 2006

Source: *Konfliktbarometer 2006*, Heidelberg Institute for International Conflict Research, December 2006.

cent.[3] This is partly due to the fact that, in the past fifteen years, more UN-mandated or UN-sanctioned interventions have taken place in violent conflicts (as in Kosovo or Congo), although they have not always been successful in the long term.

Most of the wars since 1945 have been civil wars of a post-colonial or revolutionary nature; only a quarter or so have corresponded to the classical type of an interstate conflict.

In 2006, according to the Heidelberg Institute for International Conflict Research, there were thirty-five major violent conflicts, including six wars (either international or civil, sometimes with more than two sides) (see figure 7.1). However, much depends on definitions: the Hamburg-based research project Arbeitsgemeinschaft Kriegsursachenforschung (AKUF), for its part, counted seventy-six major violent conflicts in 2006, including civil wars (as in Somalia, Darfur and Sri Lanka) and a smaller number of 'interstate wars' (in Afghanistan, Chechnya, Iraq, Kashmir).

Classical interstate wars are not currently being stoked up on a major scale, but three tendencies might change this:

1 International commodities markets and supply infrastructure (especially gas pipelines) are a highly sensitive area of 'global insecurity'.[4] Attacks on pipelines, refineries, bridges, and so on, are among the tactics of international terrorism, and local rebel groups (most notably in Nigeria and Iraq) pose a further threat. Similar scenarios are not unlikely to arise in Eastern Europe, where gas pipelines cross a number of countries.

2 Conflicts over basic materials such as water will become a major phenomenon in the future: it is estimated that at least 2 billion people will suffer from water shortages by the year 2050, and the gloomiest predictions set the figure as high as 7 billion.[5] New conflict scenarios are also appearing in connection with the drying up of lakes that lie across frontiers; in some cases (Lake Chad or the Aral Sea, for example) it suddenly becomes unclear which state or regional authority controls the new territory.[6]

3 Melting of the Arctic and Antarctic ice cover offers further scope for violent conflict. The vast natural resources suspected to lie beneath the ice will soon become accessible, and it has long been disputed who has the right to exploit them. The Russian 'Akademik Fyodorov' expedition staked sovereignty claims in summer 2007 by planting a titanium seabed marker to a depth of 4,200 metres; its self-declared mission was to declare the territorial limits of the Russian shelf in the area between the Novosibirsk islands and the North Pole.[7] This drew an immediate response from the United States, Canada and Denmark, which all rejected the Russian claims. Britain staked a claim to a million square kilometres of Antarctica, which brought it into conflict with Argentina and Chile.[8] The melting of ice also opens us new transport routes and associated economic opportunities, as in the case of the

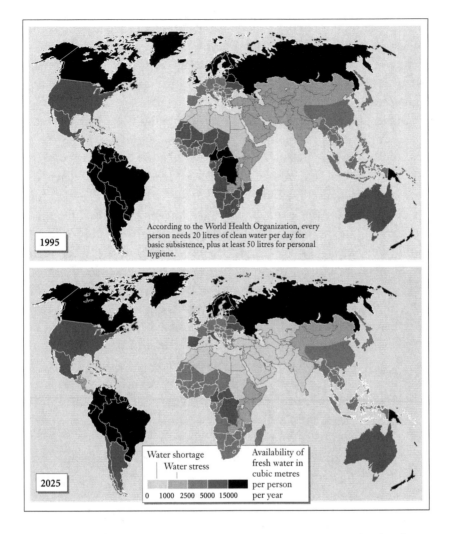

Figure 7.2 Regions affected by water shortage, 1995 and 2025 (predicted)
Source: Philippe Rekacewicz, from UNESCO/GRID.

Northwest Passage to Asia, which became navigable for the first time in summer 2007. Both Canada and the United States have established a military presence in the region.

The potential for conflict within and between states will therefore not diminish in the decades ahead. But, in addition, climate change may lead to new forms of warfare that the classical theories of war did not envisage.

NEVER-ENDING WARS

Extreme violence establishes forms of behaviour and experience for which the largely peaceful Western hemisphere of the post-Second World War period offers no frame of reference. Thus, any analysis should start by recognizing that much about extreme violence is *unintelligible* from the outside and cannot be explained in conventional theoretical terms. Gérard Prunier, one of the leading authorities on African wars and genocides, stresses at the beginning of his book on Darfur that not all the extreme violence perpetrated there makes sense; retrospective constructions of an inherent necessity are a big mistake that is best avoided.[9]

One of the hallmarks of a process of extreme violence is that it may generate social conditions and spaces at odds with the need for meaning, or the attribution of meaning, that academic analysts bring to it. Our instruments, methods and theories are calibrated to the assumption that social processes involve causal sequences of action which are capable of explanation. But this may prove mistaken, since – as Joseph Conrad learned from experience – there are social conditions in which meaning as we understand it is completely suspended, but in which social relations persist and people continue to act.

Another important point made by Prunier is that processes of extreme violence are discerned from outside only when they can be associated with a specific interest. The involvement of European politicians in the Yugoslav wars of succession played no small part in the slide into extreme violence, in parts of the country intended to become NATO allies and fellow EU members in the aftermath of the Cold War. The resulting disaster directly affected the interests of Western European states, whose reaction was correspondingly focused. In Africa and other parts of the world such interests may not come into play – for example, when Hutus started massacring Tutsis – and it may take decades for a war to come to the attention of the Western public. Prunier notes tersely: 'There are no big political, economic or security stakes for the developed world in these conflicts – just the deaths of human beings. The element which could draw wider attention to the problem, the fear of radical Islam, is not even there. Muslims killing Muslims – it is not a subject to arouse passions.'[10]

This 'attention economics'[11] is a two-way business. While Western societies become involved only if old colonial ties are still a factor or if a vital alliance or source of materials is affected, the local combatants in protracted wars gamble more and more on triggering mass poverty and refugee flows to spur the West into relief initiatives that can be fed back into the economy of violence. This too is a social interaction that finds no place in the theoretical models.

The brief euphoria after the East–West confrontation came to an end in 1989, as well as the related expectation that force would disappear in interstate relations, meant that people tended to overlook the long conflicts that had kept flaring up and dying down in the shadows of the Cold War, sometimes for decades, coming to notice only when they could be interpreted as 'proxy wars' between the USA and the Soviet Union. But the examples of never-ending conflict (Afghanistan, Tajikistan, Colombia, Sierra Leone, etc.) suggest that the classical war between states – in which one or both sides declare war and regular armies fight according to the rules of war and international law – may have been given too much prominence in reflections about the presence and importance of war in the contemporary world.

It is highly questionable whether this form of war, the dominant reference in the West, was ever actually the standard model. It may have applied to the First World War, although that has since come to be seen as the primal catastrophe of the twentieth century, whose regular beginning and formal ending conveyed none of the destructive persistence that would repeat itself in even greater horrors two decades later. The Second World War deviated in at least two respects from the classical model: Germany, the chief actor, systematically violated the laws of war to achieve its goals of colonization and annihilation of various human groups; and the concept of 'total war' struck at every member of society, erasing the distinction between combatants and civilian population. The violence of this war knew little regulation and few boundaries, and the far-reaching effects, beyond the 50 million killed, lingered on in a trans-generational half-life that reproduced national and international tensions such as those between Germany and Poland or Estonia and Russia.

Neither the so-called liberation wars of Mao Zedong or Pol Pot nor those which the communist regimes then waged against their own peoples can be described in the categories of classical warfare. Nor does the annihilation of whole cities, culminating in Hiroshima and Nagasaki, fit that model. The distinction between 'old' and 'new' wars, which has been in vogue in recent years,[12] therefore appears somewhat questionable. If the references are the Geneva Convention, the Hague Convention and Clausewitz's theory of war, then earlier regulated conflicts should be seen as an exception associated with particular processes of European state-building, rather than a rule that would make it appropriate to describe them today as 'old'.

And what of all the violent conflicts that have been, or still are, fought over many decades between Irish Protestants and Catholics, Chinese and Nepalese, Turks and Kurds, Israelis and Palestinians? 'Low intensity wars' by no means represent a new dimension of warfare. Rather, everything suggests that heterogeneous forms of violence have existed alongside one another. And if this testifies to anything, it is that violence is always available as an option for social behaviour, a latent or manifest core element of social relations. Members of societies with a stable monopoly of violence usually like to overlook this, but there the violence is simply embedded in a different social relationship; it has become *indirect*, and is employed only in special punishable cases, but that does not mean it has disappeared. Moreover, when a regulated form of warfare has lasted for a long historical period, it has been, as Keegan points out, the warfare of a 'primitive' people, whose violent disputes were contained within highly ritualized practices.[13] This all shows that we tend to consider a violent confrontation as war if that corresponds to our historical experience, overlooking the fact that elsewhere violent relations of a different intensity and duration determine the social reality.

But, regardless of whether the new/old distinction holds water or not, one cannot but agree with Mary Kaldor that in the last thirty years, especially in Africa, a type of organized violence has taken shape in which no sharp boundary can be drawn between war and peace,[14] still less between legitimate and criminal violence. Similarly, the line of divide between regular and irregular soldiers has gone by the board, and fighting has, as Münkler says, become 'asymmetrical': that is, it takes place not between opponents of equal status but between semi-state or private entrepreneurs and populations. Private warlords, close to the government or the opposition, organize violence that helps groups with financial muscle to maintain power and furthers the criminal exploitation of raw materials such as diamonds, precious woods and oil or the production and export of drugs. As a result, the warlords actually have an interest in the continuation of war rather than its conclusion.[15]

Here the 'monopolists of war' are not states and trained experts but semi-state or non-state players who, in pursuing their particular interests, kill part of the population in order to sow fear and terror among the rest. Münkler argues that such asymmetrical wars will shape the twenty-first century. There is much to be said for this, since fragile or failed states are more vulnerable to the effects of climate change, and the erosion of state power and the privatization of violence will become more frequent and affect more countries. Climate wars such as the Darfur conflict are thus harbingers of the future, but this does not at all mean that similar processes will engulf the OECD countries, for example. On the contrary, the power, welfare and security gap between first world countries and fast-developers, on the one hand, and the countries of the third world, on the other, will widen still further, resulting in the entrenchment of global inequality and discord.

According to Mary Kaldor, five groups of armed players appear in these protracted wars. First of all are *regular armies*, whose weakness may mean that their role is highly problematic in the context of fragile or failing states. Poorly trained and equipped, often receiving little or no pay, such soldiers are more likely to be recruited by private entrepreneurs than to serve as loyal representatives of the public weal; national armies then turn into an undisciplined force displaying symptoms of breakdown. At the same time, they overburden the state budget with weapons purchases, produce sizeable military elites and lower the threshold of violence in society. As Keegan writes, 'Western "technology transfers", a euphemism for selfish arms sales by rich Western nations to poor ones that could rarely afford the outlay, did not entail the transfusion of culture which made advanced weapons so deadly in the hands of the West.'[16] Not infrequently, parts of the regular army put themselves up for sale, or split off under the command of an officer who has decided to set up in business on his own account. Such developments were seen in Yugoslavia, as in Tajikistan and Zaire.

These split-offs then become indistinguishable from *para-military groups*, which, like the *Janjaweed* in Darfur, consist of discharged or turncoat soldiers, youth gangs, criminals and assorted adventurers, often too of children and teenagers. Such paramilitaries may be close to either the government or the opposition. In the first case, they undertake actions that serve the purposes of the government but for which it cannot accept responsibility; in the second case, their task is to fight against the existing government. These roles may be reversed, of course, if circumstances change.

Self-defence units are the third group of armed players. Formed in response to attacks by regular troops or paramilitaries, they do not have an effective military potential and do not usually remain in existence for long.[17]

Of greater significance are the *private military companies* (PMCs) and *foreign mercenaries*, usually veterans from West and East European armies or mujahideen from Afghanistan, or 'often recruited from retired soldiers from Britain or the United States, who are hired both by governments and by multinational companies and are often inter-connected.'[18] Such professionals of violence, rooted in the private sector of the economy, play an especially important role in tasks such as torture and blackmail, which governments are reluctant to take on directly because of the potential for scandal. PMC personnel have also operated in the latest wars in Iraq and Afghanistan, performing guard duties, pursuing terrorists, training local police and militias, and so on. In 2003 alone the US government signed 3,512 contracts with companies for security functions.[19] In Kenya there are some 40,000 policemen in comparison with 300,000 employees of private security firms.[20] The number of non-state armed players on the American side in the Iraq War stood at roughly 50,000. 'Most private contractors do support jobs such as logistics, training, communications and intelligence, catering and laundry; ... when the scandals about torture in the Abu Ghraib prison became public, it was evident that private contractors had carried out some of the most dubious practices.'[21] The killing of civilians is also often attributed to them.[22]

A fifth group of players is *regular foreign armies*, acting under the umbrella of the UN, the African Union or NATO, which are supposed to prevent genocide or ethnic cleansing, provide security at elections or monitor ceasefire agreements. Often numerically weak, they are also in the precarious situation of not being accepted by the local population and having a limited mandate to use force. Other players may deliberately target them to provoke an overreaction or attacks on civilians, which can then be used as a weapon against the intervention force in the global media. An extreme case of failure on the part of an intervention force was the withdrawal of Dutch UN troops from Srebrenica in 1995, which opened the way for a massacre of approximately 8,000 adult men and youths.

VIOLENCE MARKETS

Never-ending wars generally involve heterogeneous, fragmented groups of players which, with the exception of intervention forces, use less violence against other such groups than against the civilian population. The late social anthropologist Georg Elwert described the social spaces in which they do this as 'violence markets' – a term which emphasizes that privatization and economic factors of violence are a central element of never-ending wars, and that the economic strategies in question 'appear thoroughly profitable to the entrepreneurs of violence that pursue them'. The 'appeal to culture, ethnic traditions and religion is here one resource among others' for stirring up and maintaining the armed conflict, as are emotions such as hate or fear, which were not a structural element in the origination of the conflict.[23] Indeed, such emotions often appear first with the outbreak of violence, but then have a tendency to become self-perpetuating and to fuel new sources of violence.

As we have seen, the lack of a stable monopoly of violence offers niches and opportunity structures for the private deployment of violence. Such spaces are 'open to violence', and it is the coupling of these with market interests that establishes the violence market. In Elwert's analysis, this is a field of action defined by acquisitive goals, involving the exchange of goods (weapons, drugs, food, local raw materials, hostages), theft and various combinations of the two, such as road tolls, protection money and kidnapping for ransom money. 'Protection money (also called tolls) and hostage-taking develop as intermediate forms between trade and robbery. . . . Diamond smugglers in present-day Zaire, khat dealers in Somalia, emerald smugglers in Colombia, and not least the convoys carrying food relief in Somalia and Bosnia make this the main economic sector by income in certain periods.' Here too it is clear that kidnappings, as in Iraq or Afghanistan, are very rarely attributable to the political calculations that serve to camouflage them, but are part of an economy of violence in which politics, faith and ideology are tools rather than ends in themselves.

The production of violence itself takes place within an economic perspective. If the fighters supply themselves, by robbing and pillaging, this reduces costs for the warlords and assists their strategy of implanting violence in the region: the aim is to sow fear, to trigger refugee flows and to facilitate the recruitment of fighters or forced labour. The instruments of violence are not expensive: handguns, Kalashnikovs, simple rocket launchers and light trucks do the brunt of the work; Darfur showed how easily ordinary petrol cans may be turned into fire-bombs. So, one is speaking of low-tech means, which have the advantage of costing little and requiring no special operational skills. Murder or intimidation can be practised cheaply and efficiently.

The fact that violence is directed less against another armed party than against civilians is one of the key features of never-ending wars. The unleashing of refugee flows, the speedily erected camps and the ensuing relief operations by the international community are important resources for the economy of violence. Relief convoys can be used to supply one's troops with weapons and food, and it is even possible, as it were, to order the delivery of provisions from abroad by means of targeted actions against the civilian population. Considerable sums can also be raised in tolls and protection money for allowing aid convoys to pass unhindered, and almost intact, along the road to a refugee camp. The camps themselves become arenas for political or religious agitation, and not least for the recruitment of new fighters and all kinds of labour. There are subtle and not so subtle ways of exploiting international aid in crisis situations.

Wars in certain regions of the third world have something disturbingly opaque about them, and even the war in Yugoslavia, so close to

the West geographically, had an uncanny exoticism not unlike that of
Rwanda or Darfur. In Africa it could be put down to a 'tribal conflict',
while here the special culture of the Balkans was supposed to account
for the astonishing escalation of violence.[24] Such explanations serve to
reduce the dissonance that open violence, injustice and human rights
violations produce in those who live in better worlds and have made it
their political and cultural task to enforce human rights globally or, in
the event of breakdown, to provide material assistance.

So, in order to reduce the moral dissonance that Rwandan genocide
produces in Germany, every effort is made to help the victims – or
anyway those who have escaped with their lives. Mobile hospitals, doctors and nurses, medicine, blankets, tents and food: all these have to be
transported, often with considerable difficulty, to the affected region,
and that costs a lot of money and involves a lot of 'wastage' along the
way. The armed combatants exploit this Western mode of dissonance
reduction, to such an extent that they deliberately add to the West's
moral dissonance; they sow violence and reap the harvest.

In a different context, Erving Goffman called this exploitation of
institutional structures 'secondary adaptation'[25] – and this is precisely
the parasitic manner in which violence markets relate to other economies. But by now the system of secondary adaptation has become so
routinized that protection money and wastage quotas are built into the
calculations of aid agencies and the strategies of the entrepreneurs of
violence. This two-way link between aid and violence is an interesting example of how the conditions and consequences of action can be
interconnected in ways that are unexpectedly straightforward.

To be sure, this is not the only resource that the entrepreneurs of
violence utilize. Along with robbery of civilians, exploitation of raw
materials, organized smuggling and dealing in drugs and weapons,
hostage-taking and subcontracted violence, the respective diasporas
pump in money from outside to support their 'we group' in the esca-
lating conflict. This was particularly striking in the wars in the former
Yugoslavia.[26]

Violence markets are a radical form of free market economy, in
which goods are purchased, used and passed on where the potential
for violence is greatest. Its spread usually weakens traditional sectors
in the region: trade, industry and agriculture fall into crisis, as they

are unable to obtain supplies from outside or to reach sales outlets. It is therefore not surprising that the entrepreneurs of violence have sometimes engaged in other economic activities, before branching out in accordance with the new structure of the market. The same is true of the practitioners of violence, who may have previously been employed in small-scale industry.

Such forms of organization have consequences for the processes and dynamics of development. First, it may be completely unclear who took a particular decision or initiated a particular situation, and when and under what circumstances this happened. Second, in the development of violence, conditions come about that did not exist previously, and which perhaps no one had foreseen or intended; interviews with killers caught up in a mass escalation of violence repeatedly display confusion about how they actually came to kill, rape and plunder.[27]

According to Georg Elwert, violence markets have a strong tendency to stabilize, since persistent violence and threats of violence have removed other possibilities of reproduction. 'Violence markets do not arise or exist in a vacuum. They grow out of self-organizing social systems, which as such are geared to exchange with their environment, and they partly continue this exchange in altered forms.' Violence markets emerge when the state monopoly of violence breaks down, with the result that any conflicts that arise over resources in short supply (land or water, for example) are settled not by the state (the law courts) but by the use of force.

Elwert illustrates the catalytic effect with reference to an older study of events in Somalia by the anthropologist Marcel Djama.

The beginning seemed banal: pastoral communities in the research region had for some time been arming themselves with firearms, so that they could clarify access rights to watering places without having recourse to clan courts, state courts or notaries. This was a cheaper alternative, both for the state and for those directly involved. The state tolerated this development because it relieved it of a burdensome task. Clan systems, which so often feature in journalistic analyses of the Somalia conflict, had little to do with this development. For the accumulation of weapons signalled the breakdown of the clan system and its form of judicial process. At first the state tolerated only low-grade use of arms. But when the state failed to defend pastoral interests after the closure of borders with neighbouring states, access to wells and food aid from Ethiopia became the problem. (Until then, food diverted from international aid to Ethiopia had been marketed cheaply in Somalia.) Those who suffered as a result were not only the nomadic herdsmen but also traders who had made a handsome profit by export- ing the livestock in large quantities to Yemen and Saudi Arabia. Yemen in particular was almost completely dependent on these meat imports. As the traders' business collapsed, they supplied the nomads with large quantities of weapons, so that they could use force to ensure the repro- duction of their herds. This is how the so-called Gadabursi militia arose. It soon discovered that it could obtain food almost cost-free at the point of a gun, and that hostage-taking, food convoy 'taxation' and protection for drug dealers were lucrative activities.

Here, as under a magnifying glass, we can see how the dynamic of violence first sprang up and meandered its way through the country. It is this progression of violence in societies with a weak or virtually non-existent state which is so difficult to perceive from outside.[28] It combines particular interest with collective irrationality. The result is never-ending war.

An Oxfam International study showed that, between 1990 and 2005, wars in Africa cost a total of €211 billion – which corresponds quite closely to the amount of development aid that flowed into the continent during the same period.[29]

Never-ending wars are a form of violence with a future. We have not yet built the exacerbating consequences of climate change into the picture. But, from the case of Darfur, it is evident that phenomena such as rapid desertification may become new sources of violent con- flict, to be channelled and exploited in many ways by groups with an interest. This may be termed the self-catalysing dynamic of the forma- tion and occupation of spaces open to violence. De-statification and the growing fragility of existing states intensify this dynamic, so that the opening of further spaces for violence brings international players onto the scene, increases the resources available for violence, and so forth. The war in Iraq provides the clearest contemporary example of this process.

ADAPTATION

These are all attempts to adapt to changing environmental situations, and the adaptation is expressed in the shape of violence markets and experts, refugees, camps and dead people. Anyone who thinks this formulation too dry should bear in mind that the West's adaptation strategy for the predicted climate change consists of evoking and forcing a third industrial revolution – a strategy which, as Nicholas Stern has impressively calculated, would be considerably cheaper in the long run than failure to adapt proactively. In fact, adaptation will probably turn out to be profitable for the national economies of the West: a problem will be converted into a locational advantage, because education, technology and funding are available for the transformation. The choice of means and the legitimacy of the strategy are rather different from when a Somali warlord uses his muscle to snatch at the economic opportunities presented by a resource conflict; the latter is, of course, also regarded as *morally* more questionable than the West's response to climate change. But what the two strategies have in common is an attempt to convert a problematic situation into a particular advantage. Each can also be given a high-sounding name: the former described as 'reduction or avoidance of CO_2 emissions', the latter as 'support for freedom fighters'.

The points made here about never-ending wars only relate to the visible, though also obscure, part of the total configuration of violence. But the role of international aid agencies and intervention forces has made it clear that external players are also part of the configuration. Moreover, aid agencies and UN soldiers are themselves only the visible part of a system of external players that mostly remains unnoticed. We are these invisible players.

To sum up, we may say that the phenomenon of never-ending wars and violence markets will become more widespread and dramatic as the consequences of climate change (desertification, salinization, shrinking water supplies, etc.) make themselves felt. The question then, in a context where violence markets are expanding all the time, will be what scope international agencies have to intervene against genocidal violence, ethnic cleansing, and so on. It is already likely that international troops and special forces will be unavailable on a sufficient scale. For intervention itself is a scarce resource, which, reason tells us, can be distributed only in the interests of those who intervene. Or, to put it more simply, if such interests are not affected – if people fight *among themselves* and power politics, strategy or resources are not the issue – then the countries in the grip of violence will be left to get on with it.

Any moral dissonance related to this can be reduced in many different ways. It can be argued that it is wrong to meddle in the internal affairs of another country, that it is more important to play an active role in other crisis regions, that the risks for one's own troops are too high, that intervention might lead to 'mission creep', that local forces on the ground are better able to handle conflicts, that mistakes can be made, as in the past, and the wrong groups supported, and so on. Of course, it might then be further argued that the entrepreneurs of violence should no longer be given the opportunity to exploit humanitarian relief operations, and that a halt should be called to investment in the violence market economies. That would be another stage in the adaptation to climate change.

ETHNIC CLEANSING

For expulsion is the method which, so far as we have been able to see, will be the most satisfactory and lasting. There will be no mixture of populations to cause endless trouble as in Alsace-Lorraine. A clean sweep will be made. I am not alarmed at the prospect of the disentanglement of population, nor am I alarmed by these large transferences, which are more possible than they were before through modern conditions.[30]

These matter-of-fact words of Winston Churchill referred to the postwar situation of the so-called ethnic Germans in Poland and Czechoslovakia. When, as prime minister, he spoke of expulsions to the House of Commons on 15 December 1944, it was already taken for granted that there would be no *mixed populations* in the territories formerly occupied by Germany. Once the war was over, this idea of ethnically homogeneous states turned as many as 14 million ethnic Germans into refugees and expellees; roughly 2 million lost their lives in the process, and several hundreds of thousands were deported and made to engage in forced labour.[31]

That was probably the largest population movement of the twentieth century, but it was not the only one. All the transfers, whether in the form of expulsions, ethnic cleansing, deportation or official population exchanges, were the result of a path to modernity that ran through the creation of ethnically homogeneous states; they were one aspect of modern nation-building. Heterogeneous populations, causing 'endless trouble', were always regarded as a potential or actual obstacle to national development, and Churchill's view that even extensive resettlement would pose no special problems harked back to the 1923 Treaty of Lausanne, which provided for large-scale population transfers of Greeks from Anatolia and Turks from Greece following the end of the Greco-Turkish War. This exchange of approximately 1.5 million Greeks and 350,000 Turks, which took place under the auspices of an international commission, did not count as inhumane but was seen as a rational strategy for the homogenization of nation-states that would reduce the risks of future conflict.

The modern age has witnessed a whole series of ethnic cleansings, some of which (as in Armenia or in Stalinist strategies for the building of a new order) turned into genocide. These cases of mass killing did not always involve an escalation of violence; they could also be due to indifference or a lack of planning, as when tens of thousands of Chechens and Ingush died in Soviet deportation wagons or 100,000 more perished in the first three months after deportation, abandoned without food or accommodation because no one had thought it necessary to provide such things.[32]

The outcome of Yugoslavia's break-up wars was the transformation of constituent republics of a federal state into ethnically homogeneous nation-states. Here too the means to the end was ethnic cleansing, and in Kosovo or Bosnia conflicts smouldered on until internationally monitored ceasefires finally took effect. Michael Mann, in his extensive history of ethnic cleansing in the twentieth century, came to the sobering conclusion that it was not the result of failed modernization processes but a sign that modernization had been successful. All Western societies, with the exception of Switzerland, Belgium, Britain and Spain, owe their present nation-state form to a policy of ethnic homogenization, of which ethnic cleansing is the other side of the coin. This is the dark side of the development of democracy, and people simply forget it when they look with horror at the violence in Bosnia.

Against this background, the globalization process has evidently added more than a little to the violence. The more that post-colonial, post-socialist or post-autocratic societies were drawn into the OECD model of nation-state building, the more the potential for violence grew within them, and the more tendencies developed to direct the violence outwards. Radical Islamism, with its violent refusal to join the global process, is only one expression of how this modernization pressure has been experienced.[33] The point here is that never-ending wars, refugee flows, ethnic cleansing, and so on, are not the antithesis of modernization but simply part of its costs.

If, Mary Kaldor writes, globalization denotes 'the intensification of global interconnectedness – political, economic, military and cultural', then forms of violence such as never-ending wars and ethnic cleansing must be seen in this light.[34] The potential for violence arises through changes *within* the existing structures, not through the clash of intrinsically antagonistic forces such as the current counterposition of radical fundamentalism and Western liberalism suggests. Samuel Huntington's 'clash of civilizations' argument is not fundamentally wrong, because violent conflicts between cultures do exist, but it points only to what *others* do and fails to see the role of one's own culture in the action context that the different cultures *jointly* constitute, and whose conflicts they *jointly* wage. What is involved is an interaction, partly violent but certainly not as metaphysical and subjectless as a 'clash of civilizations'; that kind of thing does not exist in the world of the social. Conflicts are interactions, and they connect up the perceptions, interpretations and actions of the various parties.

The greater interconnectedness of cultures changes living conditions for very different human groups. A decisive role is played in this by the rapidly changing information landscape; communication across all cultural differences and geographical distances links together the most diverse cultures and regions of the world, while leaving their life chances and conditions as far apart as ever. Globalization therefore leads to 'both integration and fragmentation, homogenization and diversification',[35] universalism and nationalism. These consequences are evident in the phenomenon of never-ending war: information about any local skirmish can potentially be communicated and instrumentalized with the greatest dispatch, allowing any number of state, non-state and trans-state players to find pretexts for intervention or business alongside the local antagonists. This is what lies hidden behind concepts such as 'global interconnectedness, political, economic, military and cultural', and at the end of these links are human beings in flight, or being killed or rescued, and international criminal courts whose unenviable task it is to unravel the causes of murder and genocide and to judge those responsible for them.

Here a deadly modernization gap opens up. On one side are 'members of a global class who can speak English, have access to faxes, the Internet and satellite television, who use dollars or euros or credit cards, and who can travel freely'; on the other side are 'those who are excluded from global processes, who live off what they can sell or barter or what they receive in humanitarian aid, whose movement is restricted by roadblocks, visas and the cost of travel, and who are prey to sieges, forced famines, landmines, etc.'[36]

At the upper end of the scale, wars and persistent expulsions may generate moral dissonance, but at the lower end 'stuff like that happens', and it would be wrong to understand it as 'tribal' or 'primitive'. That may be how it seems, but the causes do not lie there. As the twentieth century showed, there is a close link between modernization and mass violence, and, as Michael Mann put it, ethnic cleansing spreads together with democratization, not against it.

Ethnic rebellions have risen in the South of the world ever since the 1960s and 1970s, the period of its ostensible democratization. They remain low in the North, dominated by institutionalized democracies and the politics of class. During the 1950s they declined greatly in the Communist states, authoritarian and dominated by the politics of class. They fluctuated in the Middle East and North Africa, increased steeply in sub-Saharan Africa after 1960 amid democratizing states, rose after 1965 in Asia, and rose after 1975 in South and Central America. After 1975 all the southern regional trends rose until about 1995. The curve rose as a result of the collapse of the Soviet Union and Yugoslavia. After 1995 the trend may have declined a little, except in sub-Saharan Africa, though the overall trend is not yet back to pre-1991 levels.[37]

In a context of changing spheres of political influence, system break-downs or implosions of authoritarian rule, the most diverse factors may be interpreted in ethnic categories, especially if they are obscure or downright incomprehensible. Shifting political interests linked to geography, power and resources define an extensive, increasingly global force field, in which environmental factors have until recently scarcely been taken into consideration. However, it is not uncommon for an earthquake, floods or wildfires to lead to looting, demonstrations, revolts or even uprisings; recent examples include the forest fires in Greece[38] and the earthquakes in Peru[39] and Pakistan.[40] In each of these cases, the failure of state-led disaster relief led to unrest, and Greece and New Orleans showed that law and order can quickly break down even in societies with an intact state structure.

ENVIRONMENTAL CONFLICTS

But if climate change affects population distribution and redraws the boundaries of agrarian and waste land, variously producing water short-ages and flooding, then this upsets the geopolitical balance and fuels international tensions at the level of power and resource politics. Thus, there is every sign that the twenty-first century will see an increased potential for tensions and a major danger of violent solutions. Michael Mann lines up a number of likely candidates for the next conflicts:

> Indonesia will be unable to assimilate or repress Aceh or West Papuan autonomy movements; India will be unable to assimilate or repress Muslim Kashmiris or several of its small border peoples; Sri Lanka will be unable to assimilate or repress Tamils; Macedonia will be unable to assimilate or repress Albanians; Turkey, Iran and Iraq will be unable to assimilate or repress Kurdish movements; China will be unable to assimilate or repress Tibetans or Central Asian Muslims; Russia will be unable to repress Chechens; the Khartoum regime will be unable to contain South Sudanese movements. Israel will be unable to repress Palestinians.[41]

Conflicts are to be expected in the Baltic too, since ethnic Russians are in a majority in many industrial regions that have suffered extreme environmental damage.[42]

Existential problems linked to climate change will sometimes feed the dynamic for violence, sometimes play no role at all, and perhaps sometimes even calm tensions. But, in each case, the twentieth-century practices that involved the formation of ethnically homogeneous states and the use of ethnically targeted violence will continue to function, possibly on a greater scale than before. Global warming accelerates changes in the configuration of states, raises tensions and creates pressure to find quick solutions. Table 7.2 shows that this is not a gloomy prediction but a part of present reality.

Table 7.2 Violent environmental conflicts

Region	Country/countries (year)	Conflict level	Resource
North America	Canada – Spain (1995–present)	International	Fish
North America	USA (Hawaii) (1941–90)	Local	Water, soil
North America	USA – Mexico (present)	International	Water
Central America/ Caribbean	Mexico (2005)	Local	Land/soil
Central America/ Caribbean	El Salvador – Honduras (1969–80)	International	Land/soil
Central America/ Caribbean	Belize (1993–present)	National	Forest/wood, water
Central America/ Caribbean	Mexico (1995–present)	Local	Land, forest
Central America/ Caribbean	Guatemala (1954–present)	National	Land
Central America/ Caribbean	El Salvador (1970–92)	National	Land
Central America/ Caribbean	Haiti – USA	International	Land
South America	Brazil (2005)	Local	Land
South America	Chile (2005)	Local	Water
South America	Ecuador – Peru (1995)	International	Land
South America	Peru (1996)	National	Land
South America	Brazil (1960–present)	Local	Land
South America	Chile (1960–present)	Local	Land
South America	Peru (2001)	Local	Land
South America	Bolivia (2000)	National	Water
South America	Uruguay (2005)	Local	Soil

Table 7.2 Violent environmental conflicts *(continued)*

Region	Country/countries (year)	Conflict level	Resource
South America	Colombia (1992–present)	Local	Soil, water, biodiversity
Europe	France (1995–present)	International	Water, soil
Europe	Greece – Turkey (1987–99)	International	Fish
Europe	Russia – Norway (1955–90)	International	Water, fish
Europe	Hungary – Slovakia (1989–94)	International	Water, fish, biodiversity
Europe	UK (1971–present)	Local	Land, biodiversity, fish
Africa (North)	Ethiopia (present)	Local	Land, wood, water
Africa (North)	Eritrea (1991–present)	Local	Land, wood, water
Middle East	Iraq (1991–2003)	Local	Soil, land, water
Middle East	Israel – Lebanon (1967– present)	International	Water
Middle East	Israel – Palestine (1967–present)	International	Water
Middle East	Jordan – Lebanon (1948–99)	International	Water
Africa (North)	Morocco – Spain (1948–99)	International	Fish
Africa (North)	Somalia – Ethiopia (1886–1991)	International	Soil
Africa (North)	Sudan – Egypt (1992–9)	International	Water
Africa (North)	Sudan (1987–present)	National	Land
Middle East	Turkey – Syria – Iraq (1990–9)	International	Water
Africa (North)	Mauritania – Senegal (1989–2001)	International	Water
Middle East	Jordan – Saudi Arabia (1990–present)	International	Water
Africa (North)	Mali (1970–96)	National	Land, water
Africa (North)	Niger (1970–95)	National	Land, water
Africa (North)	Ethiopia (2000–present)	Local	Land, water
Africa (North)	Ethiopia (1990)	Local	Water
Africa (North)	Senegal – Mauritania (1989–93)	International	Land, water
Africa (North)	Niger (1990–1)	Local	Water, soil, land
Sub-Saharan Africa	Kenya (2005)	National	Water, land
Sub-Saharan Africa	Chad (2005)	Local	Water, firewood
Sub-Saharan Africa	Lesotho – South Africa (1955–86)	International	Water
Sub-Saharan Africa	Rwanda (1990–4)	National	Land
Sub-Saharan Africa	Zimbabwe (1980–present)	National	Land

Table 7.2 Violent environmental conflicts *(continued)*

Region	Country/countries (year)	Conflict level	Resource
Sub-Saharan Africa	Nigeria (1978–80)	Local	Land, water
Sub-Saharan Africa	South Africa (1984–present)	National	Water, land
Sub-Saharan Africa	Botswana (1985–91)	Local	Water, land
Sub-Saharan Africa	Kenya (1991–5)	Local	Land
Asia/Oceania	China (2006)	Local	Land
Asia/Oceania	China (2004–present)	Local	Land
Asia/Oceania	China – Vietnam (1973–99)	International	Water, air, soil
Asia/Oceania	Indonesia (1996)	Local	Land
Asia/Oceania	Pakistan (2006)	Local	Water
Asia/Oceania	Philippines – USA (1991–present)	International	Water, air, soil
Asia/Oceania	India (1974–present)	Local	Water
Asia/Oceania	North Korea (1994–present)	National	Soil, land
Asia/Oceania	Uzbekistan – Kazakhstan (1970–present)	International	Water, soil
Asia/Oceania	Japan – USSR/Russia (1945–99)	International	Fish, biodiversity
Asia/Oceania	Japan – South Korea (1997–present)	International	Fish
Asia/Oceania	India – Bangladesh (1951–present)	International	Water
Asia/Oceania	Philippines (1971–present)	Local	Fish, land
Asia/Oceania	India (1985–present)	Local	Water, land, biodiversity, fish
Asia/Oceania	China (1980–present)	Local	Water, land
Asia/Oceania	Thailand (1985–present)	Local	Water, land
Asia/Oceania	Pakistan (1995)	National	Water, land
Asia/Oceania	India – Bangladesh (1980–8)	International	Land
Asia/Oceania	Philippines (1970–86)	National	Land

Of course there are no 'pure' environmental conflicts, only ones in which several different factors are present. But the WGBU-commissioned research team that prepared this overview, using a definition of environmental conflicts as 'conflicts that are sharpened or accelerated by the destruction of renewable resources',[43] suggested a fourfold regional typology. The main role in conflicts is played by land use and soil degradation in Central America, soil degradation in South America, water supplies in the Middle East, and both water and soil degradation in sub-Saharan Africa.[44] In the first two of these regions, government incapacity and migration are not exacerbating factors; conflicts are driven by poverty, population pressure and the unequal distribution of power. In the Middle East, population pressure, migration, poverty and ethnic tensions dictate the shape of water conflicts, while in sub-Saharan Africa, as we have already seen in some detail, failing states, population pressure, poverty, migration and ethnic tensions are the principal factors. Land use conflicts in Central and South America are far from innocuous. Apart from the effects of deforestation, expulsion takes place on a large scale: 70,000 people in El Salvador, and 200,000 in Guatemala, have lost their lives in the wake of such conflicts.[45] Moreover, extreme weather events add to the conflict potential: 'floods and droughts, in which other existing forms of environmental conflict come into the open, have been on the rise in these regions, with more than 500 victims.'[46]

A different way of looking at past, present and future conflicts clearly reveals the importance of environmental changes for the development of violence. Previous research has concentrated mainly on economic, ideological and ethnic factors, but a change of focus brings home the role of basic resources such as water, soil and air.

To repeat: violence is never the result of one factor alone. The very phenomenon of modernization pressure, which globalization produces throughout the world, explains the close, though not deterministic, connection between violence (internal or international) and disparities in life or development chances. Every country drawn into the globalization process forms an area of tensions, which are not confined to the level of the state but are also experienced by individuals or groups that economic development puts at an advantage or disadvantage. Direct changes in people's circumstances are not necessarily the trigger; other factors may have the same effect. The lasting character of modern terrorism, for instance, is due to the fact that it is a child of modernization processes. Flourishing in the global age, it expands both quantitatively and qualitatively into military-style operations, which, like all modern trans-individual forms of violence, are directed mainly at civilian targets; and its protagonists, when they do not come from central locations in the society they attack, are mostly second-generation immigrants or people who have studied or worked in the West. Of course, climate change is only directly linked to anti-Western terrorism and will depend in future on real and perceived asymmetries in the world that global warming induces. As a self-empowering form of substitute warfare, terrorism is therefore likely to grow and has a place in any discussion of killing tomorrow.

Terror spreads with the growth of worldwide migration. The modernization of further societies confronts more and more people with the exigencies of freedom and problems of meaning, especially if it creates a sense that the world is divided into winners and losers. For this reason societies like China or India, in the throes of radical modernization, are already preparing for the time not many years ahead when they too will have a major terrorist problem. Islamist terrorism will have fewer recruitment problems as global communications shrink space, and as the gap in standards of living widens. Climate change may not be a cause of violence, but its unequal consequences are certainly a spur for it – hence questions of justice will become increasingly important in relations both between countries and between generations.

ENERGY CONFLICTS

The role of energy in future scenarios of violence is the reverse side of the carbon emissions problem. In a bizarre equation, the limitless energy hunger of the industrial countries, both old and new, sharpens the struggle for the resources whose depletion endangers the survival of humanity. But the deadliness of this equation is not much talked about. Michael Brzoska points out that, whereas territory used to be the main resource over which states waged war, 'industrialization meant that raw materials such as coal and oil became *casus belli*'.[47]

All debates about the future of fossil fuels revolve around the magical 'peak oil' formula, the point in time after which supplies can only diminish. It may seem surprising that we still do not know how much oil remains beneath the earth's surface, but it is safe to assume that the quantity is finite and that, squeezed between rising demand and growing difficulty of access, *the* central resource of industrial societies will become more expensive and subject to more intense competition.

The Energy Watch Group calculates that the maximum output of 81,000 barrels of oil a day was reached in 2006, so that we are already past the peak, while the International Energy Agency (IEA) assumes that further increases will be possible in the future as soaring oil prices fill the corporate coffers and encourage new investment in exploration. Whatever the reliability of these predictions, one cannot fail to be disturbed by the general lack of clarity about existing reserves and the scope for future use. After all, 80 per cent of global primal energy use comes from coal, oil and gas, and the figure is rising by a yearly average of 1.6 per cent. Oil consumption alone, which accounts for a third of the total, will rise from 84 million barrels a day in 2005 to 116 million barrels in 2030[48] – in conditions where, as we said, access will become increasingly difficult. Oil, according to Wolfgang Sachs,

> is more important than gold ever was. The industrial system would break down without it: industry and jobs rely extensively on the use and processing of crude oil; transport and mobility, by land, air and water, are essentially dependent on refined oil products; and so too are plastics, medicines, fertilizers, construction materials, dyes, textiles and much more else besides. The dependence on oil has been continually increasing since the middle of the last century; it has become a politically, economically and even culturally irreplaceable resource. Oil, more than any other material, has put its stamp on lifestyles all over the world.[49]

Not only does this generate emissions on a horrific scale; it also increases political dependence on the producer countries (Iran and Russia together dispose of half the world's natural gas reserves). Of the twenty-three countries 'that derive a clear majority of their export income from oil and gas, not a single one is a democracy.'[50] Wolfgang Sachs is right when he says that 'conventional economic development based on fossil fuels has become a great risk for security in the world'.[51] Here too the changed power configuration of world society plays an important role; China's trade with Africa will be worth $100 billion by 2010, and thirteen out of fifteen oil companies active in Sudan are Chinese.[52] The economist Dambisa Moyo contrasts China's strategy with Western development aid: 'In five to ten years the Chinese model has created more jobs and infrastructure in Africa than the West did in sixty years.'[53]

Lastly, international commodities markets and supply infrastructure (above all, gas pipelines) are a highly sensitive field of 'global insecurity'.[54] Attacks on pipelines, refineries, bridges, and so on, are among the tactics of international terrorists and local rebel groups: Nigeria and Iraq are the most telling examples to date. Similar scenarios are not unlikely wherever pipelines cross a series of countries.

The Russian–Georgian War of 2008, in which a pipeline was bombed in the early stages, was a sign of the role that the struggle for fossil energy will play in future conflicts. A resolution at the Christian Democrat congress in November 2006 showed that politicians in Germany are aware of the risks ahead and are preparing to confront them: 'In the global age, the German economy relies more than before on free access to the world's markets and raw materials. The Bundeswehr, as part of its task of ensuring the country's safety, can help to secure trade routes and raw materials in the framework of international operations.'[55]

AENEAS, HERA, AMAZON AND FRONTEX: INDIRECT BORDER WARS[56]

More and more people are trying to enter Western Europe or North America illegally. Most of the refugees who want to get to Europe come from Africa across the southern maritime borders of Portugal, Spain or Italy. Other major entry points are eastern land frontiers and international airports within the EU. But at present the refugee flow is most conspicuous on the southern coasts, and that is where the five key tasks involved in securing the EU's external borders are mainly concentrated:

1 sealing the frontiers by means of technology and a police and military presence;
2 transferring measures to deter would-be refugees to their countries of origin and transit;
3 integrating countries of origin and transit into European measures to block refugees. A number of intergovernmental agreements have been signed that make it easier for EU border guards to operate in African coastal waters, and pressure is exerted on transit countries to crack down on illegal migrants;

4 building camps for the reception and processing of refugees, both in the EU and in transit countries;

5 deporting illegal migrants to their country of origin if they are not given the right to stay in Europe.[57]

THE MOROCCO-SPAIN ROUTE

In 2002, with EU support, the Spanish government began to establish its 'Integrated System for External Surveillance' (SIVE), initially concentrating on the Canary Isles and the Straits of Gibraltar,[58] where refugees from Morocco had been crossing to the EU and corpses of those who failed had been regularly washed ashore. In 2005, after refugees turned to other routes, the SIVE was extended to the whole of Spain's southern coast.[59] The system consists of several dozen watchtowers, from which infrared cameras can pick out a human corpse as far as 7.5 kilometres away, and radar devices can detect a 6 x 6 metre refugee boat from a distance of 20 kilometres. In addition the Spanish coastguard carries out regular patrols with ships and helicopters.[60] At first the electronic surveillance was a big success: the number of refugees reaching the shore fell sharply, as did the number of floating corpses. In 2004 a similar system was installed on the Greek islands.[61] But then the refugees began to take different routes and headed more often for the Canary Isles – where in 2006, for example, 31,000 Africans landed on Fuerteventura, Tenerife and Gran Canaria. Some avoided Morocco altogether, sailing directly from Western Sahara or Mauritania and, increasingly since 2006, braving the 1,000 kilometres or more from Senegal in boats that are usually not fit for the high seas.[62]

In spring 2006 the Spanish government also decided to deploy surveillance satellites, and in May the French firm Spot Image and the University of Las Palmas came up with a pilot project.[63] In June the British newspaper *The Independent* reported plans by the EU Commission to deploy unmanned drones to monitor the Mediterranean;[64] the BSUAV (Border Surveillance by Unmanned Aerial Vehicles) corporation subsequently devised a plan for this, under the direction of the French company Dassault Aviation.[65] Italy had already bought five 'predator drones' from the United States in 2004, intending to use them to track irregular migrants as well as terrorists –

as Leonardo Tricario, then head of the Italian air force, announced in October of the same year.[66]

In September and October 2005, after the SIVE had closed down the Straits of Gibraltar route, the refugee problem on the EU's southern coast hit the headlines when hundreds of refugees in Morocco repeatedly tried to scale the border fences of the Spanish enclaves of Ceuta and Melilla with home-made ladders.[67] These are barbed-wire fences, three deep at some stretches, patrolled by guards with motion detectors, night vision devices and directional microphones.[68] In summer 2005 preparations were under way to raise the fence around Melilla from 3.5 to 6 metres.[69] Moroccan and Spanish border guards used truncheons, tear gas and rubber bullets against the rush of refugees, who fought back with sticks and stones.[70] Fourteen refugees lost their lives during the events.[71] As spokesmen for Médecins sans Frontières observed, the Moroccan police took 500 refugees (some of them injured) to the desert near the Algerian frontier and released them there.[72] After the incidents, Morocco received EU emergency aid of €40 million to strengthen its border security.[73]

In a report published in September 2005, Médecins sans Frontières complained about the 'extreme violence of the countermeasures' used by the Moroccan border guards, but also about the EU's sealing-off strategy. The organization estimated that there had been 6,300 fatalities on the coasts over the past ten years; the official figure of 1,400[74] does not include the thousands presumed drowned at the turn of 2005–6. (In March 2006 the Spanish government itself spoke of people 'dying in droves' off the Canaries.)[75] 'Torture and humiliating treatment' added to the sufferings of the refugees. Doctors from Médecins sans Frontières reported treating a total of 9,350 migrants from sub-Saharan African countries between March 2003 and May 2005 at several places in Morocco; 2,193 of them (23.5 per cent) bore marks of torture.[76]

CAMPS

The building of reception and deportation camps inside and outside the EU is another part of the strategy. In February 2003, in a paper entitled *New Vision for Refugees*, the Blair government in Britain proposed creating a 'worldwide network of safe havens' (later called 'regional protection areas') in the vicinity of countries from which people were fleeing. In March it added a network of 'transit processing centres' (TPCs) outside the EU's frontiers, designed to hold refugees applying for asylum until a decision had been taken whether to admit them or to send them back to their country of origin. These plans were backed by the governments of the Netherlands, Austria and Denmark, but the protests from sections of the European public proved too strong. Shortly afterwards, the United Nations High Commission on Refugees (UNHCR) submitted a variant of this model.

At an intergovernmental summit meeting held in Greece in mid-June 2003, the European Council asked the EU Commission 'to examine ways and means to enhance the protection capacity of regions of origin' and noted 'that a number of Member States plan to explore ways of providing better protection for the refugees in their country of origin, in conjunction with the UNHCR'.[77] In 2004 the German interior minister Otto Schily and his Italian counterpart Giuseppe Pisanu revived the plans to build camps, especially in North Africa. In October, after an informal meeting in Scheveningen, EU justice and interior ministers made it known that they planned to have 'reception centres for asylum-seekers' built in Algeria, Tunisia, Morocco, Mauritania and Libya, under the administration of the respective countries.[78]

There are also refugee camps in Ceuta and Melilla,[79] on the Italian island of Lampedusa (where just under 2,000 refugees came ashore in 2004),[80] on the Italian mainland and on various islands in eastern Greece.[81] After the great surge of refugees towards the Canaries, Madrid sent a delegation to Mauritania with an offer of financial and technical assistance; thirty-five army engineers soon followed to build a camp at Nuadibu.[82] Italy has extra-territorial camps in Libya and Tunisia; and in October 2004 and March 2005 the Italian authorities deported hundreds of refugees from Lampedusa to Libya.[83] In Libya itself, half a million to a million people without valid papers are waiting for an opportunity to cross to Italy or Malta. In 2006 a total of 64,000 illegal immigrants were flown or trucked out of the country, quite a few of them probably released in the desert.[84]

The funding of extra-territorial camps and the tightening of border controls go together with political pressure on African countries to take active measures themselves against the flow of refugees.[85] Between 2004 and 2006 the EU Commission allocated €120 million under its AENEAS Programme for 'financial and technical assistance to third countries in the area of migration and asylum matters'.[86] This is intended especially to cover 'management of migratory flows, return and reintegration of migrants in their country of origin, asylum, border control, refugees and displaced people'.[87]

Many people use traffickers to help them cross from Africa into the territory of the EU, and the profits increase with the difficulty and expense of the journey. When an interviewer asked Wolfgang Schäuble, Germany's interior minister, what was the right way to deal with refugee boats on the high seas, he replied that 'the traffickers' organizations must be destroyed'; only then would there be a 'way out of the dilemma'.[88]

FRONTEX AGAIN

As mentioned earlier, the European Union has reacted to the increased flow of migrants by establishing a common border control, which is supposed to be the responsibility of the Frontex agency.[89] Regulation (EG) 2007/2004 of the European Council, issued on 26 October 2004, provided for the establishment of a 'European Agency for the Management of Operational Cooperation at the External Borders of the Member States of the European Union'. In its own words, the agency was to

- coordinate operational coordination between Member States in the field of management of external borders;
- assist Member States on training of national border guards, including the establishment of common training standards;
- carry out risk analyses;
- follow up the development of research relevant for the control and surveillance of external borders;
- assist Member States in circumstances requiring increased technical and operational assistance at external borders; and
- provide Member States with the necessary support in organizing joint return operations.[90]

The agency began its work in October 2005, with a budget of €6.2 million for the first year. This rose to €19.2 million for the second year, and for 2007 Frontex put the figure at €35 million[91] and the German interior ministry at €42 million.[92] However, this budget covers only the running of the Warsaw-based agency itself; the costs of employing and equipping border control officials fall on the Member States that make them available to Frontex.[93] At the time of writing Frontex's own administrative staff numbers 105 employees.[94]

On 26 April 2007, the European Parliament issued a directive for the formation of 'Rapid Border Intervention Teams' (RABITs), a joint initiative of the EU's then commissioner for justice, freedom and security, Franco Frattini, and the German interior minister. These teams are supposed to be available for 'a limited period of time' and in 'exceptional and urgent situations' – that is, if 'a Member State was faced with a mass influx of third-country nationals attempting to enter its territory illegally'.[95] At first it was intended that the pool would consist of 500 to 600 officers.[96] In 2007 a joint equipment pool (or 'toolbox') was created, whereby member states inform Frontex of the equipment they can make available to RABITs. According to the German interior ministry, this consists of 'more than twenty aircraft, almost thirty helicopters and well over a hundred ships, plus extensive further equipment'.[97]

Frontex was set up as a largely autonomous supranational agency. When some Free Democrat deputies enquired about its accountability, the German government replied on 13 April 2007: 'The executive director of Frontex [the Finnish brigadier-general Illka Laitinen] has a duty to keep the governing board of Frontex informed. The European Parliament or Council may ask the executive director to provide a report about the performance of his duties. Frontex does not have an obligation to provide information to Member States.'[98] Frontex itself emphasizes that its activity is 'intelligence driven'[99] – which means that it cooperates and pools information with the secret services of member states. Some of the first Frontex deployments in 2006 took place in collaboration with EUROPOL.[100]

According to its report for 2006, the agency directed a total of fifteen 'operations'. In June and July, for example, it drew on border guards from Austria, Italy, Poland and Britain to strengthen controls on the Greek–Turkish frontier and the Greek coasts, apprehending a total of

422 illegal migrants. But Frontex remains discreet about the details of its local work. The fifteen operations included 'Hera I' and 'Hera II' in the Canary Isles, which became the flash points for illegal immigration from Africa after the clampdown on Spain's southern coast and in the Spanish enclaves in Morocco. In the framework of Hera I, international experts gave the Canary Isles authorities key assistance in determining the citizenship of the refugees they apprehended.

With Hera II, beginning on 11 August 2006, Frontex took on direct responsibilities for maritime surveillance and border control. Along with the Portuguese coastguard, it was reported to be using one Portuguese and one Italian ship, and one Italian and one Finnish aircraft. For the first time, activities were organized in Senegalese and Mauritanian territorial waters, in collaboration with the local authorities. During its nine weeks, the operation apprehended 3,887 refugees on fifty-seven fishing boats, and another 5,000 were prevented on the African mainland from taking to the high seas. A total of seven Schengen countries took part.[101]

In February 2007 Frontex got Hera III under way: this involved questioning refugees in the Canaries about the routes they had taken there and then attempting to cut those routes as close as possible to the African coast.[102] In 2006 and 2007, Frontex's 'Amazon' and 'Amazon II' operations gave it experience on the European mainland, checking for illegal immigrants at the international airports of Frankfurt, Amsterdam, Barcelona, Lisbon, Milan, Madrid, Paris and Rome. Twenty-nine border officials from seven EU countries vetted 2,161 people during the seventeen-day exercise.[103] Since May 2007 Frontex has been coordinating joint patrols by border police forces in the Mediterranean.[104]

ILLEGAL ALIENS

The US has a frontier of 8,891 kilometres with Canada and 3,200 kilometres with Mexico. Although Washington and Ottawa cooperate on immigration and border control, the US northern frontier poses relatively minor problems, since Canada's geographical position makes it difficult for illegal immigrants to reach. Current estimates put the number of people living illegally in Canada at approximately

200,000.[105] In the last fifteen years, the North American Free Trade Agreement (NAFTA) has led to progressively tighter control of the US–Mexican frontier, with a doubling of patrols and the installation of fences and walls, especially in the vicinity of transport hubs and cities, where illegal immigrants can easily blend into the crowd. In the late summer of 2006, for example, a triple steel wall 4.5 metres high was erected around the busy highway linking San Diego with the Mexican city of Tijuana. There are similar structures in Arizona and Texas.[106] Each year several hundred people die in an attempt to enter the USA illegally from Mexico,[107] and the dangers are increasing as border security measures become tighter.[108] Among the causes of death are snake and insect bites, drowning, cactus wounds, accidents and thirst.[109]

In response to the terror attacks of 11 September 2011, President Bush created a special office in the White House to develop a 'National Strategy for Homeland Security', and in November 2002 the resulting Department of Homeland Security (DHS) took over responsibility for border protection. The strategy paper submitted in July had already shown a tendency to highlight the terrorist threat in border control and, at least officially, to organize around that priority. Here is a typical quote: 'America historically has relied heavily on two vast oceans and two friendly neighbors for border security, and on the private sector for most forms of domestic transportation security. The increasing mobility and destructive potential of modern terrorism has required the United States to rethink and renovate fundamentally its systems for border and transportation security.'[110] As early as October 2001, the so-called Patriot Act had made it easier to hold non-citizens for investigation and to deport immigrants.[111]

The Department for Homeland Security also took over responsibility for the US Coastguard and the newly created 'US Customs and Border Protection' (CBP).[112] Since then controls have also been tightened on legal entry. Visa-free travel – from EU countries, for example – is now possible only with machine-readable passports, and fingerprints or photos are taken at the point of entry. In future people intending to enter the United States will have to register online forty-eight hours in advance. The German foreign office already advises travellers to be at the departure airport at least three hours before take-off in order to allow time for security clearance.[113] The USA is pioneering the collection and recording of biometric data: travellers from visa-free countries will soon have prints taken of all ten fingers; and a DHS representative has announced that future checks may include retina scans. The collected data will be fed into a central bank, to which the FBI and the CIA will have access.[114]

The privatization of security services is an interesting aspect of this. In 2006 the US government spent $545 per head of the population on homeland security, and in the 22-month period ending in August 2006 awarded more than 100,000 contracts to private firms for security functions.[115] Border collaboration between the US and Canada intensified after September 11, with the compiling of joint 'passenger analysis lists', and in December a 'Smart Border Declaration' provided for increased exchange of information ('Project Northstar'). The Royal Canadian Mounted Police now has access to the FBI's fingerprint database, and each country's data about refugees and asylum-seekers is shared and closely monitored.[116]

The main responsibility for border control lies with the US Customs and Border Protection (CBP), which began work in March 2003. With a staff of 42,000, including 18,000 officers at the 325 frontier posts at airports, seaports and land crossings and a further 11,000 for border surveillance, the CBP reports having a fleet of at least 8,000 motor vehicles, 260 aircraft and 200 ships.[117] Since 2005 two unmanned drones have been patrolling Arizona, and by the end of 2008 four more were due to come into service to monitor stretches of coast and parts of the border with Canada.[118] On an average day nearly 1.2 million people legally cross the US borders, 870 are turned away at entry points, and just under 3,500 are caught trying to evade checkpoints ('illegal aliens'). For every successful attempt to enter illegally, there are eight failed attempts.[119]

November 2005 saw the 'Secure Border Initiative' (SBI) come into force – a brainchild of the secretary of homeland security, Michael Chertoff. According to the CBP, this is designed to tighten not only border controls but also the implementation of customs and immigration procedures, and to oversee the official 'Temporary Worker Program'. A 'critical part' of the SBI is 'SBInet', a border modernization programme reliant on high-tech surveillance and communication.[120]

In September 2006, the Bush administration awarded Boeing a \$2.5 billion technology contract for a 'virtual border' in the Southwest; hundreds of 30-metre high watchtowers, fitted with radar and cameras and linked to aerial observation and physical patrols, were supposed to make it impossible to cross the border unnoticed. Nine towers were ready by July 2007, each with an observation radius of 16 kilometres. The development, the construction and, to some extent, the running of these systems were entrusted to private subcontractors, nearly one hundred firms working under Boeing. A 45-kilometre pilot project in the Arizona desert west of Nogales ('Project 28') was due for delivery to the government in June 2007, at a cost of \$20 million. But it ran into technical problems, and after just a few months the anticipated costs of SBInet in the Southwest had risen to \$8 billion.[121] In September 2007 Michael Chertoff threatened that, if necessary, he would abandon SBInet and look for other solutions. An improved system was scheduled for testing in the autumn, after which a final decision would be made about its future.[122] The Arizona desert is a focus of illegal immigration from Mexico, involving 438,000 out of the estimated 1.13 million arrests made in this connection in 2005. It is also where the 'Minutemen' are active: a vigilante force that keeps watch at the border and notifies the authorities of anything suspicious.[123]

In late September 2006, after years of discussion, the Senate approved President Bush's plans to build a 1,123-kilometre fence on the border with Mexico, at a cost of \$1.2 billion. Mexican politicians sharply criticized the project.[124] Only 30 kilometres had been built by September 2007, and a Homeland Security spokesperson listed 'virtual fences' (such as SBInet) under the Secure Fence Act of September 2006.[125] As of January 2010, roughly 1,035 kilometres of the US–Mexican border were protected by fences.[126]

As in Europe, attempts are made to stop refugees before they reach a land border, by projecting border controls outwards. According to a Caritas report, Mexico is watching its own southern border more closely at the instigation of the United States, since it is a transit country for migrants from Guatemala and other parts of Central and South America. Forty-one US-funded deportation holding centres already exist in Mexico, under bilateral agreements such as 'Plan Sur' and 'La Repatriación Segura'.[127]

In 1985, for the first time in recent history, Ronald Reagan made illegal immigration a major public issue by speaking of an 'invasion' and claiming that the United States had lost control of its borders. The following year, an Immigration Reform and Control Act provided for the strengthening of the southern borders, the fining of employers who hired illegal immigrants, and an amnesty for those who had been living in the country for some time.[128] In 1994 the Republican governor of California, Pete Wilson, proposed a law barring illegal immigrants from public services such as schools and healthcare. He obtained a majority for this in a referendum, but then the Latinos mobilized against the plans and ended up turning California into a Democratic stronghold. This brought it home to the Republicans that, because of the large size of the Latino population, a policy that was too hostile to immigrants (even illegal immigrants) would cost them heavily at the polls.[129]

This political situation, together with the conservative character of the core Republican electorate, may explain why a longstanding consensus on the need for immigration reform has not yet led to tangible results. Draft legislation that came before the House of Representatives in December 2005 (H.R. 4437) provided for a tighter system of border controls, and in May 2006 the Senate passed a draft that would increase the scope for legal immigration and the acquisition of American citizenship. Yet neither the one nor the other has yet gained the necessary approval of Congress.[130] Moreover, the first proposal led in spring 2006 to the largest mass protest in the history of the United States: between half a million and a million demonstrated in Los Angeles alone on 25 March against a tightening of immigration laws and the erection of frontier barriers.[131] Finally, in June 2007, the Senate failed to approve an immigration reform bill which, as well as allocating further human and technological resources to the southern borders, would have introduced an annual quota of 200,000 temporary visas for immigrant workers and made it easier for people working in agriculture to gain residency rights.[132]

REFUGEES AND ASYLUM POLICY

Anyone subject to political persecution in their home country can request permission to enter the United States; and anyone already there who fears persecution in their home country can apply for asylum. In 1980 an upper limit of 231,700 a year was set for the number of refugees who could be admitted into the United States, but since 2004 this figure has been held at around 70,000, and in practice the granting of refugee status has been even more restrictive. In the 1990s an average of 100,000 a year were admitted, but between 2000 and 2006 only 50,000. In 2010, a total of 73,293 refugees entered the United States legally; the commonest countries of origin were Iraq (24.6 per cent), Burma (22.8 per cent) and Bhutan (16.9 per cent). Asylum was granted to 21,113 people, the most strongly represented being Chinese (31.7 per cent), Ethiopians (5.2 per cent), Haitians (3.9 per cent) and Venezuelans (3.1 per cent).[133] Between 1995 and 2004, 46 per cent of people granted asylum in Canada came from China, Colombia, the Democratic Republic of Congo, Hungary, India, Iran, Mexico, Nigeria, Pakistan or Sri Lanka. Between 2002 and 2004, the two main countries of origin were Mexico and Colombia.[134] The tighter entry restrictions in the United States mean that the refugee flow from Mexico is likely to shift increasingly from the US to Canada.[135]

Europe and North America, the most attractive regions for refugees and illegal immigrants, pursue border control strategies that resemble each other in at least two respects: their border installations and personnel are equipped with advanced technology, and there is a tendency to project the borders outwards (more pronounced in the EU than the USA). The question arises as to how the reactions to migration will evolve if the pressure increases as a result of climate change.

EXTRA-TERRITORIAL BORDERS

The outward projection of borders seems the most effective way of keeping undesired immigrants at a distance – and also the least conspicuous. For if European security forces are not involved, and if the EU authorities do not concern themselves with administrative action and the repatriation of refugees, the problem comes to public attention only on the occasions when corpses show up on the beaches of Sicily or the Canary Isles. And that is not enough to establish a link in people's minds between a restrictive homeland security policy and the deaths of refugees; the latter seems to be unrelated, though certainly a problem for the relevant authorities.

Many attempts to seal the borders take place behind the political scenes. The extra-parliamentary status of Frontex, which carries out sovereign tasks, is a good illustration of this. One remarkable feature of the border control activities is an expectation that the problems will become serious in the years ahead, so that preventative measures will be necessary against eco-migration, a central consequence of climate change. Also interesting is the imaginative choice of names for particular operations or teams: many of them hark back to Greek mythology, as if to emphasize that they are essentially innocuous and serve to protect a valuable cultural tradition. In all this, the basic paradigm is to tackle the problem of border violations as far as possible outside the territory of the EU.

Not only do migrant camps and protected zones have unwholesome historical precedents; the number of existing and planned camps indicates a determination to meet the coming surge of refugees by means of indirect violence, which does not pit refugees and European security forces against each other but delegates the responsibility for handling the problem to authorities in North Africa or elsewhere. Political and economic power is being deployed to make countries like Morocco or Libya partners in this displacement of violence. Legally and morally, this frees the EU of responsibility for violence. For if the Moroccan or Algerian authorities abandon refugees in the desert, this takes place far outside the competence of European security agencies; the EU can even lodge a complaint about human rights violations.

The scale of the new measures and the expected numbers of future refugees make it possible to speak of a new type of conflict, which is characterized by the delegation of violence and a technical lack of culpability. Only the organizational advantages of the core countries, financial, political and technological, allow the use of violence to be invisible and unidentifiable on European soil.[136] The visible players are the refugees, 'smuggling gangs' and 'human traffickers', the African authorities, and perhaps the families who put up money for the journey. The EU's border security officials appear mainly as a humanitarian force doing their utmost to reduce the suffering on the high seas.

Nowadays, it would seem, no one considers whether quotas might be allowed for climate refugees, on the grounds that the early industrial-ized countries caused the existential difficulties facing people in Africa and should therefore be made to shoulder some of the responsibility. The WGBU's point that climate policy is security policy may be seen as a recommendation that the former should be more efficient, and not only that the latter should be more restrictive.

In terms of social psychology, this raises the question of how far migration pressures generate a sense of threat and insecurity among the European public, leading to demands for a tighter policy on secu-rity. Fewer freedoms in exchange for greater security is an option that many embrace in the aftermath of a terrorist attack – which would sug-gest that a sense of personal threat expresses itself above all in a desire for more efficient protective measures. Threats from outside produce greater cohesion within.

Development policy therefore pushes for border protection meas-ures to be introduced *outside* the EU, in order to prevent the build-up of pressure on its frontiers. But up to now there has been no idea of what will happen when refugee numbers reach the level predicted for the middle of the century. A tenfold increase will put democratic societies under major strain and produce perceived problems that clamour for solutions.

RAPID SOCIAL CHANGE

The twentieth century witnessed a series of processes involving rapid social change: for example, the Russian Revolution (1917), the Nazi takeover of power (1933), the South American revolutions and counter-revolutions of the 1960s and 1970s, the collapse of Yugoslavia, and so on. Amazingly, however, neither sociology nor politics nor history has a theory, or even concepts, to describe and explain such accelerations. This is especially curious because all who think and work in these disci-plines have lived through at least one process of rapid social change with which no politician, academic or journalist had reckoned. The collapse of the Eastern bloc gathered momentum over a few months, before the breakthroughs of November and December 1989. Afterwards the world – or at least Europe – looked very different. Such short sharp change is not allowed for in modern theories of society: it is simply not supposed to happen. 'Madness' was the label that attached itself to those heady days, which, apart from the downfall of the Romanian dictator couple, were at first surprisingly free of violence.

The lack of a theory of *self-dynamizing social transformation* blocks the registration, interpretation and eventual guidance of radical changes in one's own society. In this regard it is symptomatic that, although Western countries were quick to characterize post-1989 Eastern Europe as 'transformation societies', they still do not recognize that the new international configuration, with all its economic, social and ecological implications, has changed Western countries too into transformation societies.

Processes of rapid change usually become apparent only when they involve force or result in outbreaks of collective violence. For example, if we think of the speed with which ethnicization drew Yugoslavia into an extremely brutal war, complete with ethnic cleansing and mass shootings, or of the incredibly short time it took for German society to turn Nazi after 1933, we realize how unstable and sluggish the institutional safeguards and psychological structures of modern societies really are.

It is becoming clear not only that abstract analytic categories such as 'society' or 'forms of rule' can change in the space of a few months, but also that the individuals who shape society and experience its forms of rule can adjust surprisingly quickly their moral compass, values and identities, even the way in which they interact with other people. This is most striking where real or perceived threats restrict the range of possible action and seem to make quick decisions necessary. An important factor here is whether the threat is abstract or concrete. That which cannot be visualized cannot be mastered either: it lies outside one's control.

LARGER-THAN-LIFE CLIMATE CHANGE

Climate change is larger than life, in several respects. It is the first truly global manmade event. Regardless of whose emissions caused it, when and where, their influence is felt and endured by different generations in other parts of the world. Cause and effect have drifted far apart in the case of climate change: those who brought it about are not contemporaries of those who have to deal with its consequences. One problem with attempts to regain control is that a *lack of responsibility* is built into the situation. The temporal, regional and biographical mismatch between cause and effect cuts across the allocation of responsibility, and also of obligations to do something to avert catastrophe. Since the climate is slow to respond, any new influences on it will take time to make themselves felt; what might be done today would have no visible or tangible result for a number of decades. The most that could be achieved would be a slowing of CO_2 concentrations, incapable of measurement by any procedures that might be imagined today, but the glaciers would continue to melt and the polar bears would continue to die out.

The sheer scale of the consequences makes it impossible to counter their unevenness: half the population of Africa cannot be resettled if people from Bangladesh and inhabitants of the Arctic have lost their habitat. Unlike disasters such as the Christmas tsunami of 2004 or Hurricane Katrina in summer 2005, climate change is not eventually over and finished. And if the consequences of a particular flood or storm already overstretch the public imagination as well as the plans and capacities of relief and protection agencies, how can people visualize a disaster, known about but not perceptible, which is likely to turn human existence upside down in at least some parts of the world? Do the Western faith in progress and the related belief that there is a solution to everything permit a radical assessment of the scale of the problem? And if they do, what would be the practical consequences for people's lives?

There have already been unexpected technological, natural[137] and social disasters that have exceeded the capacity to visualize and master them. The nuclear reactor meltdown at Chernobyl in April 1986 was a *technological* disaster which, according to statistical calculations, could not have happened,[138] and which, when it did happen, filled the world with complete bewilderment. The reasons for this were the unexpectedness of the accident, the lack of any idea as to how it could be brought under control, and the fact that radioactive fallout affected polluters and victims alike, wherever the wind took it, in Sweden, Finland, Poland and beyond. Chernobyl was thus a harbinger of the global ecological disasters that lie ahead. It was also a debacle for the control fantasists who, having switched to outdoor-grown organic food, were now only too happy to fall back on Dutch greenhouse vegetables unexposed to the fallout. But the greatest blow to morale for the safety-conscious inhabitants of a technological civilization was the primitiveness of the solution that was eventually found in Chernobyl; the derisory concrete cover on the molten reactor core, which is again becoming brittle and will have to be supplemented with a second layer, is the most vivid symbol of the fact that *some technological disasters cannot be remedied*.

Things are rather different with a *natural* disaster such as the earthquake-driven tsunami that crashed ashore at Christmas 2004. That too came out of the blue, but it could be understood as an uncontrollable stroke of fate, less shaming and demoralizing than a disaster due to banal human error.[139] But the tsunami too was a global disaster, not only because of its media impact but also because it struck so many international tourists. It completely overstretched the capacities of local governments and permanently shook the sense of security felt by long-distance travellers. The disaster could be overcome, of course, in the sense that people were able to mourn the dead and set about restoring the beaches and hotels.

The *social* catastrophe of the Holocaust took place much longer ago, but its effects are still with us today. The thought that the Western Christian world gave birth to a social crime that neither literary Cassandras nor political cynics could have imagined is still disturbing, six decades later, to anyone who considers the nature and dialectic of the civilizing process. To have carried the principle of rational problem-solving so far that the building of human extermination camps could appear logical was foreseen neither in theories of modernity nor in the minds of those who lived in it. The Holocaust too had a global character, because the world war in which it was situated fed it with victims from the most diverse social and national origins (a total of twenty nations)[140] and because the Nuremberg trials, which tried to bring the law to bear upon hitherto unimaginable crimes, marked the birth of today's concept of human rights and international criminal law.

The social, political and psychological consequences of this catastrophe have also proved *impossible to remedy*: there are still international tensions and trans-generational effects which go back to that paroxysm of violence. The Holocaust was also a social catastrophe, which permanently shook people's faith in the world, at least in the secular West. It was the first systematic display of what human beings could do to other human beings in an enlightened world – of what seemed to them proper and rational because no transcendent power could lay down obligations that limited the free use of their own reason.

Technological, natural and social disasters may thus turn out to be *unimaginably* large, with no prior frame of reference capable of comprehending them. Climate change, as a *social* problem, has something in common with these larger-than-life disasters: its threat is global, its consequences unpredictable, its countermeasures ineffectual, its psychological impact disorienting; all these elements will intensify the basic sense of helplessness in the event of a flood or hurricane, famine or urban devastation. We have to do with a qualitatively and quantitatively *new* problem, for the control of which there are no master plans and no guidelines. A normal psychological reaction to something threatening and uncontrollable is avoidance: one reduces the dissonance by ignoring the danger or making it out to be smaller than it is. The possibilities for this are manifold, ranging from scepticism about science to the interrogative shrug: mankind's long been finished, so why shouldn't it be now too?

Since the consequences of disasters are socially uneven and often reveal governments to be incapable of handling unexpected events, the burial of the victims and the itemization of the damage may be followed by looting and mass protests. The floods in New Orleans in 2005 were no different in this respect from the Peruvian earthquake in 2007. Even system change can be accelerated by environmental events; the overthrow of the Somoza dictatorship in Nicaragua, for example, followed the earthquake of 1972.[141]

In other words, uncontrollable events lead to discontent among those who suffer from them most: their expectations that the state will protect and care for them are dashed, and they express their disappointment in often violent protest. The resulting unrest is especially severe if the disaster has made it clear that the worst affected are poor people with few means to fend for themselves. The potential for violence may then become more virulent in later disasters, if they too have asymmetrical consequences for society.

Social disasters destroy social certainties: things that used to be taken for granted in everyday life suddenly become undependable; formulas for behaviour prove unworkable, rules cease to be valid. The outcome is a deep 'shaking of confidence in one's own culture and in the manageability of risks, but also in the reliability of planning and predictive action'.[142]

The shorter horizon of planning, narrower room for manoeuvre and loss of everyday certainties may result in violence if there are no stable institutions for the regulation of conflict, or if the ones that do exist are in crisis following some uncontrollable event. Technological, natural and social disasters – nuclear or chemical accidents, earthquakes or tsunamis, revolutions or acts of genocide – may demonstrate with amazing speed that instability is the rule and stability the exception.

In dissolving relatively sluggish traditional relations and production conditions, modernity has ensured that ways of life become more flexible and relationships more complex. But, beside the instability of individual life, today's institutions appear – and usually are – relatively lasting and dependable. Many ways of producing predictability and stability have been shifted to the direct responsibility of the individual: the task of caring for the sick and elderly has been transferred from the family to social welfare systems, conflict resolution is the business of the state rather than clans and families, and the handling of risks has been taken over by insurance companies. This is the normal way of things in functionally differentiated societies, and if all goes as expected such delegation of responsibility to institutions mostly guarantees continuity, stability and predictability.

The other side of the coin, however, is that the causal chains from decisions through interventions to effects become longer and their actual functioning becomes less visible, since 'supply, transport, communications and other infrastructural networks ideally remain in the background, operating without friction behind the functional systems'.[143] In a crisis these guarantees may prove illusory – it is crises that suddenly make perceptible what is normally part of the inconspicuous functioning of society. The grey areas of the functional system become visible at the moment of failure, revealing that 'risks and dangers are systematically left out of account in everyday action and decision-making'.[144] Self-reinforcing effects of insecurity, wrong decisions, panic reactions, and so on, then make a return to normality more difficult or impossible – which is why the disaster follows no inner logic and is open in terms of its outcome. If it is large enough, no one knows what will happen.

Nevertheless, more than two generations of peace and prosperity in the West have meant that people expect stability to last. If you have grown up without ever seeing your world torn apart by war, earthquake or mass hunger, you will think of large-scale violence, chaos and poverty as a likely problem *for others*. The frameworks that take shape in periods of relative stability are not calibrated for disasters, but at most for minor irregularities such as forest fires or floods. That is why any bursting of a river's banks there becomes a 'flood of the century'.[145]

This carries the danger that the potential for rapid social changes may fail to be noticed even when it is before people's eyes. In 1989, for example, people who had until then lived in either the GDR or the Federal Republic assumed that conditions in the two countries would not radically change; many Jews in Nazi Germany were of the same view up to the moment of their deportation; and people living in the vicinity of Chernobyl refused to believe that anything major would happen. A number of studies have shown that people express fewer feelings of insecurity the closer they are to a nuclear power station.[146] The more unavoidable a danger is, the greater is the degree of dissonance and the more necessary its reduction by means of lethargy, mental repression or defence mechanisms. It is not possible to live well otherwise with dangers outside one's control.

Man's superior adaptability to environmental changes is based on a capacity for cultural inheritance: new generations grow up with knowledge and techniques developed by their ancestors, and can begin their problem-solving strategies at a level that the previous generation had to develop by itself.[147] To be sure, the theories that deal with this fascinating side of human life easily overlook the fact that, over the generations, failed social-evolutionary strategies can develop and spread globally as much as successful ones can do. Moreover, success in the short term – for example, the breathtaking gain in personal security and living standards in the early industrialized countries, based on resource exploitation and possible only as a result of growth – can turn to disaster in the medium term. If *all* societies are drawn into the wake of industrial modernity, the principle of raising prosperity through exploitation and growth soon runs up against natural limits. Human beings are psychologically constituted in such a way that they register only abrupt changes in their lifeworld, not ones that creep up on them.

So, two psychological aspects come together in relation to a larger-than-life problem against which nothing much can be done: an anachronistic feeling, based on previous experience, that nothing spectacular will happen; and a need to conjure away dissonances. Norbert Elias describes this inertia as a 'drag effect', whereby individual habitus lags behind developments in reality, such that perception fails to keep step with social transformation.[148] We still *are* what we believed of ourselves yesterday, writes Günther Anders; attitudes are not synchronized with changing threat scenarios. Anders attributes 'apocalypse blindness' – an inability to weigh up and respond appropriately to real dangers – to 'a belief stretching back generations in the supposedly automatic progress of history'.[149] The other side of this inertia in relation to processes of change is the phenomenon of 'shifting baselines': perceptions and their interpretations shift imperceptibly together with changes in reality.

8

CHANGED REALITIES

In the rolling present, it is difficult to decide whether one has reached a critical point in a process: When does a decision become irreversible, and when does the further pursuit of a strategy spell disaster? When was that point reached on Easter Island? From today's vantage, we can give an answer: it was when so many trees had been felled that the forest could no longer regenerate. At the time, the state of environmental knowledge – the mental framework that dictated how to deal with nature – probably meant that people could not have 'known better'.[1] Jared Diamond is therefore on the wrong track when he asks what Easter Islanders thought when the last tree came crashing down. The fateful moment is not at the end of a process of destruction, but at the point when no one can see that what they are doing is destructive.

The Easter Island disaster did not begin when the last tree fell, any more than the Holocaust began when the last gas chamber was installed at Auschwitz. Social disasters commence when false decisions are taken: that is, in the case of Easter Island, when distinction and status rules required the use of wood to produce statues, or, in Nazi Germany, when pseudo-scientific assumptions about human inequality passed into laws and directives. But how present could the fate of the Jews have been in people's minds, at a time when no one had yet thought of developing systems for the annihilation of groups of human beings?

SHIFTING BASELINES

Besides the storms, it was the year that the rainforests got no rain. Forest fires of unprecedented ferocity ripped through the tinder-dry jungles of Borneo and Brazil, Peru and Tanzania, Florida and Sardinia. New Guinea had the worst drought for a century; thousands starved to death. East Africa saw the worst floods for half a century – during the dry season. Uganda was cut off for several days and much of the desert north of the region flooded. Mongol tribesmen froze to death as Tibet had its worst snows in fifty years. Mudslides washed houses of the cliffs of the desert state of California. . . . In Peru, a million were made homeless by floods along a coastline that often has no rain for years at a time. The water level at the Panama Canal was so low that large ships couldn't make it through. Ice storms disabled power lines through New England and Quebec, leaving thousands without power or electric light for weeks. The coffee crop failed in Indonesia, cotton died in Uganda and fish catches collapsed in the eastern Pacific. Unprecedented warm seas caused the tiny algae that give coral their colour to quit reefs in their billions across the Indian and Pacific Oceans, leaving behind the pale skeletons of dead coral.[2]

A report from the future, say 2018, when the planet has warmed by another degree? Wrong. All the above events took place in one year in the past, in 1998, and were associated with a particular climate event, El Niño. They were not the result of global warming, although it is assumed that such things will occur more often in the future on account of climate change. The events of 1998, to which one might add many more – from 1999, 2000, 2001, and so on – serve mainly to demonstrate that people develop a forgetful attitude to disasters that did not affect them and were seen only in the media.

There have been other media events in the last ten years, such as the massive fire in the Borneo rainforest that created a smog over a provincial capital, Palangkaraya, for months in 1997–8 and discharged 800 million to 2.6 billion tonnes of carbon dioxide into the atmosphere;[3] or the series of tornadoes that devastated Oklahoma in May 1999, killing forty, injuring 675 and causing damage estimated at $1.2 billion. There have also been spectacular hurricanes: Mitch, for example, cost 10,000 lives in Central America in 1998; Katrina buried a large Western city in water for the first time when it hit New Orleans in 2005; and Wilma broke three records, as the last in the 2005 season of twenty-two storms (the largest number ever known), the most powerful Atlantic hurricane ever measured, and the most costly in terrestrial damage ($29 billion).

Such extreme weather events are not new, but in recent years they have become more frequent and larger in scale. Yet people come to see them as normal, their attention slackening as the events become less newsworthy. Something that has little to do with nature is increasingly seen as 'natural'.

'Shifting baselines' is how environmental psychologists refer to the fascinating phenomenon that people always consider 'natural' the surroundings that coincide with their lifetime experience. Perception of changes in the social and physical environment is never absolute but always relative to one's own observational standpoint. So, the present generation has at best a vague or abstract notion of the fact that, in previous generations, not only the constructed lifeworld and infrastructure but also the natural environment was different; that, for example, meadow and heath landscapes are products of bygone deforestation, or that erosion problems in Central Europe have been known ever since the massive clearances of the Middle Ages.[4]

But we do not have to go back so far in time; the passage from one generation to the next is usually enough to display massive changes in how the environment is perceived. We have already mentioned the pioneering study of fish stocks and fishing grounds in different generations of Californian fisherfolk, the results of which are quite astounding. The researchers asked a sample from three generations where they thought that stocks had dwindled, which species they mainly caught in their nets, what was the size of their largest catch, and how large was the mightiest fish they had ever hauled aboard. The youngest group of respondents was aged between fifteen and thirty, the middle group between thirty-one and fifty-four, and the oldest fifty-five and above.[5] A full 84 per cent agreed that stocks had been declining, but there was blunt disagreement about which fish species were disappearing and where. Respondents in the oldest group named eleven species and the middle group seven, while the youngest mentioned only two that were no longer appearing in their fishing grounds.[6]

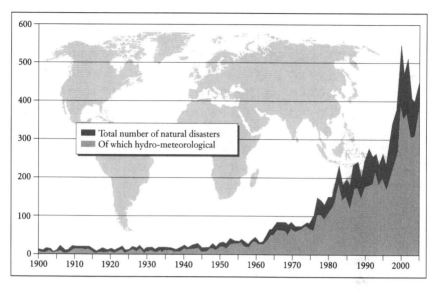

Figure 8.1 Number of extreme natural events and percentage involving weather-driven disasters

Source: EM-DAT (the OFDA/CRED international disaster database) (www.emdat.be/database), 3 April 2006.

The youngest also had no idea that, where they went every day to fish, there had not long ago been an abundance of great white sharks and goliath grouper, as well as pearl oysters. The same differences were apparent in relation to fishing grounds. The oldest respondents said that, whereas they had once not gone a long way to fill their nets, they now needed to sail far out to sea for a reasonable catch. Among the youngest, no one had any idea that it had once been possible to fish off the coast, so no one thought of such areas as overfished. In their frame of reference, there *were no fish* in coastal waters.

In the 1930s, travel guides would recommend the Gulf of California to anglers for its wonderful and easy-to-catch goliath grouper. Today the oldest fishermen can remember catching as many as twenty-five a day some fifty or sixty years ago; by the 1960s the number was down to ten or twelve a day, and by the 1990s to one at the most. Whereas nearly everyone in the oldest and the middle group had caught goliath groupers, less than half of the youngest had ever set eyes on one. Especially amazing is that only 10 per cent of the youngest thought that the stocks of this fish had disappeared; most thought there had never been any in the first place.[7] Similarly, the size of the largest fish ever caught became smaller and smaller as the age of the respondent declined.

The authors of the study concluded that these rapid changes in the perception of the environment (the 'shifting baseline') explain why most people are fairly laid back about the decline in biodiversity.[8] This is naturally a depressing finding for ecologists, since it also means that it is an uphill struggle to make the public aware of the need for stock protection, which, from a scientific point of view, has become an urgent necessity.

In terms of social psychology, the study offers an excellent example of the fact that people's evaluations change together with changes in their environment. It is like when two trains run on parallel tracks and seem motionless in relation to each other. Shifting baselines naturally have implications for how people perceive and evaluate threats or losses, and hence for what they regard as normal and abnormal.

Shifting baselines do not concern only the biological domain. Indeed, it may be easier to describe them in the context of social processes. If we think back to the uproar in the early 1980s over the plan to hold a census in Germany (when people denounced the drift to a 'total surveillance state' or 'the baring of every detail of our lives'), and if we compare that with today's carefree attitude to credit cards, mobile telephones, internet connections, and so on, then we find ourselves with a perfect example of shifting baselines in the sphere of the social. Every user of these technologies leaves electronic traces of his or her activity that can be reconstructed at any time, and the whole concept of a private life has radically changed. Yet scarcely anyone seems to feel that this restricts or 'bares' their personal life, probably because it does not involve a deliberate heightening of 'transparency' but is a collateral effect of innovations in which data protection or personal rights appear on the surface to be of little or no significance. The technology increases the ease of communication but at the same time leads to considerable normative changes, although, because of the shifting baseline, this is not really noticed.

Shifting social baselines may also feature in the acceptance of legislative changes – for example, those relating to Bundeswehr intervention abroad. This may make itself felt in a sense that such measures require less discussion, or even none at all. In the ecological sphere, increased environmental protection and higher energy costs have led in the last few decades to more fuel-efficient car engines, while at the same time a greater emphasis on safety and status has tended to make vehicles larger and heavier. The result has been a continual rise in cylinder capacity and engine performance, which largely eats up or even reverses the efficiency gains.

Shifting baselines are also a factor in the norms and beliefs, therefore the reference frameworks, which provide the bearings for what is true or false, good or bad.

REFERENCE FRAMEWORKS AND THE STRUCTURE OF IGNORANCE

On 2 August 1914, Franz Kafka wrote in his diary in Prague: 'Germany has declared war on Russia. Swimming class in the afternoon.' This is only a particularly striking example of how events that posterity learns to regard as historic are seldom experienced as such at the time. If they come to people's knowledge at all, it is as one among countless other incidents in everyday life that take up their attention, so that even an exceptionally intelligent individual may find an outbreak of war no more worthy of note than his attendance at a swimming class. So, when does a social catastrophe actually begin?

At the moment when history is taking place, what people experience is 'the present day'. Events acquire their importance only subsequently, when they have produced lasting consequences or, as Arnold Gehlen put it, have proved to be *Konsequenzerstmaligkeiten* – original events with profound consequences for everything that follows. This creates a methodological problem if we ask what people actually perceived or knew about the dawning event, or what they *could* have perceived and known. For original events usually escape perception, precisely because they are unprecedented; people try to insert what is happening into their available reference framework, even though its novelty means that it can only be a reference itself for later comparable events.

This is the very reason why German Jews did not grasp the scale of the exclusion process to which they would fall victim. In its first five years, many saw the Third Reich as a short-lived phenomenon 'that one had to live through, or a setback to which one had to adjust, or at worst the threat of a narrowing life that was nevertheless more bearable than the uncertainties of exile'.[9] The bitter irony is that, although the Jews' reference framework certainly included painful historical experiences of anti-Semitism, persecution and robbery, this itself made it impossible for them to see that what was happening was something different, something utterly murderous.

Thus, what people can know depends first of all on what they perceive. But this is not the only reason why it is so difficult to investigate what people did or did not know at an earlier point in time. Since history is perceived from shifting baselines, it is a *slow* process for human perception, which only concepts such as 'collapse of civilization' later crystallize into a sudden event – once the far-reaching consequences are known. To interpret what people saw of a process that only later turned to catastrophe is therefore an extremely tricky business, apart from anything else because they, unlike we, could not possibly have known how things would develop. In looking from the end of a history at its beginning, we have to suspend our historical knowledge, as it were, in order to grasp what people actually knew at the time. Norbert Elias was not wrong in saying that one of the hardest tasks in social science is to reconstruct the structure of ignorance in an earlier period.[10]

Conversely, those living at the time of an event know nothing of how a future observer will see what is today's present and tomorrow's history. The paradoxical task, then, is to gauge what was not visible in contemporary conditions yet played a decisive role in shaping the future. There is only one source on which such a heuristics of the future can base itself: the past.

KNOWING AND NOT-KNOWING ABOUT THE HOLOCAUST

You know, the horror we felt at first – that a human being could treat another human being like that – somehow abated.
That's how it is, no? And I saw in myself that we really became quite cool about it, as they say today.

Former prisoner in Gusen concentration camp

Every genocidal process begins at a point when no one has murder in mind, but when a majority of the population feels a perceived problem. On the other hand, it is hard to identify the moment when analysis of a social cataclysm like the Holocaust got under way, although this exerts a major influence on one's findings. In any case, analysis of the Holocaust cannot begin when the event itself began, especially if the starting point is itself doubtful. Was it the so-called Kristallnacht of 9–10 November 1938? The introduction of the Race Laws in 1935? The victory of the Nazi Party in the elections of 1933? The enabling law of 1933 that gave it full powers? The introduction of forcible 'euthanasia' in 1939? The onslaught on Poland in September 1939? The first systematic 'Jewish operations', the mass shootings of summer 1941? Or the moment when Rudolf Höss, the commandant of Auschwitz, having been introduced to the effects of Zyklon B, thought himself lucky that mass murder could now proceed without undue bloodshed?

As we see, the historian's beloved search for 'starting points' in a causal chain must end in failure. Causality is not a category that applies to social relations; contexts of interdependence may involve striking tensions and concentrated processes of change, but nothing like a decisive cause to which all else can be traced back. Thus, for example, the quest for a Führer Directive ordering the murder of the Jews is beside the point; a social process such as the Holocaust has a dynamic towards results and solutions that no one reckoned with, probably not even the 'Führer' himself. Social developments refer to changes in the figurative connections that people forge with one another, not to someone's saying B because he has said A. Social processes – as in the case of 'body counts', which we considered earlier – therefore often lead to results that no single participant intended, but which do shape reality. It is true that the consequences of yesterday's action are conditions for today's action – but the reverse is not true. One cannot always infer back from the consequences to the preconditions, and never to the underlying ideas and intentions.

Nevertheless, the social reality of the 'Third Reich' is usually seen through the prism of the Holocaust, and there everyday life looks peculiarly static and hermetic. But the genocide was only the end result of an immensely accelerated eight-year process of social transformation. As we now know, support for the system grew continually from

1933 until the invasion of the Soviet Union. We are therefore talking of a normative 'shifting baseline': most citizens would have thought it unthinkable in 1933 that just a few years later, with their own active involvement, the Jews would not only be robbed of their rights and property but shipped off en masse to be murdered. These same citizens saw the deportation trains begin to leave in 1941; quite a few bought 'Aryanized' kitchen furnishings or living-room suites; and some thought it perfectly normal to run businesses or live in homes that had been confiscated from their Jewish owners.

All stages in the exclusion of German Jews took place in public. From the day of the Nazi takeover, a fundamental change in values made it seem increasingly normal that different standards of human interaction, and therefore of legislation and judicial process, should apply to human groups that were essentially different from each other.[11] To reconstruct this axiological 'shifting baseline', we can draw on contemporary sources on everyday life such as the notes of Sebastian Haffner, the journals of Victor Klemperer or Willy Cohn, and the letters of Lilly Jahn. These show how, in a startlingly short space of time, the Jews and other human groups were radically excluded from the binding social norms of justice, empathy or love of one's neighbour that still operated in the rest of society. It is often overlooked in analyses of the Third Reich that, although it was an unjust and arbitrary system, the arbitrariness and injustice were directed almost exclusively at those who 'did not belong'; members of the *Volksgemeinschaft* continued as before to enjoy legal security and state protection in large areas of society.

A survey of 3,000 individuals, conducted in the 1990s, showed that nearly three-quarters of those born before 1928 knew no one who had been arrested or interrogated for political reasons during the Nazi period.[12] Even more respondents stated that they had never felt personally threatened, despite the fact that, in the same survey, a large number said they had listened to illegal radio broadcasts, joked about Hitler or expressed criticism of the Nazis.[13] Another remarkable result was that between a third and more than a half of respondents confessed to having believed in National Socialism, admired Hitler or shared Nazi ideals.[14] A survey conducted in 1985 by the Allensbach polling organization produced similar findings. Of the respondents, who had to have been aged at least fifteen in 1945, 58 per cent confessed to having believed in National Socialism, 50 per cent thought that it had embodied their ideals, and 41 per cent had admired the Führer.[15]

This perceived lack of personal threat or repression rested on a strong sense of belonging, the other side of which was the daily demonstration that other groups, especially the Jews, did not belong. Immediately after 30 January 1933, the exclusion of Jews began to gather enormous momentum without meeting significant resistance from the majority of the population – although some might turn up their noses at the 'SA or Nazi rabble' or feel that the cascade of anti-Jewish measures was uncouth, improper, exaggerated or simply inhumane. Saul Friedländer gives an idea of what I mean by this 'enormous momentum':

The city of Cologne forbade the use of municipal sports facilities to Jews in March 1933. Beginning April 3 requests by Jews in Prussia for name changes were to be submitted to the Justice Ministry, 'to prevent the covering up of origins'. On April 4 the German Boxing Association excluded all Jewish boxers. On April 8 all Jewish teaching assistants at universities in the state of Baden were to be expelled immediately. On April 18 the party district chief (Gauleiter) of Westphalia decided that a Jew would be allowed to leave prison only if the two persons who had submitted the request for bail . . . were ready to take his place in prison. On April 19 the use of Yiddish was forbidden in cattle markets in Baden. On April 24 the use of Jewish names for spelling purposes in telephone communications was forbidden. On May 8 the mayor of Zweibrücken prohibited Jews from leasing places in the next annual town market. On May 13 the change of Jewish to non-Jewish names was forbidden. On May 24 the full Aryanization of the German gymnastics organization was ordered, with full Aryan descent of all four grandparents stipulated.[16]

Such measures, which affected *others* but were naturally not unknown to the rest of the population, were an everyday phenomenon in the Third Reich. Scarcely a day passed without one more being added. The keynote was the 'Law for the Restoration of the Professional Civil Service' (7 April 1933), which provided *inter alia* for the retirement of all non-Aryan officials. In the same year 1,200 Jewish professors and lecturers were dismissed, without a single protest from any of the faculties concerned. On 22 April non-Aryan doctors were excluded from the health insurance schemes that oversaw public healthcare.[17] On 14 July 1933 the Law for the Prevention of Genetically Diseased Offspring was passed.

However the various measures appeared to individuals in the '*Volk* community', it should be noted that even in these early stages – which implied a considerable value change in relations between people – there was little or no expression of discontent. As things got worse for some, others felt so much the better. It was a radically changed existential situation, which registered at the level of perception and reflection for the better-off, but did not seem at all radical – a normative shifting baseline. Not for nothing do people who were alive at the time still largely agree that the Third Reich was a 'wonderful period', at least until the invasion of the Soviet Union; some think it remained that until even later in the war.[18] In this 'shifted' normative universe, even the deportation of erstwhile fellow humans to places about which nothing was known appeared part of normality.

A little thought experiment will make the scale of the value change clearer. If the deportations had begun in February 1933, immediately after the Nazi takeover, the deviation from what the majority considered within the bounds of normality would have been too great to have proceeded without friction. It would even have exceeded most people's capacity to imagine it (quite apart from the fact that the Nazis themselves had not yet thought through the sequence that led from exclusion through deprivation of rights and property to deportation and annihilation). Only eight years later, that way of treating others was already part of what people had come to expect; it therefore did not strike them as out of the ordinary. As we see, a shift in fundamental social baselines did not require even a generational changeover or decades of evolution; a few years were enough.

And the participants did not notice how their perceptions of reality and their conceptions of what was right and wrong, social and antisocial, were changing. In view of this phenomenon of shifting baselines, we should not delude ourselves that moral convictions will make people pause at any point in an anti-human process and take a better direction. This is true not only of the Nazi period but also of quite different problems and situations.

SHIFTING BASELINES ELSEWHERE

People can find meaning in actions which, from the outside, seem incomprehensible, unspeakably cruel, sometimes even self-damaging or self-destructive. The example of Islamist suicide bombers shows that it can even make sense to blow oneself up and kill as many others as possible. Of course the decision to do this is not taken alone: it is embedded in a social frame of reference and is preceded by a shifting of baselines. For suicide bombing is a normative innovation within the history of Islamic fundamentalism, and even the bombers' families would have thought it inconceivable a few decades earlier that they would feel joy at their son's or daughter's action. The Koran forbids the taking of one's own life.

Once again a value shift made it possible, within quite a brief space of time, to regard a person's readiness to blow themselves up as highly positive and desirable. In his work on terrorism, Bruce Hoffman has investigated the religious coding of political acts of violence and the role played by the traditional posture of the 'martyr'. 'The images of suicide terrorists emblazoned on murals and wall posters, calendars and key chains, postcards and pennants throughout Palestine are but one manifestation of this deliberate process', whereby social value is attached to self-destruction. 'Similarly, the suddenly elevated and now highly respected status accorded their families is another. The proud parents of Palestinian martyrs, for instance, publish announcements of their progeny's accomplishments in local newspapers not on the obituaries page but in the section announcing weddings.'[19]

Modern media play an important role in this value change – for example, when Palestinian television carries publicity that urges young people to sign up for terrorist organizations.

One such segment broadcast in 2003 depicts the image of a young Palestinian couple out for a walk when suddenly IDF [Israeli] troops open fire, shooting the woman in the back and killing her. When visiting her grave, her boyfriend is also shot dead by the IDF. He then is shown ascending to heaven, where he is welcomed by his girlfriend, who is seen dancing with dozens of other female martyrs, portraying the seventy-two virgins – the promised 'Maidens of Paradise' – who reputedly await the male martyr in heaven.[20]

Evidently such broadcasts are closely linked to suicide attacks that take place shortly afterwards. (A reader who feels haughtily superior about such actions would do well to pause and ask himself whether it makes more sense to die for a 'Leader', without any prospect of reward in the afterlife.)

The families of suicide bombers receive financial support (some-times as much as $25,000 per family member killed), in addition to things such as television sets, furniture or jewellery. Terrorist organi-zations or their funders also help to supply infrastructure that the local state does not provide – for example, healthcare, education and social welfare. All terrorist organizations gain recruits as a result of the loyalty that such forms of practical aid generates, but in the process they weed out those who seem to represent false values or who merely care about other people's problems. This is as true of Hamas as it is of the IRA or ETA. Ideology plays scarcely any role in this *practical transformation of social space*. People change their values because their world changes, not vice versa.

Video messages that suicide terrorists recorded before their mission provide further information about the value shift in Palestinian society, which means that, according to survey evidence, more than 70 per cent of Palestinians approve of suicide attacks.[21]

As norms have changed within Islamic fundamentalism, establishing forms of violence unthinkable two decades ago, social norms have also changed in another part of the configuration: that is, among those on the receiving end of suicide attacks. This concerns the value of free-dom relative to security, the willingness to put up with manifold forms of restriction and surveillance and to support military intervention abroad.

Changes in one part of the societal field of tension set up pressure to change in quite different parts of the field. This feedback mechanism is particularly evident in the case of terrorism, where actions on one side generate pressure on the other side. Thus, any successful attack not only kills random victims but, as *a communicative act*, shakes the sense of security of countless other people. The shifting baselines are then almost complementary: every terrorist attack generates a need for greater security among its potential targets and makes them more willing to restrict their own freedom in return for at least a sense of security.

In Germany, following the 9/11 attacks in New York, anti-terror legislation valid for a five-year period provided for a number of adjustments to existing laws (on defence of the constitution, police powers, security vetting, passport and identity card regulations, air traffic control, the central criminal register, energy security), so that the security forces would have the means to improve their exchange of information, surveillance operations, border control, and so on. In particular:

– The internal intelligence agency (*Verfassungsschutz*) may gather information about money transfers and bank accounts of suspicious organizations and about individuals in banks and finance companies. It also has powers to monitor air transport companies and telecommunications operators and service providers.
– The Federal Criminal Police Department (*Bundeskriminalamt*) received greater powers to investigate computer sabotage, including on grounds of 'initial suspicion'.
– The federal police were given powers to deploy security agents on board aircraft and to carry out wider checks on individuals.
– New provisions were introduced to deny a visa or residence permit to individuals who endanger the security of the Federal Republic, take part in acts of violence, publicly call for the use of violence or belong to a terrorist association. Identity and residence papers were further protected against falsification.
– In the context of asylum procedures, powers were created to record applicants' voices as a way of determining their country of origin. Identity materials (e.g., fingerprints) would be kept for ten years after the decision on asylum, and data could be passed on to the Bundeskriminalamt.
– The Register of Aliens law permitted better checks on incoming traffic. Police access to the register was supposed to flag immediately whether someone was residing in Germany legally. The data

could be accessed online and not, as before, released only on postal application to the central register.

– As regards passports and identity papers, provision was made for computer-supported identification of individuals (photograph, signature and biometric features).

Germany's anti-terror legislation was reviewed in 2005, and supplementary provision was made for the *Verfassungsschutz* to gather information about activities not previously considered anti-constitutional. It may now also require airlines to provide information about flight bookings by suspicious individuals.

However, in a ruling on 31 January 2007 (StB 18/06) the Federal Court prohibited the kind of secret online searches that the security services and the interior minister had been urgently requesting. Until then Trojans and backdoor programmes had been used under §102 of the Code of Criminal Procedure to conduct searches without the target's knowledge where there was suspicion of a serious criminal offence. But the Federal Court based its decision on the fact that computers are also part of the sphere of private life (in which searches must be carried out in the presence of suspects or witnesses). At the time of writing, however, the interior ministry is apparently ready to deploy new spyware, in the shape of mini-programmes that can trawl through a user's hard disk and search for data movement pointing to the preparation of a terrorist attack.

A new anti-terror database, for which the go-ahead was given in December 2006, makes it possible to link IT systems to intelligence agencies, security forces and the police. This contains information about individuals under suspicion (membership of terrorist associations, possession of weapons, telecommunications data, bank accounts, education and occupation, family status and religion, place of residence and journeys abroad), as well as reported losses of identity papers. Of course not only terror suspects but all kinds of other people are in danger of ending up in this database.

In September 2007 a 'Forum for Collaboration between Security Authorities and Industry' was created in Brussels. According to a report of its meeting, 'the European Union will release a total of €2.135 billion by 2013 for the development of new security technologies, which are intended to give member states far-reaching possibilities of surveil-lance and investigation.'[22] Two aims will be the development of devices that can detect explosives in private homes and video cameras that can detect unusual movements in a crowd. Even the vice-president of the European Commission, Günter Verheugen, described these as tech-nologies 'which are fundamentally changing our societies'.[23] The newly founded forum is, moreover, independent of the European Union.

Most other European countries have made similar moves in security legislation and technology: a million surveillance cameras were due to be deployed in France by 2009,[24] and their ubiquitous presence is already a fact of life in Britain. In the United States, as we have seen, a special ministry was created for 'homeland security' after the 9/11 attacks. All the related watering-down of data protection and computer privacy seems to have raised scarcely any objections – on the contrary, the new laws and technologies find wide public support, especially after a terrorist attack has taken place or been foiled. Opinion surveys in Germany point to a growing fear of terrorism,[25] whose place on the scale of perceived threats has risen considerably in relation to classical issues such as epidemics, accidents or unemployment.[26]

There is also a new level of support for tighter security policies. Whereas in 2005 only 37 per cent of the German public thought that 'more needs to be done against the terrorist threat', the figure had risen to 46 per cent a year later. More than two-thirds of Germans approve of greater video surveillance at railway stations, for example;[27] and 65 per cent thought in 2007 that not enough was being done in the fight against crime.[28]

One interesting point is that two-thirds of survey respondents do not consider that anti-terror measures involve a restriction of civil liberties.[29] A European Commission study showed that, in general, only people over forty-five feared that data protection was inadequate, whereas the under thirties saw no problem in the existing state of things.[30]

Such findings indicate that baselines are shifting on the other side too. In the event of a further rise in the perceived terrorist threat (fol-lowing another major attack, for example), the priority may shift still further from freedom to security – not without reason, since only the living are in a position to enjoy freedom. Demands for the protection of personal liberties have clearly weakened in comparison with the 1970s and 1980s, and survey results are already evidence that citizens will not only condone but demand stronger security measures in the future. So, values and standards of normality are shifting within democratic societies.

How will conceptions of a normal and measured response to external threats change if growing numbers of environmental refugees pose security problems at state frontiers? How will the trade-off between freedom and security develop if terrorist attacks become more frequent and more violent? What calls for orientation and stability will appear if a catastrophe hits European cities? There is much historical evidence that unsatisfied expectations of stability and security lead to outbreaks of violence, and that a sense of increased population pressure can turn against refugees or others who are held responsible for it. The willingness to exchange freedoms for security also requires no further demonstration. Faith in stable values and standards of normality and civilized behaviour therefore seems unwarranted. Radical consequences of climate change may bring a radical value shift in their wake.

Real or perceived threats from outside generate a deeper sense of internal belonging; the terrorist threat is thus conducive to the strengthening of we-group identity,[31] which in turn involves establishing who 'the others' are. Thus, threat–reaction configurations increase the need for 'we' and 'they' identification; it then depends on the scale of the perceived threat whether reactions of an excluding or aggressive kind are directed against members of 'they-groups'. As Mary Kaldor puts it, identity politics gains a new importance in the age of globalization.

To sum up: a change of values in one part of the transnational field of tension does not leave untouched the values which are added in another part – yet people in both parts remain convinced that they are adhering to values they have always upheld.

THE REVIVAL OF OLD CONFLICTS: FAITHS, CLASSES, RESOURCES AND THE EROSION OF DEMOCRACY

The world of Stalinism, with its ethnic cleansings, deportations, labour camps and deliberately induced famines, was a radical departure from anything that might have been expected in Western Christian thought or in the Enlightenment tradition, for which everything was in principle rationally explicable. Yet that world held out for much of the twentieth century, and a few offshoots, in North Korea, Burma or Laos, survive to this day. This is of interest to our argument only because twentieth-century trends in state systems show that *unexpected* developments can suddenly appear and persist, generating social realities with which no one had previously reckoned. In this light, the belief that all societies will sooner or later follow the OECD model proves to be a mere illusion, and an ahistorical one at that. For the Western experiment has been going on for just 250 years, and history will not come to an end when that experiment is over.

Other systems of rule existed for considerably longer and collapsed in the end. But until now – with a few exceptions – much less attention has been given to the fall of societies than to their rise, so that there are as few models of systemic implosion as there are of unexpected variants of development. Which theory of the state allows for capitalist autocracies such as Russia or China, or for a modern fundamentalist state such as Iran? And which has room for the 'anachronistic' intrusion of seemingly old causes of conflict into modern processes of development?

The major conflicts of the twentieth century appeared to take place under an imperial and, later (in the Cold War), ideological aegis. But since the brief post-1989 period of Euro-American euphoria came to a rude end, we have seen a revival of fault lines that one would have thought more typical of the nineteenth century than the twenty-first.

What today look like religious wars undoubtedly belong to an earlier time in history, and although they involve reactions to modernization and globalization they are real and tangible conflicts that have arisen under the aegis of religion, in which highly charged terms such as 'Crusaders' or 'failed states' are used to label the two antagonistic sides. Once a conflict is defined in such a way that the groups stand radically opposed to each other as 'us' and 'them', mediation is no longer possible and the hostilities will last at least until one side or the other is victorious. This is the logic common to jihad and the 'war on terror': a peace agreement between equals is ruled out in *faith wars*. The opposing sides constantly reinforce the attitudes and claims that each has about the other.

Faith wars therefore impact on the reference frameworks that are part of the hostile configuration. Mirror-image fundamentalisms emerge, such as the sects in the United States which, exploiting pseudo-scientific disputes over creationism and evolutionism, have spilled over into Europe too. It is still hard to say what value shifts might develop out of these mirror reactions, but if, in the thoroughly secular 1960s (the age of civil rights movements, anti-colonial liberation wars, growing liberalization in the West and occasional stormy weather in the East), anyone had predicted that violent conflicts would soon be dominated by religion, he or she would certainly have been pronounced ignorant of earthly reality.

Yet that is how things are today, four decades later. And just as religious wars are back, so too are *class conflicts*, albeit in a new form. With globalization and the supranational operations of companies and hedge funds, class society too has emancipated itself from nation-state boundaries. The chief executive of an automobile corporation, the manager of an investment trust, the IT specialist, the manual worker from a low-wage country and the illegal migrant worker – all represent, in their very different ways, the global asymmetry of opportunities for economic activity. Whereas transnational business has for a long time operated outside narrow legal frameworks, using national regulations only as opportunity structures for technological, fiscal or political decisions as to location, both skilled and unskilled labour can follow in the same direction and achieve income levels that would be utopian in their place of origin. The return of class society thus happens in a space beyond the nation-state, outside the traditional institutions for conflict resolution that were often the product of long and hard struggles in the past. At the same time, there are no international trade unions or supranational economics or social ministries capable of taking effective action to moderate the disparities. It is not yet possible to see the kind of conflicts that will emerge in this new class society.

Finally, there is the revival of *resource conflicts*, and, as we have already seen, these are likely to become more intense as the world's reserves of oil, uranium, water, and so on, dry up. Disputes over resources thought to lie beneath the Arctic Ocean or the Antarctic ice give a foretaste of the return of resource imperialism, which was thought to belong to history. The fight to conquer and divide has already begun (see pp. 93–95 above).

The dominant conflicts of the twenty-first century are therefore global *class, faith and resource conflicts*. And, in the absence of effective transnational players or a monopoly of force in relations between states, we may say that there is scarcely any scope to regulate these new-old conflicts. To be sure, judging by recent cases of violence linked to the environment and resources, it can be assumed that such conflicts will never be one-dimensional but will either involve interdependent factors at the outset or come to do so as they progress. Here issues such as justice, ethnicization, revenge, and so on, also play a role in sharpening the conflict.

The Cold War age of system rivalry and competing utopias, which seems almost idyllic in retrospect, is over for the time being. What is now at stake, after a peculiar turn in history, is a series of hot conflicts over space and resources, which over the coming decades will have a fundamental impact on the shape of Western societies. We know from the totalitarianisms and genocides of the last century how quickly an attempted solution to social problems can turn into sharply divisive formulas and deadly actions.

DISPLACEMENT OF VIOLENCE

Of course, history does not repeat itself. Formats for the resolution of security problems will look different in the twenty-first century, if only because new communications media have triggered a competitive spiral between terrorists and security services and shifted the locus of international tensions. The scale of the violence has also changed things, especially since (quite apart from Iraq and Afghanistan) Western countries have deployed their means for the internal and external use of force to regions where this makes direct confrontation inevitable. Two clear cases in point are the prevention of illegal migration, where the control of borders is being de-territorialized, and the increasing efforts in internal security matters to make 'pre-criminal activity' liable to punishment.[1]

The return of private armed forces in national and international conflicts seems curiously pre-modern, but paradoxically it is closely linked to the modernization of violence. After the end of the Second World War, and at the latest by the end of the Cold War, the dawning of something like a post-heroic age placed classical forms of offensive warfare and the use of torture and other such means under increased legitimation pressure. But since, even in the post-heroic age, particular interests still require violence to assert themselves, there has been a trend in recent years to turn both military and police functions over to private companies. It has been predicted that in future private companies will also intervene in conflicts over raw materials.[2] Such shifts in the use of force to the private sector have hollowed out the state monopoly of violence and parliamentary control over military action, representing a retreat from the levels of control achieved in the previous period.

A similar delegation of power takes place when potential frontier violators are arrested in buffer countries, thereby avoiding incidents in border regions and the violence that is often associated with them. In such cases, too, the use of force is turned over to another party – not a private agency, though, but the authorities of another state.

An analogous trend is visible in attempts to make certain actions punishable even before a crime is committed – for example, strategic or technological activity in the field of terrorism. Though desirable in the eyes of the authorities, this has dire implications for democracy: it changes the law-based state into a preventive state (as Heribert Prantl put it), automatically placing its citizens under suspicion. But if 'the boundary between the innocent and the guilty, the suspicious and the unsuspicious, is removed',[3] so that telephone and internet data can be routinely recorded, bank accounts monitored and an individual's daily movements followed, irrespective of any suspicion, then the result is an erosion of the rule of law.

Both these sets of reactions to real and perceived problems are changing the face of Western democracies. But the less the rule of law is observed in crisis situations, the weaker are the weapons of civilization against arbitrariness and violence, and the more radical the attempted solutions to social problems will become.

10

MORE VIOLENCE

We had to destroy the city to save it.

US army officer, South Vietnam, 1968

Against this background, climate change has been underestimated and indeed, up to now, largely unconceptualized as a danger to society. It appears inconceivable that such a phenomenon defined by natural science might produce social disasters such as system breakdown, civil war or genocide, especially at a time when everything still seems to be in order. Yet no great flight of the imagination is needed to visualize such things, and a number of present-day social conflicts, wars and security measures can already be attributed to environmental factors.

1 Climate wars are already occurring in regions where de-statification and privatized 'violence markets' have become the norm. Here, any negative change in environmental conditions creates further scope for entrepreneurs of violence and makes it more likely that armed conflict will become permanently entrenched and spill across international frontiers.

2 Such consequences of climate change as soil degradation, flooding, water shortages or hurricanes limit the possibility of making a livelihood and deepen the problems already present in the region.

3 Outbreaks of violence in vulnerable societies, which are the most likely to suffer from climate changes and to be the hardest hit, will increase the flow of refugees and migrants, both within and between countries. And this will bring further violence in its train.

4 Cross-border migration is reaching the islands of prosperity and stability in Western Europe and North America, causing their state authorities to tighten security policy and to strengthen their security apparatuses. In external policy, this involves strategies that seek to shift conflict from border control posts to the authorities in other countries and to increase the measures available for use against border violators.

5 The terrorism that has grown in step with global modernization processes is legitimated and strengthened by inequalities and injustices resulting from climate change.

6 This constantly raises the surveillance needs of the state, restricting the spaces of freedom in society and increasing the level of state-monopolized violence.

7 New spaces outside the rule of law, such as those established in the war against terror, increase the level of state violence and expand the area behind the scenes of society. The use of force is displaced; the arm of the state hits at people before any crime is committed.

8 Shifting baselines change the perception of problems and increase the public acceptance of new security measures and proposed solutions. Norms of conduct and standards of normality are redefined.

9 These processes interact with one another. Growing numbers of refugees, more intense security efforts, international resource conflicts, and so on, generate autocatalytic effects. Sudden environmental disasters stretch the capacities of OECD and developing countries to the limit, and have a totally devastating impact on failing societies. The resulting stress and fear of new threats lead to unpredictable reactions.

The scenario that is taking shape is one that puts the global configuration of societies under pressure, resulting in tensions and violence of varying forms and intensity. The social climate is more complex than the physical climate, but this does not mean that we cannot identify the potential threats and violence that may become a reality in the future.

Climate changes work in two directions: they may provoke violent conflicts or deepen existing ones; but they may also interact, accumulate and set up indirect chains that produce *unexpected consequences*. It is high time that environmental effects were taken into account in the description and analysis of social conflicts. Most of the changes outlined above have long since passed the stage of hypotheses and are already shaping the reality of human societies: there are climate wars here and now; people are already being killed, dying from other causes and taking the road of flight. Empirically, there is not the slightest reason to believe that the world will remain as we know it.

11

WHAT CAN AND CANNOT BE DONE – I

Whether radical solutions to social problems will be blocked in the future will be another test of how much societies have learned from their history. This is not an academic but a political question.

To be sure, political theory in the age of global danger cannot concentrate on models for the future, not only because the imagination for that is lacking, but also because the utopian social promises of the twentieth century turned out to be totalitarian nightmares. On the other hand, that is precisely why a revival of political theory is necessary, and why it must prove its worth in *a critique of any limitation of survival conditions for others*. It also needs to be considerably more future-oriented than it has been in recent decades. Societies with no experience of the huge dangers ahead are like an oil tanker steaming towards an iceberg, no longer able to avoid it although it has long been in their field of vision.

After all that has been said about the social consequences of climate change, it should not be hard to imagine that the world will look markedly different in a few decades from now. Indeed, it is to be feared that in quite a few regions the conditions for human life will have considerably worsened. The question that suggests itself is therefore: What can be done for the author of this book to be proved wrong?

GOING ON AS USUAL

One option is as simple as it is obvious: to go on as usual. This would mean a continuation of economic growth, requiring further imports of fossil fuels and other raw materials and systematically reducing the medium-term capacity to help or support societies that fall into major difficulties. Such a strategy accepts, for example, that car fuel will have to contain an increasing bio-element, in order to extend the time before oil reserves run out. But this implies in turn that rainforests will have to be destroyed, so that land can be cleared for oil-bearing plants to provide the biofuel. This is already happening in many countries in Asia and South America;[1] and it often goes together with forcible land expropriation and the expulsion of local people.

To go on as usual means a policy of securing supplies through agreements with countries that neither respect human rights nor observe environmental standards. It must also accept that the means for humanitarian intervention in crises will be more limited than they are today, because the number of conflicts and the flow of refugees will increase and the sources of livelihood will diminish.

Aid will therefore have to be more targeted; some countries and regions will have to be excluded from it. Negative developments of this kind will unfold not in the public spotlight but in backstage departments that contain no potential for scandal and raise no obstacles to action. Such a strategy may thus seem rational, until the painful consequences of climate change spread to initially unaffected regions – either directly or in the form of economic shockwaves from other countries' wars and conflicts, terrorism or migration pressure; or else in the form of social conflict between new generations who have no chances in life and older generations responsible for the effects of past pollution who did enjoy many opportunities. Nevertheless, things might go on for a few more decades, during which 'business as usual' might seem the most rational strategy to today's middle-aged, the core group of the functional elites.

Another reason why this seems a neat solution is that it raises no obvious ethical problems. For the nation-state is a player that acts on behalf of others not as an individual, and in relations between states such categories as egoism, inconsiderateness or indolence are irrelevant. Any state can play dirty, but that does not change by one iota its bargaining power in the international arena.

If one were to imagine the 'go on as usual' strategy at the level of individuals, one would immediately think of a sociopath who has no problem consuming seventy times more than anyone else[2] while largely relying on their raw materials – or someone who uses fifteen times more energy, water and food than the less well-off and discharges nine times more pollutants into the atmosphere. Such a personality would also be totally unconcerned about the lives of his children and grandchildren, accepting that, because of him and his kind, 852 million people worldwide go hungry and more than 20 million are refugees.

All normative criteria would classify such a person as a social misfit or, more bluntly, a dangerous parasite, whose game should be put a stop to sooner rather than later. But collective players escape such moral attributions because in this case they are simply representatives of states, institutions, associations or corporations, who shape action structures from which they can distance themselves subjectively at any moment;[3] immorality is simply not an issue in international politics. This is why a category such as 'failed state' – which Washington introduced to bolster its use of 'pre-emptive strikes' – sounds so out of place: so long as one is not dealing with personal attributes, morality is of no relevance to action. Individuals can think of themselves as acting morally even if the community they help to shape behaves 'immorally'.

This makes the inequalities and injustices of the globalized world appear nondescript and unexceptional, so that someone who feels responsible for the poverty of people at the other end of a chain that he and others like him originated cuts an irrational figure in the eyes of the West. For this reason, it is extremely unlikely that a strategy other than 'business as usual' will be chosen in the lands of affluence.

Someone who, in the name of species survival or justice between generations, finds this an unacceptable solution has three possible (and not mutually exclusive) ways of trying to change things for the better. The first and most popular is to individualize the problem and the solutions. A recent book on climate change, for example, offered a hundred tips on how to save the world, which ranged from educating children in environmental protection (tip 10) through using one's dishwasher only when it is full (tip 35) to forming car-sharing clubs (tip 56) and separating refuse for recycling (tip 95).[4]

Such tips not only fall grotesquely short of the scale of the problem but, by individualizing it, grossly understate the level and complexity of the responsibilities and obligations in relation to climate change. The false, but highly attractive, assumption that social changes begin with the little things in life becomes ideological if it frees corporate or political players of their obligations, and irresponsible if it claims that the problems associated with climate change can be tackled at the level of individual behaviour. When the oil industry flares off 150 to 170 billion cubic metres of natural gas every year[5] – as much as the industrial countries Germany and Italy combined – the savings made by individual households become little more than a footnote.[6] It is certainly true that the cleanest energy is that which is never used, but this has little relevance in a global context of pollution and resource consumption in the growth-oriented newly industrializing countries. On the other hand, the psychological effect of the emphasis on individuals is all the greater, since it suggests that it is within their power to effect a solution. We can all do our bit, it seems, even when we next switch on our dishwasher.

Table 11.1 Emissions of emerging economies (in millions of tonnes)

Emerging economies	China	India	South Africa	Mexico	Brazil
Total emissions 2004 (with % change since 1990)	5,253 (+48%)	1,609 (+50%)	453 (+18%)	487 (+30%)	905 (+35%)
Emissions per capita (with % change since 1990)	4.2 tonnes (+34%)	1.6 tonnes (+25%)	10.5 tonnes (−1%)	4.9 tonnes (+9%)	5.3 tonnes (+18%)

Source: Bundeszentrale für politische Bildung: M 02.07 CO_2-Emissionen Schwellenländer (www.bpb.de/popup/popup_grafstat.html?url_guid=7825TW).

The second level of action concerns the initiatives taken by various states since the IPCC reports – from the climate protection programme of the German environment ministry to the Australian proposal to replace all conventional light bulbs with low-energy ones. Measures such as home insulation undoubtedly lead to energy savings, and the

German government's target of a 40 per cent cut in CO_2 emissions by 2020 is ambitious but certainly on the right track. Even if international disparities in climate policy, and the fact that emissions do not stop at frontiers, limit the effect of national solutions, such moves by individual collective players are certainly helpful. Innovative strategies change the configuration that societies create together, at least gradually, and the role of the pioneer may be inspirational. Here too the psychological effect is considerable: the feeling that nothing anyone does can make a difference is reduced. On the other hand, one should not lose sight of the limits built into such strategies. National solutions cannot 'turn the climate round', because their quantitative impact remains too exiguous.

It is at the international level that the complexity is greatest and the loss of control most evident. There is no supranational organization that can order sovereign states to emit lower amounts of greenhouse gases than they think reasonable. The same is true of river pollution, dam construction or deforestation. Nor is there an international monopoly of force that can sanction individual countries – for example, in relation to population resettlement or expulsions, land confiscation or human rights violations accompanying a ruthless environmental policy. A division of powers certainly exists within states, but not between them; only international criminal law offers the first rudiments of supranational regulation, with the possibility of putting on trial individuals responsible for massacres or genocidal acts.[7] A major development of supranational institutions, especially of ones with real teeth, is still a long way off and currently has no effect on the problem of global warming. It may be hoped that the problem will give a further impetus to the creation of such institutions; international criminal law has its roots in the social disaster of the Nazi crimes, which the Nuremberg trials defined as 'crimes against humanity'. But at present international agreements on environmental questions are limited to self-imposed obligations, and any failure to meet these does not make a country liable to sanctions. Here too, then, the upshot is that everything is good which serves climate protection at international level, but it is an illusion to believe that emissions can be cut sufficiently by 2020 to contain global warming.

These are the levels of social action available in the current state of play. It must therefore be assumed that the problem of climate change is *unsolvable* – which means that the earth will warm by more than the extra 2 degrees that are still considered manageable.

FUTURE PASTS

For a long while I stood on the bridge that leads to the former research establishment. Far behind me to the west, scarcely to be discerned, were the gentle slopes of the inhabited land; to the north and south, in flashes of silver, gleamed the muddy bed of a dead arm of the river, through which now, at low tide, only a meagre trickle ran; and ahead lay nothing but destruction. From a distance, the concrete shells, shored up with stones, in which for most of my lifetime hundreds of boffins had been at work devising new weapons systems, looked (probably because of their odd conical shape) like the tumuli in which the mighty and powerful were buried in prehistoric times with all their tools and utensils, silver and gold. My sense of being on ground intended for purposes transcending the profane was heightened by a number of buildings that resembled temples or pagodas, which seemed quite out of place in these military installations. But the closer I came to these ruins, the more any notion of a mysterious isle of the dead receded, and the more I imagined myself amidst the remains of our own civilization after its extinction in some future catastrophe. To me too, as for some latter-day stranger ignorant of the nature of our society wandering about among heaps of scrap metal and defunct machinery, the beings who had once lived and worked here were an enigma, as was the purpose of the primitive contraptions and fittings inside the bunkers, the iron rails under the ceilings, the hooks on the still partially tiled walls, the showerheads the size of plates, the ramps and the soakaways.[8]

W. G. Sebald's ghostly impressions, as he visits a former military establishment on the Suffolk coast, involve a curious telescoping of his own times. Something similar may be felt at the remnants of the vast underground site for V-2 rocket production at the Mittelbau-Dora concentration camp, or at certain abandoned locations in Eastern Europe. What one sees there are infrastructures built with a huge input of energy and often at the cost of thousands of human lives. At Mittelbau-Dora the construction work had to be done so quickly that many a labourer, having been worked to death, was cemented without further ado into the lining of the tunnels; one can still find the corpses there today. In many cases, these vast projects that looked with such confidence towards the future lasted only a few years; they now stand as futile witnesses to bygone plans that can be decoded, if at all, only with difficulty. Sometimes, historians or archaeologists look in vain for a meaning that is simply not there.

Sebald's monuments at Orford Ness, like the Nazi factories for the production of aircraft, rockets and dead bodies, are peculiar islands of time in an advancing present, relics of a *past future*. Just as the military research establishments worked on future wars, the aim of Mittelbau-Dora was to prepare the way for Nazi world domination. And the fallow lands of communism testify to dreams of a future in which the new man would have come of age. Its rusty ruins, grown over and serving no purpose, harbour not only the past but also a future that never became reality.

Human beings live in the present, but mentally they can also travel through time into the past and the future. Man's distinctive capacity to situate personal existence in a space–time continuum, looking back at a past that preceded the present, serves the purpose of giving the bearings for future action. It is also possible to look ahead to the future. The grammatical form for this is the future perfect ('will have been'); its mental form is what Alfred Schütz called 'anticipatory retrospection'.[9] This plays a central role in human behaviour: any outline, plan, projection or model involves looking ahead to a state of affairs that will one day have come to pass. Human motives and energy feed off such anticipation – from the desire to reach a state that is different from the one existing today.

This fascinating capacity has given human beings the evolutionary advantage of being able to play through beforehand any actions that will change the shape of the world, and to weigh up their various pluses and minuses. More generally, it has endowed them with a mind that draws energy not only from what is given but also from what is desired and dreamed.

This involves a certain dialectic, of course, and anticipatory retrospection in the style of Hitler or Speer[10] – whose utopian self-assurance produced the grandiose plans for a rebuilt capital, Germania, complete with a museum of the extinct Jewish race[11] – represents the dark side of futuristic certainties, as well as of all totalitarian variants associated with the Marxist utopia of an emancipated society. But it is precisely horrific cases such as National Socialism which demonstrate the mental energies that the promise of a seemingly attainable future can release, provided that everyone goes along with it. This 'feel good dictatorship'[12] not only brought out the vast destructive energy that would eventually leave behind 50 million dead and a half-destroyed Europe, but also enlisted feverish support for a societal project that promised a rosy future to everyone who belonged – until late in the war, that is, 'when the vanguard of the Sixth Army had reached the Volga and not a few were dreaming of settling down there after the war on an estate in the cherry orchards beside the quiet Don'.[13]

Anticipatory retrospection regularly becomes deadly if its initiators seek to shape the whole world in its image. For every social utopia inevitably presupposes a view of what *man* is: the error of utopianism, argues Hans Jonas, is its conception of the 'human essence'.[14] If there is such a thing as the human essence, then it lies in plurality and its constitutive potential – its cooperative way of life and its capacity to anticipate future opportunities and threats. And this openness to potentiality is all the greater, the better the conditions of life are in the present: only the freedom of a secure livelihood permits the luxury of exploring the possibilities for a better existence; and, conversely, that luxury can be curtailed at any time, or even vanish without trace, if existential security comes under threat.

This implies that the scope for developing one's potential, the availability of future opportunities, is highly unevenly distributed. But, for a society that places itself culturally and politically within the Enlightenment tradition (including all its postmodern and post-postmodern variants), such inequality is not acceptable. It means that another approach must be found to the problem of climate change, not only for the sake of one's livelihood but also for the sake of one's *identity*. What we are talking about, then, is social self-presentation.

THE GOOD SOCIETY

Global warming has come about because of the thoughtless use of technology, so any attempt to fix things through more and 'better' technology is part of the problem, not of the solution. Since the qualitative and quantitative scale of the problem is such that no one knows what a rescue strategy would be like, it is necessary to get away from a 'business as usual' mind set. To rise above responses to immediate stimuli and pressures is precisely what makes human existence unique and purposive action possible. In principle, then, new mental horizons are necessary to find a way out of crises. Overhasty thinking can prove fatal; the perception of a huge problem should give pause for thought, in which mental space can open up to determine what is involved and what can be done about it. Only freedom from illusions makes it possible to escape the deadly force of circumstance, such as one sees in the false alternative of coal-fired stations or nuclear power as a response to climate change.

This is a false alternative, because the two energy technologies each rest upon limited resources and have proven to have unforeseeable consequences. The climate change debate is full of such traps. Another example is whether societies behind in modernization should be allowed the same pollution rights that early industrialized countries had in an age when no one gave a thought to such matters. In the present day, when the consequences of a heedless attitude are known, a question like that expresses nothing other than a kind of forced stupidity. There are definitely better contexts in which to consider the case for global justice than one of further limitations on the opportunities that human beings will have in the future. If there is to be debate about that, it should centre on fair distribution of the burdens attached to cuts in energy use; ethics commissions should work out proposals for the wealthy high-tech nations to provide less modernized countries with cost-free technology for the reduction or avoidance of noxious emissions – although even that begs the question as to whether it is desirable for everyone to achieve Western levels of modernization.[15]

Another false alternative is whether the growing numbers of environmental or climate refugees should be parked temporarily in third countries or left to drown in the sea. Here the 'objective constraints' show their totalitarian logic, and it should be made clear that such people are deported or perish because the Schengen countries have agreed that they do not want them. This is not a moral point but a simple statement of fact. If one feels no moral dissonance over policy decisions to treat other human beings in that way, one can happily continue to refuse them admission.

One way out of this dilemma would be to use one's native wit, not for devising ostensibly more humane strategies of exclusion at considerable public cost, but to explore participatory avenues that the early industrialized countries will anyway have to embrace in the medium term for demographic reasons. Why should societies that are also planning for future challenges stick to the ideal of an ethnically homogeneous state, which will anyway prove antiquated in the face of further modernization requirements?

And if one is trying to move beyond false alternatives and 'objective constraints', one might do well to take a fresh look at climate change and define it as a *cultural* problem. This anyway seems obvious, because climate change affects human cultures and can be perceived only within the framework of cultural techniques such as agriculture, livestock breeding, fishing or science. Nature is essentially indifferent to ecological problems; they are a threat only to human cultures.

The forms and possibilities of future human life are therefore a *cultural issue* that relates to our own society and lifeworld. This raises a series of questions. Can a culture be successful in the long run if it systematically uses up resources? Can it survive if it accepts the systematic exclusion of future generations? Can such a culture be a model for those whom it must win over if it is to survive? Can it be rational if it is regarded from outside as exclusive and predatory and rejected for that reason?

The redefinition of climate as a cultural issue, together with a move away from the fateful, often deadly, logic of 'objective constraints', would offer an opportunity for qualitative development, especially if the situation is as crisis-prone as it is at present. A fixation on ostensibly objective constraints precludes ways of thinking and acting that a more detached view of things would immediately embrace.

Let us take four examples, each very different from the others.

Norway does not invest its oil revenues in prestigious infrastructural projects or the raising of living standards, but pursues a far-sighted strategy that will enable future generations to enjoy today's high living standards and to benefit from the achievements of the social state. It therefore chooses ethical investment criteria, excluding, for example, companies involved in the production of nuclear weapons and favouring climate-friendly energy suppliers.[16] The Utsira municipality on Rogaland, a North Sea island in the south of the country, is already self-sufficient in energy thanks to its combination of wind farms and hydro-installations. It has set an example in the sustainable use of national economic resources.

Switzerland opted twenty years ago for a public transport system which ensures that every local community is connected. Trams were reintroduced in Zurich at a time when they were disappearing from many German cities, and new stretches of railway were laid when services were closing down in many other countries. Switzerland today has the densest public transport network in the world, although its frequently mountainous terrain could scarcely be less favourable. 'Post cars' link up remote villages and side valleys. The average Swiss makes forty-seven train journeys a year, compared with the EU average of 14.7.[17]

Estonia guarantees cost-free internet access as a basic right. Blanket provision with communication facilities not only reduces bureaucracy and enhances the potential for direct forms of democracy; it has also become a key driving force of modernization, which appeals especially to younger members of society.

The decision of the German government in 2003 to remain outside the military alliance against Iraq, despite considerable external pressure, has proven to be correct and far-sighted. It avoided a mistake which, by reminding everyone of Germany's negative historical role in the two world wars of the twentieth century, would have had unpredictable consequences for political life in the Federal Republic. This was a practical example of learning from history.

These four policy orientations, though relating to very different matters, had a common denominator in that they all touched on an aspect of identity. Each decision concerned not only a particular issue but the wider question of what the political community *wanted to be*: a society that was fair towards future generations (Norway); a society that offered all its citizens the same mobility (Switzerland); a republic with equal communication opportunities for all (Estonia); a society capable of learning from the past that held back from disastrous policies of military intervention (Germany). This identity level of the various decisions contained a statement about who people wanted to be (as a Norwegian, Swiss, Estonian or German) and the conditions under which they wanted to live, at least in the area to which the policy referred. It thus seems highly significant for a cultural approach to global warming. For the 'what is to be done?' question simply cannot be addressed unless an answer is first given to the question of how people want to live.

In fact, this question cannot *not* be answered. 'Go on as usual' is one possibility, pointing further down the road that led to the problems one is trying to solve. It would mean deepening the asymmetries, inequalities and injustices, between generations as well as countries, which climate change brings in its wake. And every answer rules out at least one other possibility.

How do people want to live in the society of which they are part? This is a cultural question: it forces us to discuss who counts as a member of society, what form participation should take, how material goods as well as immaterial ones such as income and education should be distributed, and so on. The setting of priorities – subsidies for fossil fuel use (coal-mining) or increased spending on education, job creation in backward industries or investment in education and training for new patterns of employment – involves answers that define the self-image of the community and whether citizens can identify with it. They are cultural issues, in which the guiding imperative is whether the *potential for future development* should be limited or not.

The premise for a participatory, open-structured model of society is, on the one hand, Western levels of material wealth and the international obligations that such wealth implies and, on the other hand, *political* thinking that goes beyond the immediate situation of the day. The world of global capitalism, devoid of orientation or transcendence, creates no sense of meaning within itself and is inadequate for such long-range purposes. What is needed, precisely in times of crisis, is to develop visions or at least ideas that have never been thought before. This may all sound naïve, but it is not really. Besides, what could be more naïve than to imagine that the train bringing destruction on a mass scale will change its speed and course if people inside it run in the opposite direction? As Albert Einstein said, problems cannot be solved with the thought patterns that led to them originally. It is necessary to change course, and for that the train must first be brought to a halt.

REPRESSIVE TOLERANCE

A serious approach to the problems of inequality and violence bound up with climate change would have to concern itself with such categories as justice and responsibility – that is, to argue in the light of value decisions and to replace cultivated indifference with a capacity for normative discrimination. This raises the question of which groups or individuals in global society are better placed than others to assert their interests. In 1965 Herbert Marcuse published a famous essay on 'repressive tolerance', which, however adventurous its drift seems today, accurately points out that 'the function and value of tolerance depend on the equality prevalent in the society in which tolerance is practised'.[18]

Technically, tolerance is a variable dependent on the level of equality achieved within and between societies. Where tolerance is practised without reference to the existing power relations, it works in principle to the advantage of those with the greatest power. So, in a society based upon inequality, tolerance is fundamentally repressive because it normatively and ideologically entrenches the positions of those with the least power. In Marcuse's time it was understood that his argument served to ground a kind of putative right of resistance (for third world liberation, for example), but, in relation to the findings set out in this book, 'repressive tolerance' might describe the lack of articulated counter-tendencies to the global asymmetry between rich and poor countries.

'Repressive tolerance' is also an appropriate term when the opportunities for people elsewhere or for future generations are restricted or even removed without arousing immediate criticism. Societies with a culture of repressive tolerance lack all possibility of critically examining themselves and moving towards a more desirable state of affairs, so that ideas about how the future should look seem reduced to the unhelpful formula: like now, only better. Such is the extent of the West's vision today, although people have a strong sense that it is based on an illusion.

THE CAPACITY FOR A HISTORICAL NARRATIVE ABOUT ONESELF

Individualist strategies against climate change have a mainly sedative function. The level of international politics offers the prospect of change only in a distant future, and so cultural action is left with the *middle level*, the level of one's own society, and the democratic issue of how people want to live in the future.

Cultural work at this level would not only create a sense of identity but also engage those who wish to make a much greater contribution as individuals to the control of emissions – for example, people in the energy supply or automobile industry. Internationally, moreover, the development of a *different* option would at least produce new interests, even if it was unable to influence a particular climate regime. It would have the psychological advantage that thinking would be less prone to illusions and more adequate to the nature of the problem, and this in turn might be another factor generating identity. The focus would be on citizens who do not *settle for* renunciation – fewer car journeys, more tram rides – but contribute culturally to changes that they consider to be *good*.

For some twenty years now, the view has been gaining ground in development policy that material aid does not produce the desired effects, and that a great deal depends upon the state structures, institutional functionality and legal system in the recipient country. Attention has therefore shifted to the concept of 'good governance', which requires the fulfilment of a number of criteria such as transparency, efficiency, participation, responsibility, market economics, the rule of law, democracy and justice. Indeed, since the 1990s development funds and other material support have been disbursed according to whether the state in question meets these criteria. It has been objected that this is an ideological approach, which insists too much upon a profile laid down in advance, and it might further be said that donor countries are assumed to fit the profile, whereas it is used as a test of rectitude for recipient countries.

We cannot here go further into the problems of this approach, but it does seem fruitful to ponder on what is involved in the idea of good governance. Similarly, one might develop criteria for a *good society* that reflect the concept of good governance. First of all, a good society would have to maintain its development potential at the highest possible level, which, given the past impact of industrialization on the environment, would also mean avoiding decisions that have irreversible consequences such as resource exhaustion or unfair burdens on future generations, as in the case of nuclear waste.

Decisions affecting social development in areas such as security, the legal system, education or welfare would also have to meet the criterion of reversibility, in order to ensure that society remains open-ended in its structure. A further yardstick of the good society is the opportunities it offers for participation, including immigration issues such as the right to asylum and the involvement of citizens in debates and decision-making on questions of importance for the future. With today's dense networks of communication, it is by no means necessary that forms of participation should be geared to the electoral cycle. Estonian-style access to communication facilities as a basic right for all opens up the possibility of novel forms of extra-parliamentary debate and direct forms of democracy.

At the same time, greater opportunities for communication and participation would increase the extent to which citizens identify with the society they help to shape. As regards the climate problem and the proposed solutions on offer, the *cultural project* of the good society means turning away from the illusion that people would treat the world differently if they were told that it would one day be in less danger as a result. Such an argument does not work psychologically, because individuals cannot perceive the effects of their action on the environment and are left only with the experience of giving something up. The idea of the good society does not emphasize renunciation, but rather social involvement in achieving a better climate. And a society that encourages greater participation and commitment is better placed to solve urgent problems than one whose members remain indifferent.

The individual psychological equivalent of this concept of social involvement is 'empowerment', which refers to the strategy of highlighting the individual's strengths and seeking to promote them. In this sense, the concept of the good society draws on the potential of its citizens, offers them greater participation, and makes better use of the resources of involvement and interest than traditional styles of politics do. In other words, such a society initiates a conscious strategy of reflexive modernization.[19] In contrast to the first modernity of the past and the second modernity of the present, the good society would represent the third modernity: the future. It tells a new story about itself.

The crux of functional modernity is that it has no historical narrative in which people can describe themselves as citizens and, on that basis, develop the sense of a definite collective identity, a 'we'. The good society, once created, would be able to tell such a story about itself.

Science has provided human beings with the ability to anticipate changes in their conditions of life even when these are not yet perceptible to them, and their intellectual capacities enable them to draw the appropriate conclusions. With the help of social and cultural skills, these conclusions can be translated into a changed practice. Thus, a practically oriented understanding that it is necessary to avert the worst consequences of global warming would mean that people demanded not only a radical worldwide reduction in resource use but also a whole new culture of participation; this still seems unthinkable today, but it must be urgently addressed if the outcome is to be at all different. In this perspective, 'climate change' would be the starting point for fundamental cultural change, in which the reduction of waste and violence was seen not as a loss but as a gain.

12

WHAT CAN AND CANNOT BE DONE – 2

In studying social development processes we repeatedly come across a constellation in which the dynamic of unplanned social processes is tending to advance beyond a given stage towards another, which may be higher or lower, while the people affected by this change cling to the earlier stage in their personality structure, their social habitus. It depends entirely on the relative strength of the social shift and the deep-rootedness and therefore the resistance of the social habitus whether – and how quickly – the dynamic of the unplanned social process brings about a more or less radical restructuring of this habitus, or whether the social habitus of individuals successfully opposes the social dynamic, either by slowing it down or blocking it entirely.[1]

It may be that, as a result of unchecked climate change, the unplanned and uneven process of human development has acquired a negative dynamic behind which habitus forms shaped over decades and centuries can do no more than trail passively. The largely defective capacity to see the true scale of the global threat speaks in favour of this hypothesis, as does the widespread apathy in the face of violence that is actually and potentially bound up with climate change. And in the medium term, of course, the completely disparate international interests will continue to hinder agreement on measures to check global warming. Catch-up industrialization in the emerging economies, insatiable energy hunger in the countries that industrialized early, and the worldwide spread of a social model geared to growth and resource consumption make it seem unrealistic that further warming by mid-century will be kept at or below 2 per cent. That itself is no more than a linear projection; it takes no account of autocatalytic processes, which may speed up climate change and lead to an escalation of violence.

At the geophysical level, the emergence of non-linear processes may make the problem much more acute – for example, if the thawing of permafrost cover reacts on the climate by releasing vast quantities of methane, or if deforestation or ocean acidification reaches a critical threshold and generates unpredictable domino effects. At the social level, the same point applies – for example, if disputes over raw materials trigger military conflicts and if the resulting refugee flows lead to sharper conflicts within and between states. The logic of social processes is not linear, nor are the consequences of climate change. Nothing in the history of human violence indicates that periods of peace are also periods of social stability; everything tends to confirm that massive use of force is *always* an option. 'Survival groups', Norbert Elias showed, are always also 'annihilation groups', and the social consequences of climate change seem to bear this out.

The sharpening of global asymmetries already offers examples of wars rooted in climate change and new forms of never-ending violence. Since climate effects strike hardest at societies least able to cope with them, migratory flows will dramatically increase in the course of the twenty-first century and push those societies into radical solutions in which migratory pressure is perceived as a threat. It remains to be seen whether it will be possible for the EU or the USA to keep projecting border controls, and hence anti-refugee violence, out towards other countries, when illegal immigration further overstretches countries such as Libya, Israel, Algeria or Morocco.

The other side of this is a continual tightening of internal security and the development of new policies that undermine the state monopoly of legitimate force; the keywords in this regard are extra-territorial detention centres, extra-judicial kidnapping, torture and execution, mercenary armies and privatized violence. All this stands in a two-way association with the growth of terrorism in the global age. But the build-up of reciprocal violence works to the disadvantage of heavily armed state combatants and unleashes more and more surrogate attacks on the population of established societies.

In the twenty-first century there will be less killing for ideological reasons than in the twentieth century, and less too on account of pseudo-scientific visions that prescribe how the world should be organized, and who exterminated, in accordance with the laws of nature. For want of a future-proof model of society, the twenty-first century steers clear of utopias and keeps its nose to the ground of natural resources; people will be killed because the killers will claim resources that their victims have or would like to have.

Can one really suppose that things will take a turn for the better? As climate effects become more extensive and visible, and as hunger, migration and violence grow in intensity, the pressure to find solutions will be more acute and the space for reflection will be narrower. The likelihood of irrational and counter-productive strategies will become greater, especially in relation to the problems of violence exacerbated by climate change. All the historical evidence makes it highly probable that 'superfluous' people who seem to threaten those already enjoying relative prosperity and security will lose their lives in increasingly large numbers, whether from lack of food and clean water, from frontier wars, or from civil wars and interstate conflicts resulting from changed environmental conditions. This is not a normative statement; it simply corresponds to what has been learned from solutions to perceived problems in the twentieth century.

All this will not look like a repetition of the Holocaust; history does not repeat itself. But people will perceive certain problems, and if they see them as threatening to their own existence they will tend towards radical solutions that they *never dreamed of before*. It must be said that Western cultures have not learned this lesson from the twentieth century. Rather, they give too much credit to humanity, reason and law, although historically these three ways of regulating behaviour have succumbed to attack whenever it has been strong enough. These cultures will not exist for much longer – maybe another two or three generations – if they stick to their habitual problem-solving strategies. In comparison with other cultures, their life span will then prove to have been absurdly short.

'The institutions, morals and customs that I have spent my life noting down and trying to understand', writes Lévi-Strauss at the end of his most melancholy book *Tristes tropiques*, 'are the transient efflorescence of a creation in relation to which they have no meaning, except perhaps that of allowing mankind to play its part in creation.'[2] Indeed, culture has no meaning in itself – only as a technique for raising the survival chances of social groups. It is still an open question whether this uniquely human capacity to keep improving survival chances by means of cultural tradition will continue to be successful in the medium term. The world as a theatre for experiment has existed for only 40,000 years. Of those, the Western variant has been with us for only 250 years, and in that speck of time more has been done to destroy the conditions for life than in the whole of the preceding 39,750. Destroyed conditions of life mean lost opportunities, not only in the present but also in the future.

Man's restless activity, Lévi-Strauss continues, consists in gradually dissolving a complex structure and narrowing the gap between different cultures (that is, different ways of organizing human 'survival groups').

> As for the creations of the human mind, their significance only exists in relation to it, and they will merge into the general chaos, as soon as the human mind has disappeared. Thus it is that civilization, taken as a whole, can be described as an extraordinarily complex mechanism, which we might be tempted to see as offering an opportunity of survival for the human world, if its function were not to produce what physicists call entropy, that is inertia. Every verbal exchange, every line printed, establishes communication between people, thus creating an evenness of level, where before there was an information gap and consequently a greater degree of organization.[3]

This too is a way of describing globalization – as an accelerating process of social entropy, which dissolves cultures and finally, if things turn out badly, leaves behind only the bare, undifferentiated will to survive. Such would be the apotheosis of the violence that the Enlightenment and Western culture thought it had found the key to abolishing. To be sure, in the actual course of its history – from modern slave labour and ruthless exploitation of the colonies to early industrial destruction of the conditions for human life, which had nothing to do with the project – the free, democratic, enlightened West eventually wrote its counter-history of unfreedom, repression and counter-enlightenment. With the future impact of climate change, the Enlightenment will not be able to free itself from this dialectic. It will fail because of it.

NOTES

Chapter 1 A Ship in the Desert

1 Jan Bart Gewald, 'The Issue of Forced Labour in the *Onjembo*: German South West Africa 1904–1908', *Bulletin of the Leyden Centre for the History of European Expansion*, 19 (1995), pp. 97–104; here p. 102.

2 Medardus Brehl, *Vernichtung der Herero: Diskurse der Gewalt in der deutschen Kolonialliteratur*, Munich, 2007, p. 96.

3 Ibid., p. 98.

4 Jürgen Zimmerer, 'War, Concentration Camps and Genocide in German South-West Africa', in Zimmerer and Joachim Zeller (eds), *Genocide in German South-West Africa*, London, 2008, p. 49.

5 Ibid., pp. 51ff.

6 Quoted ibid., p. 41.

Chapter 2 Climate Conflicts

1 See www.frontex.europa.eu.

2 The initial signatories to the Schengen Agreement were Belgium, France, Germany, Luxembourg and the Netherlands, which agreed to ease travel across their borders while simultaneously strengthening external controls. The following countries (with dates of first full implementation) have since opted in: Austria (1997), Czech Republic (2008), Denmark (2001), Estonia (2008), Finland (2001), Greece (2000), Hungary (2008), Iceland (2001), Italy (1997), Latvia

(2008), Lithuania (2008), Malta (2008), Norway (2001), Poland (2008), Portugal (1995), Slovakia (2008), Slovenia (2008), Spain (1995), Sweden (2001) and Switzerland (2008). In 1997 the Schengen Agreement was incorporated into EU law.

3 A place costs between €2,000 and €4,000. Usually the refugee's family has raised this by means of a loan, in the hope that the migrant will soon pay it back through transfers once he or she has found a job in Europe. See Klaus Brinkbäumer, *Der Traum vom Leben: Eine afrikanische Odyssee*, Frankfurt am Main, 2007.

4 See www.frontex.europa.eu.

5 Cornelia Gunßer, 'Der europäische Krieg gegen Flüchtlinge', *ak – analyse und kritik*, 19 November 2004. For an update, see www. fluechtlingsrat-hamburg.de/content/eua_EULagerplaeneGunsser.pdf.

6 WGBU (Wissenschaftlicher Beirat der Bundesregierung Globale Umweltveränderungen), *Welt im Wandel – Sicherheitsrisiko Klimawandel*, Berlin 2007; expert appraisals and synopsis at www.rhombos.de/ shop/a/show/story/?1106&PHPSESSID=8398524d78686a29de09a62 fe51342d3.

7 Gérard Prunier, *Darfur: The Ambiguous Genocide*, Ithaca, NY, 2007.

8 Nicholas Stern, *The Economics of Climate Change: The Stern Review*, Cambridge, 2007.

9 Whereas new vehicle registrations in Germany are generally declining, in 2007 SUVs were up 5.2 per cent and sports cars as much as 17 per cent (Kraftfahrt-Bundesamt, *Fahrzeugzulassungen im Juni 2007*, press release no. 21, 2007).

10 See the supplement on investment funds in the *Frankfurter Allgemeine Zeitung*, 2 October 2007, p. 12.

11 Andrea Sáenz-Arroyo et al., 'Rapidly Shifting Environmental Baselines among Fishers of the Gulf of California', *Proceedings of the Royal Society*, 272 (2005), pp. 1957–62.

12 In the classic social-psychological case of cognitive dissonance, Leon Festinger and his colleagues cited members of an American sect who shed all their possessions and gathered on a mountaintop, so as to survive the end of the world as God's chosen ones. When this failed to happen, it inevitably produced major cognitive dissonance among the sect members. Festinger's team interviewed the believers, who naturally harboured no doubts that their expectations corresponded to reality; they saw the experience as further proof of the solidity of their faith and as confirmation of their elect status. The theory assumes that

people will seek to reduce the cognitive dissonance that arises when their expectations fail to coincide with reality. They may do this in one of two ways – by adapting the expectations to the reality (that is, by revising them *ex post facto*) or by interpreting reality in such a way that it corresponds to their expectations. See Leon Festinger, Henry W. Riecken and Stanley Schachter, *When Prophecy Fails*, Minneapolis, 1956.

13 Harald Welzer, *Täter: Wie aus ganz normalen Menschen Massenmörder werden*, Frankfurt am Main, 2005.

14 In his study of psychiatric asylums, Erving Goffman coined the term 'total institution' to express the fact that the rules of everyday life outside no longer have validity for their members. For example, they lack the usual accoutrements of identity: they can no longer control how they look to others, since their heads are shaven and they are given a tagged uniform or institutional clothing to wear. They are unable to regulate their daily rhythm, are addressed in a standard way, and have little or no contact with the outside world. The special set of rules within the institution is in many respects contrary to the norms prevailing outside. Other examples of total institutions include monasteries, cadet schools and army training camps. See Erving Goffman, *Asylums*, Garden City, NY, 1961.

15 For example, SS Gruppenführer Otto Ohlendorf – the commanding officer of Einsatzgruppe D – said at his trial in Nuremberg that the mass shootings 'caused infinite mental stress both to the victims and to those ordered to carry out the killing' (Internationaler Militärgerichtshof, *Der Prozess gegen die Hauptkriegsverbrecher*, vol. 4, Nuremberg, 1948, p. 355).

16 The conception of collective murder as difficult work running contrary to moral sensitivities is integral to Heinrich Himmler's speech in Poznan on 4 October 1943:

> I also want to mention a very difficult subject before you here, completely openly. It should be discussed amongst us, and yet, nevertheless, we will never speak about it in public. [...] I am talking about the 'Jewish evacuation': the extermination of the Jewish people. It is one of those things that is easily said. 'The Jewish people is being exterminated', every Party member will tell you, 'perfectly clear, it's part of our plans, we're eliminating the Jews, exterminating them, ha!, a small matter.' And then along they all come, all the 80 million upright Germans, and each one has his decent Jew. They say: all the

others are swine, but here is a first-class Jew. And none of them has seen it, has endured it. Most of you will know what it means when 100 bodies lie together, when there are 500, or when there are 1,000. And to have seen this through, and – with the exception of human weaknesses – to have remained decent, has made us hard and is a page of glory never mentioned and never to be mentioned. Because we know how difficult things would be, if today in every city during the bomb attacks, the burdens of war and the privations, we still had Jews as secret saboteurs, agitators and instigators. [. . .] We have the moral right, we had the duty to our people to do it, to kill this people who wanted to kill us. [. . .] But altogether we can say: We have carried out this most difficult task for the love of our people. And we have taken on no defect within us, in our soul, or in our character. (www. holocaust-history.org/himmler-poznan/index.shtml)

17 It is not crucial for this prognosis whether we are speaking of manmade climate change or of a 'natural' fluctuation. The answer to this controversial issue may be relevant for political strategies to reduce emissions, and so on, but not for what concerns us here: the social and political consequences of climate change.

18 Zygmunt Bauman, 'On the Rationality of Evil', an interview with Harald Welzer, *Thesis Eleven*, 70/1 (2002), pp. 100–12.

19 Heinrich Popitz, *Phänomene der Macht*, Tübingen, 1986, p. 97.

20 Thus, in September 2001 representatives of the Herero people prosecuted the Deutsche Afrika-Linien (as legal successor of the Woermann Lines that ran the *Eduard Bohlen*) for participation in genocide.

21 Jonathan Swift, 'A Modest Proposal' (1729), at www.victorianweb.org/previctorian/swift/modest.html.

22 Norman M. Naimark, *Fires of Hatred: Ethnic Cleansing in Twentieth-Century Europe*, Cambridge, MA, 2001; Michael Mann, *The Dark Side of Democracy: Explaining Ethnic Cleansing*, Cambridge, 2005.

23 Zygmunt Bauman, *Modernity and the Holocaust*, Ithaca, NY, 1991, p. 2.

24 Ibid., p. 3.

25 Ibid., p. 12.

26 See Hannah Arendt, 'Social Science Techniques and the Study of Concentration Camps', in Arendt and Jerome Kuhn (eds), *Essays in Understanding 1930–1954*, New York, 1994, p. 232. This work was also a radical attempt to consider the problematic relationship of the social sciences to the Holocaust. In Arendt's view, the reason why the

extermination camps violently shook the basic assumptions of both sociological and everyday thinking may perhaps be that the conditions they established were unforeseeable and historically unprecedented. The assumptions she had in mind were, for example, that social action develops within identifiable causal contexts, that a meaning can be attributed to them, that intersubjective agreement is possible concerning that meaning – in short, that everything in social reality takes place within a framework of thoroughly explicable motives, actions and consequences of action.

27 Martin Broszat, *Nach Hitler: Der schwierige Umgang mit unserer Geschichte*, Munich, 1987.

28 These contexts themselves undergo change with the development of violence. Killing techniques do not remain the same but become more refined as routines and know-how develop; executioners use special tools, wear special clothing and introduce various innovations. Alf Lüdtke has more than once drawn out the affinity between industrial and military labour, showing that proletarian layers in particular saw the functions of soldiers or reserve policemen as 'work'. Basing his account on what such men wrote about themselves in letters and diaries during the Second World War, Lüdtke finds analogies between warfare and work in such aspects as the internalization of discipline and the monotony of repetitive tasks, but also in the way in which 'a military action – that is, repelling or wiping out the enemy, killing other men and destroying material – is regarded as *a job well done*.' Lüdtke concludes: 'The threat and use of violence, the act of killing or causing pain, can be thought of as work and therefore experienced as meaningful, or at least as necessary and unavoidable.' Alf Lüdtke, 'Gewalt und Alltag im 20. Jahrhundert', in Wolfgang Bergsdorf et al. (eds), *Gewalt und Terror*, Weimar, 2003, pp. 35–52; here p. 47.

29 Popitz, *Phänomene der Macht*, p. 87.

Chapter 3 Global Warming and Social Catastrophe

1 John R. Logan, 'The Impact of Katrina: Race and Class in Storm-Damaged Neighborhoods', Brown University 2006, at www.s4.brown.edu/katrina/report.pdf.

2 John R. Logan, 'Unnatural Disaster: Social Impacts and Policy Choices after Katrina', in Karl-Siegbert Rehberg (ed.), *Die Natur der Gesellschaft: Verhandlungen des 33. Kongresses der Deutschen Gesellschaft für Soziologie in Kassel 2006*, Frankfurt am Main, 2007.

3 Naomi Klein has pointed out a hitherto unnoticed aspect of social disasters: namely, that they may be seen as opportunities for structural measures that would not be taken under normal conditions. The devastation in New Orleans, for instance, triggered a large-scale privatization of the educational system: only four public schools survived, instead of the 131 that had existed before the floods; and there were thirty-one so-called charter schools instead of seven (Naomi Klein, *The Shock Doctrine: The Rise of Disaster Capitalism*, London, 2007, pp. 5–6). John R. Logan, however, reports that fifty-four public schools had been reopened by the autumn of 2006 (Logan, 'Unnatural Disaster', p. 40).

During the Second World War, the planners around Albert Speer did not feel only displeasure as the Allied bombers destroyed German cities; they also ruminated that the preliminary work for postwar reconstruction was being done for them. Disasters, then, can have a positive side for those who know how to use it. Of course, the example of Speer also shows that – contrary to Naomi Klein's claims – what is involved today is not a new strategy of global capitalism.

4 Elke M. Geenen, 'Kollektive Krisen: Katastrophe, Terror, Revolution – Gemeinsamkeiten und Unterschiede', in Lars Clausen et al. (eds), *Entsetzliche soziale Prozesse*, Münster, 2003, pp. 5–24. Societies become more vulnerable, for example, as their networking becomes more complex. As Clausen shows, the fact that individuals, groups, businesses and politicians have different planning horizons may give rise not only to conflicts but also to widespread feelings of insecurity, alienation, and so on (Lars Clausen, 'Reale Gefahren und katastrophensoziologische Theorie', ibid., pp. 51–76).

5 This is clear from the amazingly small number of studies of life behind the façade of social normality – hence of the picture behind the picture that society has of itself. Prostitution, the shadow economy, violent subcultures, and so on, are the 'poor cousins' of sociological research.

6 Joachim Radkau, *Nature and Power: A Global History of the Environment*, Cambridge, 2008; Josef H. Reichholf, *Eine kurze Naturgeschichte des letzten Jahrtausends*, Frankfurt am Main, 2007; Jared M. Diamond, *Guns, Germs and Steel: A Short History of Everybody for the Last 13,000 Years*, London, 1997.

7 Fred Pearce, *When the Rivers Run Dry: What Happens When our Water Runs Out?*, Boston, 2006, p. 237.

8 Tim Flannery, *We Are the Weather Makers: The Story of Global Warming*, London, 1997.

9 Pearce, *When the Rivers Run Dry*.

10 Jill Jäger et al., *Our Planet: How Much More Can Earth Take?*, London, 2009.

11 Klaus-Dieter Frankenberger, 'Chinas Hunger nach Energie', *Frankfurter Allgemeine Zeitung*, 27 March 2007, p. 12.

12 Diamond, *Guns, Germs and Steel*.

13 Each year 150 to 170 billion cubic metres of natural gas are burned or simply released into the atmosphere by the petroleum industry – as much as two large industrial nations, Germany and Italy, consume together. Anselm Waldermann, 'Profitdenken schlägt Umweltschutz', *Spiegel-online*, 6 September 2007, at www.spiegel.de/wirtschaft/0,1518,504278,00.html.

14 Rainer Münz, 'Weltbevölkerung und weltweite Migration', in Ernst Peter Fischer and Klaus Wiegand (eds), *Die Zukunft der Erde*, Frankfurt am Main, 2006, p. 111. A population of 10 to 11 billion is predicted for the end of the century, after which the total will start to fall (ibid., p. 112).

Chapter 4 A Brief Survey of Climate Change

1 Rainer Münz, 'Weltbevölkerung und weltweite Migration', in Ernst Peter Fischer and Klaus Wiegand (eds), *Die Zukunft der Erde*, Frankfurt am Main, 2006, p. 6.

2 Ibid., p. 7.

3 Ibid., p. 8.

4 Ibid., p. 16.

5 See Eva Berié et al. (eds), *Der Fischer-Weltalmanach 2008*, Frankfurt am Main, 2007, pp. 538ff. In Angola, where only 53 per cent of the population has secure access to drinking water, 2,174 people died within a year in a cholera epidemic that began in 2006 and was mainly due to this factor (ibid., p. 55).

6 Robert S. Watson et al. (eds), *The Regional Impacts of Climate Change: An Assessment of Vulnerability: Special Report of IPCC Working Group II*, Cambridge, 1997, p. 10.

7 In 2001 the NASA Climate Institute was already predicting a considerably greater storm risk for New York. Three flood barriers have therefore been erected to protect the metropolitan area of New York City (*Frankfurter Allgemeine Zeitung*, 31 July 2007, p. 35).

8 Fred Pearce, *The Last Generation: How Nature Will Take her Revenge for Climate Change*, London, 2007, p. 354.

Chapter 5 Killing Yesterday

1 Mischa Meier, 'Krisen und Krisenwahrnehmung im 6. Jahrhundert n. Chr.', in Helga Scholten (ed.), *Die Wahrnehmung von Krisenphänomenen: Fallbeispiele von der Antike bis in die Neuzeit*, Cologne, 2007, pp. 111–25; here p. 116.
2 Ibid., p. 119.
3 Ibid., 117.
4 Ibid., p. 121.
5 Erving Goffman, *Frame Analysis: An Essay on the Organization of Experience*, London, 1974.
6 Scott Straus, *The Order of Genocide: Race, Power, and War in Rwanda*, New York, 2006, p. 154.
7 Ibid.
8 See Harald Welzer, *Täter: Wie aus ganz normalen Menschen Massenmörder werden*, Frankfurt am Main, 2005; Jacques Semelin, *Purify and Destroy: The Political Uses of Massacre and Genocide*, New York, 2007, pp. 48ff.
9 Goebbels's diaries make it clear that, for him, a Jewish world conspiracy was not just a piece of propaganda; he really believed in its existence. Himmler, Hitler, Göring and the countless other devisers and executioners of the Judaeocide shared this conviction to a greater or lesser extent, but in every case sufficiently to launch and nearly complete the huge project of annihilation.
10 See   http://law2.umkc.edu/faculty/projects/ftrials/mylai/Myl_tmead.htm.
11 'Search and destroy' operations were targeted at 'pockets of resistance', arms depots, hiding places, and so on. In 'free-fire zones' anyone could be shot who had the bad luck to be there, whether a soldier, a child or an old person. See Bernd Greiner, '"A Licence to Kill": Annäherungen an das Kriegsverbrechen von My Lai', *Mittelweg 36* (December 1998/January 1999), pp. 4–24; here p. 5.
12 Barbara W. Tuchman, *The March of Folly: From Troy to Vietnam*, New York, 1984, p. 350.
13 Compare the account that Willy Peter Reese, a young intellectual serving in the Wehrmacht, gave of how he became increasingly caught up in atrocities. Willy Peter Reese, *Mir selber seltsam fremd:*

Die Unmenschlichkeit des Kriegs: Russland 1941–44, ed. Stefan Schmitz, Berlin, 2004.

14 Bernd Greiner, *War without Fronts: The US in Vietnam*, London, 2009, p. 28.

15 Groupthink proves disastrous when the effort to agree with others in the group overshadows contradictions and blocks realistic assessments of the situation. See Elliot Anderson, *The Social Animal*, San Francisco, 1972, chapter 4.

16 Tobias Debiel, Dirk Messner and Franz Nuscheler, *Globale Trends 2007: Frieden, Entwicklung, Umwelt*, Frankfurt am Main, 2007, p. 97.

17 The ranking is based on indicators that include population trends, numbers of refugees, human rights violations and external intervention (ibid., pp. 90ff.).

18 Jan Philipp Reemtsma, 'Nachbarschaft als Gewaltressource', *Mittelweg 36*, 13/5 (2004), p. 103; English translation, 'Neighbourly Relations as a Resource for Violence', at www.eurozine.com/articles/2005-11-02-reemtsma-en.html.

19 Natalija Basic, *Krieg als Abenteuer: Feindbilder und Gewalt aus der Perspektive ex-jugoslawischer Soldaten 1991–1995*, Giessen, 2004, p. 226. In Vietnam the surest way of identifying someone as Vietcong was to treat him or her as Vietcong: 'If it's dead and it's Vietnamese, it's VC' (Bernd Greiner, '"First to go, last to know": Der Dschungelkrieger in Vietnam', *Geschichte und Gesellschaft*, 29 (2003), p. 257). Killing and defining here go hand in hand.

20 Henry Kissinger, *The White House Years*, Boston, 1979, chapter 3, p. 54.

21 This limited vision is not peculiar to post-dictatorial societies. Established polities also show a failure of imagination with regard to forms of community beyond the nation-state, although these are precisely what the globalization process will require in the medium term.

22 See Michael Mann, *The Dark Side of Democracy: Explaining Ethnic Cleansing*, Cambridge, 2005.

Chapter 6 Killing Today

1 Jared Diamond, *Collapse*, New York, 2005, p. 104.

2 Ibid., p. 109.

3 John Keegan, *A History of Warfare*, London, 1993, pp. 24–6.

4 Diamond, *Collapse*, p. 109.

5 Ibid., pp. 97–8.

6 Ibid., p. 107.

7   Ernst Bloch, *Erbschaft dieser Zeit*, Frankfurt am Main, 1973.

8   The example is borrowed from Stanley Milgram.

9   See Norbert Elias, *Involvement and Detachment*, Oxford, 1987; Norbert Elias, *The Society of Individuals*, Oxford, 1991.

10 Barbara Tuchman, *The March of Folly: From Troy to Vietnam*, New York, 1984, p. 8.

11 Keegan, *A History of Warfare*, p. 9. Adversaries who did not use this order of battle but relied on traditional hand-to-hand fighting found such forms of warfare ridiculous (ibid.).

12 For a literary account of this, see W. G. Sebald, *Austerlitz*, London, 2002, pp. 17ff.

13 Heinrich Popitz, *Prozesse der Machtbildung*, Tübingen, 1976, pp. 9ff.

14 Keegan, *A History of Warfare*, p. 26.

15 Ibid., pp. 27–8.

16 Joachim Radkau, *Nature and Power: A Global History of the Environment*, Cambridge, 2008, p. 166.

17 Catherine André and Jean-Philippe Platteau, 'Land Relations under Unbearable Stress: Rwanda Caught in the Malthusian Trap', *Journal of Economic Behavior and Organization*, 34 (1998), pp. 1–47; quoted from Diamond, *Collapse*, pp. 320–1.

18 Semelin wrongly considers it a case of dissonance reduction or verbal rationalization when the Nazis identified Jews as 'vermin' or armed Hutus described killing as 'mucking out'. It would be closer to the truth to interpret these terms as accurate descriptions of reality in the eyes of the perpetrators. Jacques Semelin, *Purify and Destroy: The Political Uses of Massacre and Genocide*, New York, 2007, pp. 252ff.

19 Anna-Maria Brandstetter, 'Die Rhetorik von Reinheit, Gewalt und Gemeinschaft: Bürgerkrieg und Genozid in Rwanda', *Sociologus*, 51/1–2 (2001), p. 166.

20 Alison Des Forges, *'Leave None to Tell the Story': Genocide in Rwanda*, New York, 1999; quoted here from www.hrw.org/legacy/reports/1999/rwanda/Geno8-10-03.htm#P432_116374.

21 Brandstetter, 'Die Rhetorik von Reinheit', p. 168.

22 The classical demonstration of this is in Benjamin Lee Whorf, *Language, Thought and Reality*, Cambridge, MA, 1956.

23 Des Forges, *'Let None Live to Tell the Story'*.

24 Ibid.

25 Gérard Prunier, *Darfur: The Ambiguous Genocide*, Ithaca, NY, 2007, pp. 99–100.

26 Ibid., p. 100.

27 Ibid., pp. 7–8.

28 Ibid., p. 97.

29 Ibid., p. 98.

30 Ibid., p. 97.

31 UNEP (United Nations Environment Programme), *Sudan: Post-Conflict Environmental Assessment*, Nairobi, 2007.

32 In the past, nomads who crossed farmland and pastured or watered their animals there had to pay compensation to the farmer. Conflicts have grown in parallel with shortages of water and of pasture for the growing numbers of livestock.

33 Alexander Carius, Dennis Tänzler and Judith Winterstein, *Weltkarte von Umweltkonflikten: Ansätze zu einer Typologisierung*, Potsdam, 2007, p. 13.

34 Prunier, *Darfur*, pp. 61f.

35 Ibid., p. 57.

36 Ibid., pp. 49f.

37 Ibid., p. 51.

38 I am following here the account of the conflict in Wissenschaftliche Dienst des Deutschen Bundestages, *Der Darfur-Konflikt: Genese und Verlauf*, Berlin, October 2006.

39 Ibid., p. 15.

40 Wolfgang Schreiber, *Sudan/Darfur*, University of Hamburg Research Group on the Causes of War (AKUF), cited ibid.

41 Cf. Mary Kaldor, *New & Old Wars: Organized Violence in a Global Era*, 2nd edn, Cambridge, 2006; and Herfried Münkler, *The New Wars*, Cambridge, 2005.

42 Cf. Georg Elwert, *Gewalt und Märkte*, at http://web.fu-berlin.de/ethnologie/publikationen/media/Georg_Elwert-Gewalt_und_Maerkte.pdf.

43 CNA (Center for Naval Analyses), *National Security and the Threat of Climate Change*, Alexandria, VA, 2007, at http://securityandclimate.cna.org/report.

44 *Climate Change and International Security: Paper from the High Representative and the European Commission to the European Council*, S113/08, 14 March 2008.

45 CNA, *National Security*, p. 37.

46 Ibid., p. 48.

47 Ibid.

48 See Nicholas Stern, *The Economics of Climate Change: The Stern Review*, Cambridge, 2007.

49 Florian Rötzer, 'Anhaltender Krieg in Afghanistan verursacht schwere Umweltschäden', *telepolis*, 23 August 2007, at www.heise.de/tp/r4/artikel/26/26020/1.html.

50 Vo Quy, 'Ökozid in Vietnam: Erforschung und Wiederherstellung der Umwelt', at www.ag-friedensforschung.de/regionen/Vietnam/fabig-voquy.html; cf. Vo Quy, 'The Wound of War: Vietnam's Struggle to Erase the Scars of 30 Violent Years', in *CERES: The FAO Review* [Rome], no. 134, March–April 1992.

51 Ibid.

52 Some parts of this section are based on the 'Failing Societies' project undertaken in collaboration with Tobias Debiel.

53 All data from UNEP, *Sudan: Post-Conflict Environmental Assessment*.

54 Tobias Debiel, Dirk Messner and Franz Nuscheler, *Globale Trends 2007: Frieden, Entwicklung, Umwelt*, Frankfurt am Main, 2007, pp. 90ff.

55 Of countries at a relatively low level of development, a half experienced one or more wars between 1995 and 2004, while the corresponding figure for the medium-developed was 29 per cent and for the highly developed 5.5 per cent. Ibid., p. 95.

56 Ibid.

57 Andreas Mehler, 'Oligopolies of Violence in Africa South of the Sahara', Institut für Afrika-Kunde, discussion paper, Hamburg, 2004; Tobias Debiel et al., 'Zwischen Ignorieren und Intervenieren: Strategien und Dilemmata externer Akteure in fragilen Staaten', policy paper no. 23, Stiftung Entwicklung und Frieden, Bonn, 2005.

58 Jon Barnett, 'Climate Change, Insecurity and Justice', paper presented at 'Justice in Adaptation to Climate Change' seminar, Zuckerman Institute for Connective Environmental Research, University of East Anglia, Norwich, 2003, p. 3.

59 See Stephan Libiszewski, 'International Conflicts over Freshwater Resources', in Mohamed Suliman (ed.), *Ecology, Politics and Violent Conflict*, London, 1999, pp. 115–38; Steven C. Lonergan, 'Water and Conflict: Rhetoric and Reality', in Paul F. Diehl and Nils P. Gleditsch (eds), *Environmental Conflict*, Boulder, CO, 2001; Joachim Blatter and Helen Ingram, *Reflections on Water: New Approaches to Transboundary Conflicts and Cooperation*, Cambridge, MA, 2001; Shira Yoffe, Aaron T. Wolf and Mark Giordano, 'Conflict and Cooperation over International Freshwater Resources: Indicators of Basins at Risk',

Journal of the American Water Resources Association, 39/5 (2003), pp. 1109–26; Geoffrey Dabelko, Alexander Carius et al., 'Water, Conflict and Cooperation', *Environmental Change and Security Project Report*, 10 (2004), pp. 60–6; Larry Swatuk, 'Environmental Security in Practice: Transboundary Natural Resource Management in Southern Africa', paper presented in Section 31 of the Pan-European Conference on International Relations, The Hague, 9–11 September 2004; Lars Wirkus and Volker Böge, 'Afrikas internationale Flüsse und Seen: Stand und Erfahrungen im grenzüberschreitenden Wassermanagement in Afrika an ausgewählten Beispielen', discussion paper, Deutsches Institut für Entwicklungspolitik, Bonn, 2005.

60 WBGU (Wissenschaftlicher Beirat der Bundesregierung Globale Umweltveränderung), *Welt im Wandel: Herausforderung für die deutsche Wissenschaft: Zusammenfassung für Entscheidungsträger*, Bremerhaven, 1996.

61 Günther Bächler, Kurt R. Spillmann and Mohamed Suliman (eds), *Transformation of Resource Conflicts: Approaches and Instruments*, Berne, 2002.

62 Cord Jacobeit and Chris Methmann, *Klimaflüchtlinge: Eine Studie im Auftrag von Greenpeace*, Hamburg, 2007.

63 Ragnhild Nordas, 'Climate Conflicts: Commonsense or Nonsense?', paper presented at the thirteenth Annual National Political Science Conference, Hurdalsjøen, Norway, 2005; Barnett, 'Climate Change'.

64 Tobias Debiel and Dieter Reinhardt, 'Staatsverfall und Weltordnungspolitik: Analytische Zugänge und politische Strategien zu Beginn des 21. Jahrhunderts', *Nord-Süd aktuell*, 18/3 (2004), pp. 525–38.

65 I. William Zartman, 'Introduction: Posing the Problem of State Collapse', in Zartman (ed.), *Collapsed States: The Disintegration and Restoration of Legitimate Authority*, Boulder, CO, 1995.

66 Jochen Hippler (ed.), *Nation-Building: A Key Concept for Peaceful Conflict Transformation?*, London, 2005.

67 Ludger Pries, 'Transnationalisierung der sozialen Welt?', *Berliner Journal für Soziologie*, 12/2 (2002), pp. 263–72.

68 Diamond, *Collapse*, pp. 313ff.; Jack A. Goldstone, 'Population and Security: How Demographic Change Can Lead to Violent Conflict', *Journal of International Affairs*, 56/1 (2002), pp. 3–22.

69 Heidrun Zinecker, 'Violence in Peace: Forms and Causes of Postwar Violence in Guatemala', *PRIF Reports* no. 76, Frankfurt: Peace Research Institute, 2006.

70 Elwert, *Gewalt und Märkte*.

71 Ken Menkhaus, 'Governance without Government in Somalia: Spoiler, State Building, and the Politics of Coping', *International Security*, 31/3 (2006), pp. 74–106.
72 Cf. Stern, *The Economics of Climate Change*, and the reports of the Intergovernmental Panel on Climate Change.
73 Nils P. Gleditsch and Ragnhild Nordas, 'Climate Change and Conflict: A Critical Overview', *Die Friedenswarte*, 84/2 (2009), pp. 11–28; here p. 22.
74 Marshall Burke et al., 'Warming Increases the Risk of Civil War in Africa', *Proceedings of the National Academy of Sciences*, 106 (2009), pp. 20670–4.
75 Oli Brown and Alec Crawford, *Rising Temperatures, Rising Tensions: Climate Change and the Risk of Violent Conflict in the Middle East*, Winnipeg, 2008.
76 See, e.g., Cullen Hendrix and Sarah Glaser, 'Trends and Triggers: Climate, Climate Change and Civil Conflict in Sub-Saharan Africa', *Political Geography*, 26/6 (2007), pp. 695–715; Clionadh Raleigh and Henrik Urdal, 'Climate Change, Environmental Degradation and Armed Conflict', *Political Geography*, 26/6 (2007), pp. 674–94; Ole Magnus Theisen and Kristian Bjarnøe Brandsegg, 'Environment and Non-State Conflicts in Sub-Saharan Africa', paper for the forty-eighth Annual Convention of the International Studies Association, Chicago, 28 February – 3 March 2007.
77 Gleditsch and Nordas, 'Climate Change and Conflict'.
78 Thomas F. Homer-Dixon, *Environment, Scarcity, and Violence*, Princeton, NJ, 1999, p. 177.
79 Günther Bächler et al., *Kriegsursache Umweltzerstörung: Ökologische Konflikte in der Dritten Welt und Wege ihrer friedlichen Bearbeitung*, Chur, 1996, p. 318.
80 Dirk Messner, 'Climate Change Threatens Global Development and International Stability', Briefing paper 7/2007, Bonn: German Development Institute, 2007.
81 Jon Barnett and Neil W. Adger, 'Climate Change, Human Security and Violent Conflict', *Political Geography*, 26 (2007), pp. 639–55.
82 Helmut Breitmeier, 'Klimawandel und Gewaltkonflikte', *Forschung DSF*, no. 17 (2009), p. 13.
83 Donella Meadows, Dennis L. Meadows and Jørgen Randers, *The Limits to Growth: Report to the Club of Rome*, London, 1972.
84 See Bächler et al., *Transformation of Resource Conflicts*; Homer-Dixon,

Environment, Scarcity, and Violence; Nils P. Gleditsch, 'Environment Change, Security, and Conflict', in Chester A. Crocker, Fen O. Hampson and Pamela Aall (eds), *Turbulent Peace: The Challenges of Managing International Conflict*, Washington, DC, 2001.

85 Richard A. Matthew, Michael Brklacich and Bryan McDonald, *Global Environmental Change and Human Security: Gaps in Research on Social Vulnerability and Conflict*, Washington, DC, 2003.

86 Fred Pearce, *When the Rivers Run Dry: What Happens When our Water Runs Out?*, Boston, 2006, p. 107.

87 Paul Collier et al., *Breaking the Conflict Trap: Civil War and Development Policy*, World Bank policy research report, Washington, DC, 2003, at http://econ.worldbank.org/.

88 Robert S. Watson et al. (eds), *The Regional Impacts of Climate Change: An Assessment of Vulnerability: Special Report of IPCC Working Group II*, Cambridge, 1997.

89 Tilman Santarius, 'Klimawandel und globale Gerechtigkeit', *Aus Politik und Zeitgeschichte*, 24 (2007), p. 20.

90 UNICEF/WHO, *Meeting the MDG Drinking Water and Sanitation Target: A Mid-Term Assessment of Progress*, 2004, at www.who.int/water_sanitation_health/monitoring/jmp2004/en.

91 Maarten de Wit and Jacek Stankiewicz, 'Changes in Surface Water Supply across Africa with Predicted Climate Change', *Science*, 311/5769 (2006), pp. 1917–21.

92 Joshua C. Nkomo, Anthony Nyong, 'The Impacts of Climate Change in Africa', supporting document for *The Stern Review of the Economics of Climate Change*, at http://webarchive.nationalarchives.gov.uk/20100909030627/webarchive.nationalarchives.gov.uk/+/http://www.hm-treasury.gov.uk/media/3/a/chapter_5_the_impacts_of_climate_change_in_africa-5.pdf.

93 Ibid.

94 Pearce, *When the Rivers Run Dry*, p. 112.

95 Ibid., pp. 194ff. Pearce calls the Six Day War the first water war of the modern age, since it left the Jordan basin almost entirely under Israeli 'hydrological rule' (p. 187).

96 Ibid., p. 107.

97 Rudi Anschober and Petra Ramsauer, *Die Klimarevolution: So retten wir die Welt*, Vienna, 2007, p. 119.

98 Eva Berié et al. (eds), *Der Fischer-Weltalmanach 2008*, Frankfurt am Main, 2007, p. 231.

 99 Jacobeit and Methmann, *Klimaflüchtlinge*, p. 2.
100 Dennis Tänzler, Achim Maas and Alexander Carius, 'Anpassung an den Klimawandel im Zeichen von Konflikten und Krisen', *Die Friedenswarte*, 84/2 (2009), p. 74.
101 Santarius, 'Klimawandel', p. 18.
102 Ibid., p. 19.
103 Astrid Epiney, '"Gerechtigkeit" im Umweltvölkerrecht', *Aus Politik und Zeitgeschichte*, 24 (2007), p. 38.
104 Barnett, 'Climate Change'.
105 Jürgen Müller-Hohagen, *Verleugnet, verdrängt, verschwiegen*, Munich, 2005; Klaus Naumann, *Nachkrieg in Deutschland*, Hamburg, 2001; Harald Welzer, Sabine Moller and Karoline Tschuggnall, *'Opa war kein Nazi!' Nationalsozialismus und Holocaust im Familiengedächtnis*, Frankfurt am Main, 2002; Hartmut Radebold (ed.), *Kindheiten im Zweiten Weltkrieg und ihre Folgen*, Munich, 2004.
106 Heinrich Popitz, *Phänomene der Macht*, Tübingen, 1986, p. 83.
107 Jean-Claude Pressac, *Auschwitz: Technique and Operation of the Gas Chambers*, New York, 1989; Harald Welzer, 'Partikulare Vernunft: Über Soldaten, Ingenieure und andere Produzenten der Vernichtung', in Aleida Assmann, Frank Heidemann and Eckhard Schwarzenberger (eds), *Firma Topf & Söhne: Hersteller der Öfen für Auschwitz*, Frankfurt am Main, 2002.
108 The 'Madagascar Plan', which was under serious consideration for a time, envisaged a 'final solution to the Jewish question' through ethnic cleansing and the forcible resettlement of Jews on the island in the Indian Ocean.
109 All social action, before it is carried through, takes into account what the other person – a conversation or business partner or a third party – is assumed to be expecting. Mutual observation is a fundamental principle of social action. Each player is not only the subject of his action but also the object of someone else's observation: this is the condition of possibility for taking another perspective, which in turn is the precondition of successful social action. Observation of one's conversation partner, for example, is not at all confined to what he or she is verbally expressing, but extends to all perceptible marks of behaviour in the situation. Gestures, facial expressions, physical reactions such as blushing or pupil dilation, excitement: all this is part of what Erving Goffman calls expressive behaviour, which is constantly taken into account in the complexity of social interaction. It should also be noted that expressive

behaviour may itself be the object of conscious control or manipulation and serve to pull the wool over the other's eyes; a shrewd poker player, for example, may calculate that other players rely heavily on what his expressive behaviour ostensibly reveals to them. Hence the object of observation has an interest in using the observer's observation of his behaviour before the observer can make use of it himself – and therefore in what Erving Goffman calls 'impression manipulation'. This model is ratcheted up in the so-called recursive problem, in which the probable assessment that the one player tries to 'suss out' in the other player must take into account the fact that his 'sussing out' attempt is itself contained in the other's assessment. This sounds complicated, but this 'mutually assessed mutual assessment' is the basis for all social action and immediately clarifies that its fundamental category is not causality but relationship (see Erving Goffman, *Strategic Interaction*, Oxford, 1970, pp. 99–101).

Chapter 7 *Killing Tomorrow*

1 John Keegan, *A History of Warfare*, London, 1993, p. 4.
2 All the following figures are borrowed from the Hamburg University Research Group on the Causes of War (AKUF), at www.sozialwiss. uni-hamburg.de/publish/Ipw/Akuf/index.htm. AKUF defines war as 'violent mass conflict that displays all the following characteristics: a) two or more armed forces, including regular government forces (army, paramilitary units, police) on at least one side, take part in the fighting; b) both sides display a minimum of central organization of the combatants and the fighting . . .; c) military operations have a certain continuity and are not only occasional spontaneous clashes – that is, both sides operate according to a strategic plan, regardless of how long the fighting lasts and whether it takes place on the territory of one or several societies.'
3 Tobias Debiel, Dirk Messner and Franz Nuscheler, *Globale Trends 2007: Frieden, Entwicklung, Umwelt*, Frankfurt am Main, 2007, p. 82.
4 Ibid., pp. 26ff.
5 Ibid.
6 Fred Pearce, *When the Rivers Run Dry: What Happens When our Water Runs Out?*, Boston, 2006, pp. 106ff.
7 Novosti news agency report, 1 August 2007.
8 *Frankfurter Allgemeine Zeitung*, 19 October 2007, p. 6.
9 Gérard Prunier, *Darfur: The Ambiguous Genocide*, Ithaca, NY, 2007, p. 1.

10 Ibid., p. x.

11 Georg Franck, *Ökonomie der Aufmerksamkeit*, Munich, 1999.

12 The distinction originates mainly in the admirable works of Mary Kaldor (*New & Old Wars: Organized Violence in a Global Era*, 2nd edn, Cambridge, 2006) and Herfried Münkler (*The New Wars*, Cambridge, 2005).

13 Keegan, *A History of Warfare*, pp. 95ff.

14 Kaldor, *New & Old Wars*, p. 32.

15 Münkler, *The New Wars*, pp. 90f.

16 Keegan, *A History of Warfare*, p. 380.

17 Kaldor, *New & Old Wars*, pp. 97ff.

18 Ibid., p. 100.

19 Naomi Klein, *The Shock Doctrine: The Rise of Disaster Capitalism*, London, 2007, p. 12.

20 *Frankfurter Allgemeine Zeitung*, 24 September 2007, p. 8.

21 Kaldor, *New & Old Wars*, p. 166.

22 In September 2007 the murder of civilians by mercenaries was one reason why the Iraqi government, supported by the US State Department, revoked the licence of the Blackwater security company.

23 Georg Elwert, *Gewalt und Märkte*, at http://web.fu-berlin.de/ethnologie/publikationen/media/Georg_Elwert-Gewalt_und_Maerkte.pdf. See also Elwert, 'Markets of Violence', in G. Elwert, S. Feuchtwang and D. Neubert (eds), *Dynamics of Violence: Processes of Escalation and De-Escalation in Violent Group Conflicts*, Berlin, 1999, pp. 85ff.

24 Wolfgang Höpken, 'Gewalt auf dem Balkan: Erklärungsversuche zwischen "Struktur" und "Kultur"', in Höpken and Michael Rieckenberg (eds), *Politische und ethnische Gewalt in Südosteuropa und Lateinamerika*, Cologne, 2001, pp. 53–95; Holm Sundhaussen, 'Der "wilde Balkan": Imagination und Realität einer europäischen Konfliktregion', *Ost–West Europäische Perspektiven*, 1/1 (2000), pp. 79–100; Maria Todorova, *Die Erfindung des Balkans: Europas bequemes Vorurteil*, Darmstadt, 1999.

25 Erving Goffman, *Asylums*, Garden City, NY.

26 See Münkler, *The New Wars*.

27 Scott Straus, *The Order of Genocide: Race, Power, and War in Rwanda*, New York, 2006; Harald Welzer, *Täter: Wie aus ganz normalen Menschen Massenmörder werden*, Frankfurt am Main, 2005.

28 Since new 'movements' constantly appear in conflicts of this kind, it is often hard to work out exactly what is going on – a fact that has

major implications for the reporting of violent conflicts. For example, a *Frankfurter Allgemeine Zeitung* article, 'Fighting in Somalia' (25 September 2007, p. 6), tried to describe the central role in the conflict of an 'Alliance for the Re-Liberation of Somalia' (ARS), founded two weeks earlier, which included Ethiopian Islamists recently driven out of Mogadishu as well as a number of 'civilian groups'. But the reader soon realizes that it is impossible to understand from the article what are the real forces at work and the real origins of the fighting.

29 See 'Afrikas Kriege verschlingen komplette Entwicklungshilfe', *Der Spiegel*, 11 October 2007, at www.spiegel.de/politik/ausland/0,1518,druck-510917,00.html.

30 Quoted from Norman M. Naimark, *Fires of Hatred: Ethnic Cleansing in Twentieth-Century Europe*, Cambridge, MA, 2001, p. 110.

31 Rainer Geißler, 'Struktur und Entwicklung der Bevölkerung', *Bundeszentrale für politische Bildung*, at www.bpb.de/publikationen/7WF4KK.html. Contrary to widespread assumptions, these are not definitive figures but are based on not always reliable estimates. The total numbers who died were probably somewhat lower. See Ingo Haar, 'Hochgerechnetes Unglück: Die Zahl der deutschen Opfer nach dem Zweiten Weltkrieg wird übertrieben', *Süddeutsche Zeitung*, 14 November 2006.

32 Naimark, *Fires of Hatred*, pp. 92–107.

33 The revival of puritanical religiosity also displays some features of modernization, in the sense that its functioning is transnational and individualist. See Claus Leggewie, 'Glaubensgemeinschaften zwischen nationalen Staatskirchen und globalen Religionsmärkten', inaugural lecture of the International Congress on Justice and Human Values in Europe, 10 May 2007.

34 Kaldor, *New & Old Wars*, p. 4.

35 Ibid.

36 Ibid., p. 5.

37 Michael Mann, *The Dark Side of Democracy: Explaining Ethnic Cleansing*, Cambridge, 2005, p. 505.

38 *Frankfurter Allgemeine Zeitung*, 30 August 2007.

39 *Tagesschau*, 20 July 2007.

40 ORF, at http://news.orf.at/051010-92154/92155txt_story.html (accessed 2008).

41 Mann, *The Dark Side of Democracy*, p. 523.

42 Alexander Carius, Dennis Tänzler and Judith Winterstein, *Weltkarte von Umweltkonflikten: Ansätze zu einer Typologisierung*, Potsdam, 2007, p. 10.

43 Ibid., p. 14.

44 Ibid., p. 46.

45 Ibid., p. 27.

46 Ibid., p. 47.

47 Michael Brzoska, 'Raubbau an Ressourcen durch Konfliktakteure', in Reiner Braun et al. (eds), *Kriege um Ressourcen: Herausforderungen für das 21. Jahrhundert*, Munich, 2009, pp. 71–84.

48 Eva Berié et al. (eds), *Der Fischer-Weltalmanach 2008*, Frankfurt am Main, 2007, p. 27.

49 Wolfgang Sachs, 'Öl ins Feuer: Ressourcenkonflikte als Treibstoff für globalen Unfrieden', in Österreichisches Studienzentrum für Frieden und Konfliktlösung (ed.), *Von kalten Energiestrategien zu heißen Rohstoffkriegen? Schachspiel der Weltmächte zwischen Präventivkrieg und zukunftsfähiger Rohstoffpolitik im Zeitalter des globalen Treibhauses*, Vienna, 2008, pp. 31–43, here p. 37.

50 Thomas L. Friedman, *Hot, Flat and Crowded: Why the World Needs a Green Revolution*, London, 2009, p. 137.

51 Sachs, 'Öl ins Feuer', p. 39.

52 Karin Kneissl, 'Die neue Kolonialisierung Afrikas: China, die USA und Europa im Kampf um die Rohstoffe Afrikas', in Österreichisches Studienzentrum für Frieden und Konfliktlösung (ed.), *Von kalten Energiestrategien zu heißen Rohstoffkriegen?*, p. 185.

53 Marcus Theurer, 'Wir Afrikaner sind keine Kinder', *Frankfurter Allgemeine Sonntagszeitung*, 12 April 2009, p. 34 [interview with Dambisa Moyo].

54 Debiel et al., *Globale Trends*, op. cit., pp. 26ff.

55 Quoted from Lühr Henken, 'Knappe Rohstoffe – Eine Quelle für Aufrüstungen und Kriegsplanungen', in Österreichisches Studienzentrum für Frieden und Konfliktlösung (ed.), *Von kalten Energiestrategien zu heißen Rohstoffkriegen?*, op. cit., pp. 218ff.

56 This section is based on research by Sebastian Wessels.

57 Deportations by no means always take place in this legal manner, and the countries to which refugees are deported are not necessarily their countries of origin. In the case of Morocco, refugees have repeatedly been taken into the desert and released there.

58 Martin Dahms, 'Der weite Weg in die erste Welt', *Das*

Parlament, 28 (2006), at http://webarchiv.bundestag.de/cgi/show. php?fileToLoad=1718&id=1149.

59 Ralf Streck, '"Massensterben" vor den Kanarischen Inseln', *telepolis*, 24 March 2006; at www.heise.de/tp/r4/artikel/22/22317/1.html.

60 Harald Neuber, 'Festung Europa: Beispiel Spanien', *telepolis*, 22 October 2004.

61 Helmut Dietrich, 'Die Front in der Wüste', *konkret*, 12 (2004), pp. 5f., at http://nolager.de/blog/files/nolager/lampedusa.pdf.

62 Dahms, 'Der weite Weg'.

63 Ralf Streck, 'Sechs Satelliten sollen Flüchtlinge aufspüren', *telepolis*, 30 May 2006, at www.heise.de/tp/r4/artikel/22/22780/1.html.

64 Severin Carrell, 'Revealed: Robot Spyplanes to Guard Europe's Borders', *The Independent*, 4 June 2006, at: www.independent.co.uk/ news/world/europe/revealed-robot-spyplanes-to-guard-europes-bord ers-481057.html.

65 Information bulletin of the EU Directorate General Enterprise and Industry – Security Research: 'Preparatory Action for Security Research: Border Surveillance UAV, 2005', at ftp://ftp.cordis.europa. eu/pub/fp7/security/docs/bs-uav_en.pdf.

66 Dietrich, 'Die Front in der Wüste', p. 6.

67 Alfred Hackensberger, 'Anschlag auf die Grenze', *telepolis*, 3 October 2005, at www.heise.de/tp/r4/artikel/21/21064/1.html.

68 Florian Rötzer, 'Ansturm auf die neue Mauer', *telepolis*, 6 October 2005, at www.heise.de/tp/r4/artikel/21/21086/1.html.

69 n-tv, 'Noch ein Zaun für Melilla', 4 October 2005, at www.n-tv. de/586970.html.

70 Hackensberger, 'Anschlag auf die Grenze'.

71 'Spanien beginnt mit Abschiebungen', 7 October 2005, at www. stern.de/politik/ausland/:Fl%FCchtlingsdrama-Spanien-Abschiebung en/547229.html.

72 Alfred Hackensberger, 'Man muss die Flüchtlinge mit allem Respekt als menschliche Wesen behandeln', *telepolis*, 16 October 2005 [inter- view with Frederico Barroela, Médecins sans Frontières], at www.heise. de/tp/r4/artikel/21/21153/1.html.

73 Michael Schwelien, 'Die Einfalltore', *Die Zeit*, 13 October 2005, at http://images.zeit.de/text/2005/42/Ceuta.

74 Médicins sans Frontières, 'Violence and Immigration: Report on Illegal Sub-Saharan Immigrants (ISSs) in Morocco', pp. 2ff., at www.aerzte- ohne-grenzen.at/fileadmin/data/pdf/reports/2005/msfmedia-3039.pdf.

75 Streck, '"Massensterben" vor den Kanarischen Inseln'.

76 Médicins sans Frontières, 'Violence and Immigration', p. 6.

77 'Thessaloniki European Council, 19–20 June 2003: Presidency Conclusions, 22 June 2003', at www.greekembassy.org/embassy/ content/en/Article.aspx?office=2&folder=168&article=11744.

78 Gunßer, 'Der europäische Krieg gegen Flüchtlinge'.

79 Leo Wieland, 'Erste afrikanische Flüchtlinge nach Marokko abge-schoben', *Frankfurter Allgemeine Zeitung*, 7 October 2005, p. 1.

80 Karl Hoffmann, 'Lampedusa: Die Ankunft in Europa', Deutschland-funk, 30 April 2006, at www.dradio.de/dlf/sendungen/transit/494 082.

81 Dietrich, 'Die Front in der Wüste', p. 3.

82 Streck, '"Massensterben" vor den Kanarischen Inseln'.

83 Anke Schwarzer, 'Das Lagersystem für Flüchtlinge', *telepolis*, 21 August 2005, at www.heise.de/tp/r4/artikel/20/20764/1.html.

84 Hans-Christian Rössler, 'In Libyens Hölle', *Frankfurter Allgemeine Sonntagszeitung*, 22 July 2007, p. 8.

85 Mike Davis, 'The Great Wall of Capital', *Socialist Review*, February 2004, at www.socialistreview.org.uk/article.php?articlenumber=8770.

86 *Aeneas Programme: Overview of Projects Funded 2004–2006*, at http:// ec.europa.eu/europeaid/what/migration-asylum/documents/ aeneas_2004_2006_overview_en.pdf.

87 Regulation (EC) No 491/2004 of the European Parliament and of the Council of 10 March 2004, at http://eur-lex.europa.eu/LexUriServ/ LexUriServ.do?uri=OJ:L:2004:080:0001:0005:EN:PDF.

88 Franco Frattini, 'Mit Hubschraubern gegen illegale Einwanderung', *Frankfurter Allgemeine Zeitung*, 29 March 2007, p. 3 [interview with Wolfgang Schäuble].

89 Frontex Annual Report 2006, p. 2, at www.frontex.europa.eu/ annual_report.

90 Regulation (EG) 2007/2004 of the European Council, at http://eur-lex.europa.eu/LexUriServ/LexUriServ.do?uri=OJ:L:2004:349:0001:00 11:EN:PDF.

91 'Frontex Finance', at www.frontex.europa.eu/budget_and_finance.

92 Bundesministerium des Innern, 'Aufgaben und Tätigkeit der Europäischen Grenzschutzagentur FRONTEX', undated, at http:// www.bmi.bund.de/SharedDocs/Standardartikel/DE/Themen/ Sicherheit/Bundespolizei/Frontex.html?nn=109632.

93 Christoph Marischka, 'Frontex als Schrittmacher der EU-Innenpolitik',

telepolis, 25 May 2007, at www.heise.de/tp/r4/artikel/25/25359/1. html.

94 Bundesministerium des Innern, 'Aufgaben und Tätigkeit der Europäischen Grenzschutzagentur FRONTEX'.

95 Regulation (EC) No 863/2007 of the European Parliament and of the Council, 11 July 2007, at http://eur-lex.europa.eu/LexUriServ/ LexUriServ.do?uri=OJ:L:2007:199:0030:0039:EN:PDF.

96 Bundesministerium des Innern, *Innenpolitik: Informationen des Bundesministeriums des Innern,* July 2007, p. 6.

97 Bundesministerium des Innern, 'Aufgaben und Tätigkeit der Europäischen Grenzschutzagentur FRONTEX'.

98 Deutscher Bundestagsdrucksache 16/5019, 13 April 2007, p. 3, at http://dip.bundestag.de/btd/16/050/1605019.pdf.

99 Frontex Annual Report 2006, p. 5.

100 Ibid., p. 15. Cf. 'Endstation Grenze', *Öffentliche Sicherheit,* 5–6 (2007), p. 25, at http://www.bmi.gv.at/cms/BMI_OeffentlicheSicher heit/2007/05_06/files/Frontex.pdf.

101 The report leaves some questions open: not only which seven countries took part but also, for example, which international agreements formed the basis for the operations in Senegalese and Mauritanian waters, and which procedures were used with the nearly 4,000 refugees in detention.

102 Frontex News Releases: 'A Sequel of Operation Hera Just Starting', 15 February 2007, at www.frontex.europa.eu/newsroom/news_releases/ art13.html.

103 Frontex Annual Report 2006, p. 11, and Christoph Marischka, 'Frontex geht in die Offensive', Informationsstelle Militarisierung (IMI), *IMI-Analyse,* 15/2007, at www.imi-online.de/2007.php3?id=1530.

104 Bundesministerium des Innern, 'Aufgaben und Tätigkeit der Europäischen Grenzschutzagentur FRONTEX'. On 24 August 2007 the *Frankfurter Allgemeine Zeitung* (p. 3) reported that Frontex had provisionally suspended Mediterranean operations, since it lacked the funds to provide 'ships, helicopters and personnel throughout the summer for teams in the waters of Southern Europe'. This announcement, which was evidently greeted with astonishment at EU level, was probably an attempt to gain additional funding for the agency.

105 Most of these were tourists, students or temporary workers who had entered the country legally but overstayed their visa. See Jennifer

Elrick, 'Länderprofil Kanada', *focus Migration*, 8 (2007), pp. 7f., at www. focus-migration.de/Kanada.1275.0.html.

106 Mike Davis, 'Die große Mauer des Kapitals', *Die Zeit*, 12 October 2006, p. 2.

107 US Customs and Border Protection, *National Border Patrol Strategy*, September 2004.

108 Davis, 'Die große Mauer des Kapitals'. For example, 'Operation Gatekeeper' in 1994 upgraded the border between California and Baja California, increasing the number of border officials, building new walls and raising the height of ones already in place. Four years later, a number of US and Mexican NGOs – including the American Friends Service Committee, the Centro de Apoyo al Migrante and the Casa del Migrante – drew up a balance-sheet in which it noted a shift in refugee flows. Most illegal immigrants now enter the USA in desert areas east of Mexicali and around Tecate, where daytime temperatures climb as high as 50 degrees Celsius (Bundeszentrale für politische Bildung, 'USA/Mexiko: Kritische Bilanz von Nichtregierungsorganisationen zu vier Jahren "Operation Gatekeeper"', *Migration und Bevölkerung*, 8 (1998), at www.migration-info.de/migration_und_bevoelkerung/ artikel/980807.htm.

109 Ibid. Cf. Achim Reinke, 'Unterwegs in die Erste Welt', November 2006, at www.caritas-international.de/10567.html (accessed November 2006).

110 Office of Homeland Security, *National Strategy for Homeland Security*, July 2002, p. viii, at www.dhs.gov/xlibrary/assets/nat_strat_hls.pdf.

111 Nicholas Parrott, 'Länderprofil: Die Vereinigten Staaten von Amerika', *focus Migration*, 4 (2007), at http://focus-migration.hwwi.de/uploads/ tx_wilpubdb/LP04_USA_01.pdf.

112 Department of Homeland Security, 'Organizational Charts', 1 April 2007, p. 1, at www.dhs.gov/xlibrary/assets/OGC_OrgChart.pdf.

113 Kai Oppel, 'USA: Unbeliebt und unvermeidlich', *Financial Times Deutschland*, 9 September 2007, at www.ftd.de/unternehmen/handel_ dienstleister/247895.html.

114 'US-Regierung verschärft Einreisekontrolle', *Handelsblatt*, 25 June 2007, at www.handelsblatt.com/politik/international/us-regierung-verschaerft-einreisekontrolle/2826782.html.

115 Klein, *The Shock Doctrine*, pp. 12–13.

116 Bundeszentrale für politische Bildung, 'USA/Kanada: Grenzsicherung-sabkommen und höhere Einwanderungsquoten in Kanada', *Migration*

und Bevölkerung, 1 (2002), at www.migration-info.de/migration_und_
bevoelkerung/artikel/020104.htm.

117 US Customs and Border Protection, 'Securing America's Borders',
September 2006, p. 1, at www.cbp.gov/linkhandler/cgov/newsroom/
publications/mission/cbp_securing_borders.ctt/cbp_securing_borders.
pdf.

118 Tim Gaynor, 'Blocking the Border', Reuters, 10 September 2007.

119 Reinke, 'Unterwegs in die Erste Welt'.

120 US Customs and Border Protection, 'Secure Border Initiative: A
Comprehensive Border Security Solution', *Secure Border Initiative
Monthly*, 1/1 (2006), p. 1.

121 Joseph Richey, 'Fencing the Border: Boeing's High-Tech Plan Falters',
CorpWatch, 9 July 2007, at www.corpwatch.org/article.php?id=
14552.

122 Chris Strome, 'Contractor Problems Hold up Border Fence
Project', *Government Executive*, 7 July 2007, at www.govexec.com/
dailyfed/0907/090707cdpm1.htm.

123 Thomas Kleine-Brockhoff, 'Ground Zero in Arizona', *Die Zeit*, 6
April 2006, www.zeit.de/2006/15/Einwanderung; see also www.minute
menhq.com.

124 Hildegard Strausberg, 'Mexikaner protestieren gegen die neue Mauer',
Welt online, 6 October 2006, at www.welt.de/print-welt/article157609/
Mexikaner_protestieren_gegen_die_neue_Mauer.html.

125 Fred Lucas, 'Border Fence "Very Doable", Engineers Say',
Cybercast News Service, 6 September 2007, at www.cnsnews.com/
node/23665.

126 'US–Mexico Border Fence', www.globalsecurity.org/security/systems/
mexico-wall.htm. According to a study conducted by the Pew Hispanic
Center in March 2006, roughly 12 million people were living illegally
in the United States – a figure that increases by another half-million
a year. One factor fuelling this growth is the positive welcoming of
unregistered immigrant labour in parts of the economy, which is all the
cheaper for being illegal. The same study estimated that 56 per cent of
these immigrants were Mexicans without a residence permit, while a
further 22 per cent came from other Latin American countries; 94 per
cent were economically active. The sociologist Mike Davis holds the
view that the purpose of US frontier policies is not to prohibit illegal
immigration but to regulate it in accordance with the situation in the
labour market.

127 Reinke, 'Unterwegs in die Erste Welt'.

128 Parrott, 'Länderprofil', p. 2.

129 Thomas Kleine-Brockhoff, 'Die Macht der Latinos', *Zeit-online*, 1 April 2005, at www.zeit.de/online/2006/14/usa_immigration.

130 Parrott, 'Länderprofil', p. 2.

131 'USA: Massenproteste gegen Einwanderungsgesetze', *Migration und Bevölkerung*, 3 (2006), at www.migration-info.de/migration_und_bevoelkerung/artikel/060308.htm.

132 Ibid., p. 7.

133 Daniel C. Martin, 'Refugees and Asylees: 2010', *Annual Flow Report*, May 2011, at www.dhs.gov/xlibrary/assets/statistics/publications/ois_rfa_fr_2010.pdf.

134 Elrick, 'Länderprofil Kanada', p. 8.

135 Joan Delaney, 'Canada Big Draw for Mexicans', *Epoch Times*, 16 August 2007, at www.theepochtimes.com/news/7-8-16/58826.html.

136 Heinrich Popitz, *Prozesse der Machtbildung*, Tübingen, 1976, pp. 9ff.

137 Strictly speaking, there are no natural disasters, since nature is completely indifferent to what happens to it. A disaster is always something that affects, and is therefore relative to, human beings, the only living species that evolution has endowed with an awareness of the future. However, the term 'natural disaster' is used here to distinguish it from manmade disasters.

138 It later turned out, however, that the statistical probability of such an accident – once in 20,000 years – had been calculated from all existing reactors and should really have been considerably higher. Nor was it ever clear to the public that the statistically unlikely event could just as easily happen on the first day of the 20,000 years as on any other day.

139 In the psychological work of coming to terms with a disaster, it makes a considerable difference whether it was in principle avoidable or controllable or came as a stroke of fate against which nothing could be done. See Julian Rotter, *Clinical Psychology*, New York, 1964.

140 Wolfgang Benz, *Dimension des Völkermords: Die Zahl der jüdischen Opfer des Nationalsozialismus*, Munich, 1991.

141 Elke M. Geenen, 'Kollektive Krisen: Katastrophe, Terror, Revolution – Gemeinsamkeiten und Unterschiede', in Lars Clausen et al. (eds), *Entsetzliche soziale Prozesse*, Münster, 2003, p. 15.

142 Ibid., p. 6.

143 Ibid., p. 12.

144 Ibid.

145 Most sociologists also live in worlds that are perceived as stable, and so it is not surprising that their theories do not allow for system collapse, outbreaks of extreme violence or a complete turnaround in social conditions, and that they define such events as 'exceptions' if they do actually happen. Whereas oceanologists, meteorologists or paleoarcheologists can easily accept that the assumptions of their models create problems, their colleagues in the cultural sciences evidently find it difficult to investigate what a 2 degree rise in average global temperatures and a 15 centimetre rise in sea levels would mean for society. They are part of the world with which they are academically involved and therefore avoid issues that might trigger feelings of threat, fear, insecurity and loss of control.

146 This is true even when an accident happens. A study at the time of the nuclear accident at Three Mile Island showed that people's faith in the assurances of the power station managers was all the greater the closer they lived to the affected reactor. See Elliot Anderson, *The Social Animal*, San Francisco, 1972.

147 Michael Tomasello, *The Cultural Origins of Human Cognition*, Cambridge, MA, 1999.

148 Norbert Elias, *The Society of Individuals*, Oxford, 1991, p. 211.

149 Günther Anders, *Die Antiquiertheit des Menschen*, Munich, 1987, p. 278.

Chapter 8 Changed Realities

1 Stephen Jay Gould has more than once discussed what humans could and could not have known at a given point in time. See, e.g., *The Lying Stones of Marrakech: Penultimate Reflections in Natural History*, New York, 2001.

2 Fred Pearce, *The Last Generation: How Nature Will Take her Revenge for Climate Change*, London, 2007, pp. 55–6.

3 Ibid., pp. 120ff.

4 Joachim Radkau, *Nature and Power: A Global History of the Environment*, Cambridge, 2008, pp. 136ff.

5 Andrea Sáenz-Arroyo et al., 'Rapidly Shifting Environmental Baselines among Fishers of the Gulf of California', *Proceedings of the Royal Society*, 272 (2005), pp. 1957–62.

6 Ibid., p. 1959.

7 Ibid., p. 1960.

8 Changing perceptions of the environment are also apparent in the interpretation of symbols. The Californian flag, for example, features

a bear not because it is such a rare creature in that state, but because there used to be so many. The same is true of the eagle in the German Federal Republic.

9 Raul Hilberg, *Perpetrators, Victims, Bystanders: The Jewish Catastrophe 1933–1945*, London, 1995, p. 119.
10 Norbert Elias, *What Is Sociology?*, New York, 1984.
11 Harald Welzer, *Täter: Wie aus ganz normalen Menschen Massenmörder werden*, Frankfurt am Main, 2005, pp. 48ff.
12 Eric Johnson and Karl-Heinz Reuband, *What We Knew: Terror, Mass Murder and Everyday Life in Nazi Germany*, New York, 2005, p. 349.
13 Ibid., p. 357.
14 Ibid., pp. 330ff.
15 Karl-Heinz Reuband, 'Das NS-Regime zwischen Akzeptanz und Ablehnung', *Geschichte und Gesellschaft*, 32/3 (2006), pp. 315–43.
16 Saul Friedländer, *Nazi Germany and the Jews*, vol. 1: *The Years of Persecution*, London, 1997, pp. 36–7.
17 Alex Bruns-Wüstefeld, *Lohnende Geschäfte: Die 'Entjudung' am Beispiel Göttingens*, Hanover, 1997, p. 69.
18 See, e.g., Lutz Niethammer and Alexander von Plato, *'Wir kriegen jetzt andere Zeiten'*, Bonn 1985; Harald Welzer, Robert Montau and Christine Plaß, *'Was wir für böse Menschen sind!' Der Nationalsozialismus im Gespräch zwischen den Generationen*, Tübingen, 1997; Harald Welzer, Sabine Moller and Karoline Tschuggnall, *'Opa war kein Nazi!' Nationalsozialismus und Holocaust im deutschen Familiengedächtnis*, Frankfurt am Main, 2002; Johnson and Reuband, *What We Knew*, p. 341.
19 Bruce Hoffman, *Inside Terrorism*, New York, 2006, p. 157.
20 Ibid., p. 159.
21 Ibid., p. 158.
22 'EU fördert Sicherheitstechnologie', *Frankfurter Allgemeine Zeitung*, 12 September 2007, p. 4.
23 Ibid.
24 *Frankfurter Allgemeine Zeitung*, 15 October 2007, p. 6.
25 *Allensbacher Berichte*, 14 (2006), p. 2.
26 *Allensbacher Berichte*, 21 (2004), p.2.
27 *Allensbacher Berichte*, 14 (2006), p. 3.
28 *ZDF-Politbarometer*, 20 April 2007. In the nature of things, people's fears are more intense where terror attacks have already occurred. There have been reports of real Islamophobia in Spain: for example,

two men were prevented from boarding an aircraft because they looked like Pakistanis (*El Pais*, 23 August 2006).

29 Ibid.

30 Ludwig Greven, 'Der Datenhunger wächst', *Zeit-online*, 39 (2007), at www.zeit.de/online/2007/39/datenschutz-simitis.

31 Allied bombing in the Second World War was based on the false assumption that it would cause demoralization and undermine loyalty to the system. But the opposite was the case: the National Socialist *Volksgemeinschaft* became more cohesive as the air raids grew more terrifying.

Chapter 9 The Revival of Old Conflicts

1 See interior minister Wolfgang Schäuble's remarks on the ARD-Brennpunkt television programme, 5 September 2007.

2 In an interview with the *Frankfurter Allgemeine Sonntagszeitung* (14 October 2007, p. 8), Herfried Münkler noted that private security companies are sometimes paid not by the state but by corporate interests: 'They then take the monopoly of legitimate force out of the hands of the state and acquire a degree of political power, which they may bring to bear in connection with oil prices or whatever is in high demand at the time.'

3 Heribert Prantl, 'Der Terrorist als Gesetzgeber', *Neue Zürcher Zeitung*, folio 9 (2007), pp. 20–4, here p. 22.

Chapter 11 What Can and Cannot be Done – 1

1 In Sumatra and Indonesian Borneo, some 5 million hectares of rain-forest have already been cleared (most by burning) for the production of palm oil, discharging a billion tonnes of CO_2 a year (15 per cent of the world total) into the atmosphere (see www.umweltschutz-news.de/266artikel1376screenout1.html?besucht=66eceb92). It should also be noted that biofuel is ecologically counterproductive: it is climate-neutral in terms of carbon dioxide, but not in terms of nitrous oxide. For example, the greenhouse effect is approximately 1.7 times higher with rapeseed diesel than with conventional diesel (*Frankfurter Allgemeine Zeitung*, 2 October 2007, p. N1).

2 In 2006, per capita GDP in more than twenty African countries was below $500 – in comparison with $35,204 in Germany and $44,190 in the United States (*Spiegel-online*, at www.spiegel.de/politik/ausland/0,1518,grossbild-991373-510917,00.html).

3   Erving Goffman, 'Role Distance', in Goffman, *Encounters: Two Studies in the Sociology of Interaction*, London, 1961, pp. 85–132.

4   Rudi Anschober and Petra Ramsauer, *Die Klimarevolution: So retten wir die Welt*, Vienna, 2007, pp. 166ff.

5   Anselm Waldermann, 'Profitdenken schlägt Umweltschutz', *Spiegel-online*, 6 September 2007, at www.spiegel.de/wirtschaft/0,1518,504 278,00.html.

6   That is, in terms of the reduction of noxious emissions. Nitrous oxide is mentioned here only as one example, since it derives from biofuels and offsets the reduction of emissions from carbon dioxide.

7   It is recognition of the individual as a subject in international law that has made it possible to bring politicians or army officers to account. Or, conversely, state attacks on individuals permit an encroachment on the sovereign rights of the state (Gerhard Werle, *Principles of International Criminal Law*, The Hague, 2009, pp. 2ff.).

8   W. G. Sebald, *The Rings of Saturn*, London, 1998, pp. 235–7.

9   Alfred Schütz, 'Tiresias, or Our Knowledge of Future Events', in *Collected Papers*, vol. 2, *Studies in Social Theory*, The Hague, 1976, pp. 277–93; here, p. 279.

10 Harald Welzer, 'Albert Speer's Memories of the Future', in Jürgen Straub (ed.), *Narration, Identity, and Historical Consciousness*, New York, 2005, pp. 245–55.

11 Dirk Rupnow, *Vernichten und Erinnern: Spuren nationalsozialistischer Gedächtnispolitik*, Göttingen, 2005; Jan Björn Potthast, *Das jüdische Zentralmuseum der SS in Prag: Gegnerforschung und Völkermord im Nationalsozialismus*, Frankfurt am Main, 2002.

12 Götz Aly, *Hitler's Beneficiaries: How the Nazis Bought the German People*, New York, 2006.

13 W. G. Sebald, *On the Natural History of Destruction*, London, 2003, p. 104.

14 Hans Jonas, *The Imperative of Responsibility*, Chicago, 1984, pp. 199f.

15 Curiously, the critique of consumption and media culture and the listing of all the collateral damage of modernization (from childhood obesity to the erosion of social relationships) do not seem to affect the belief that people in the West are living in the best of all possible worlds.

16 Königliche Norwegische Botschaft, 'Ausschluss von Gesellschaften aus dem Staatlichen Pensionsfonds', at www.norwegen.no/News_ and_events/germany/policy/politicalnews/Selskaper_utelukket_fra_olj efondet/.

17 See Informationsdienst für den öffentlichen Verkehr (LITRA), *Meldung*, 6 July 2004, at www.litra.ch/Juli_2004.html.

18 Herbert Marcuse, Robert Paul Wolff and Barrington Moore, *A Critique of Pure Tolerance*, London, 1969, p. 98.

19 Ulrich Beck's term.

Chapter 12 *What Can and Cannot Be Done – 2*

1 Norbert Elias, *The Society of Individuals*, Oxford, 1991, p. 211.

2 Claude Lévi-Strauss, *Tristes tropiques*, Harmondsworth, 1976, p. 542.

3 Ibid., p. 543.

INDEX